Rick Riolo, Una-May O'Reilly and Trent McConaghy (Eds.)

Genetic Programming Theory and Practice VII

T0143019

Genetic and Evolutionary Computation Series

Series Editors

David E. Goldberg
Consulting Editor
IlliGAL, Dept. of General Engineering
University of Illinois at Urbana-Champaign
Urbana, IL 61801 USA
Email: deg@uiuc.edu

John R. Koza
Consulting Editor
Medical Informatics
Stanford University
Stanford, CA 94305-5479 USA
Email: john@johnkoza.com

For other titles published in this series, go to http://www.springer.com/series/7373

Rick Riolo
Una-May O'Reilly
Trent McConaghy
(Eds.)

Genetic Programming
Theory and Practice VII

 Springer

Editors
Rick Riolo
Center for the Study of Complex Systems
University of Michigan
323 West Hall
Ann Arbor, MI 48109
USA
rlriolo@umich.edu

Una-May O'Reilly
Computer Science and Artificial
Intelligence Laboratory (CSAIL)
Massachusetts Institute of Technology
32 Vassar Street
Cambridge, MA 02139
USA
unamay@csail.mit.edu

Trent McConaghy
Solido Design Automation, Inc.
102-116 Research Drive
Saskatoon, SK S7N 3R3
Canada
trent_mcconaghy@yahoo.com

ISSN 1932-0167
ISBN 978-1-4614-2501-4   e-ISBN 978-1-4419-1626-6
DOI 10.1007/978-1-4419-1626-6
Springer New York Dordrecht Heidelberg London

Springer is part of Springer Science+Business Media (www.springer.com)

Contents

Contributing Authors

Peter C. Andrews is a software engineer in the Computational Genetics Laboratory at Dartmouth Medical School, USA (Peter.C.Andrews@Dartmouth.edu).

Wolfgang Banzhaf is a professor and chair of the Department of Computer Science at Memorial University of Newfoundland, St. John's, NL, Canada (simonh@cs.mun.ca).

Josh Bongard is an assistant professor of Computer Science in the College of Engineering and Mathematical Sciences at the University of Vermont, USA (josh.bongard@uvm.edu).

Caterina Cinel is a psychologist and principal research officer within the School of Computer Science and Electronic Engineering of the University of Essex, UK (ccinel@essex.ac.uk).

Luca Citi is a research officer within the School of Computer Science and Electronic Engineering of the University of Essex, UK (lciti@essex.ac.uk).

John Doucette is an undergraduate at the Faculty of Computer Science, Dalhousie University, NS, Canada (jdoucett@cs.dal.ca).

Casey S. Greene is a graduate student in the Computational Genetics Laboratory at Dartmouth Medical School, USA (Casey.S.Greene@Dartmouth.edu).

Malcolm Heywood is a Professor of Computer Science at Dalhousie University, Halifax, NS, Canada (mheywood@cs.dal.ca).

Douglas P. Hill is a computer programmer in the Computational Genetics Laboratory at Dartmouth Medical School, USA (Douglas.P.Hill@Dartmouth.EDU).

Gregory Hornby is a Senior Scientist with the University of California Santa Cruz working in the Intelligent Systems Division at NASA Ames Research Center, USA (gregory.s.hornby@nasa.gov).

Janine Imada recently completed graduate studies in Computer Science at Brock University, St. Catharines, ON, Canada (jimada@bell.net).

Michael F. Korns is Chief Technology Officer at Freeman Investment Management, Henderson, Nevada, USA (mkorns@korns.com).

Mark E. Kotanchek is Chief Technology Officer of Evolved Analytics, a data modeling consulting and systems company, USA/China (mark@evolved-analytics.com).

Peter Lichodzijewski is a graduate student in the Faculty of Computer Science at Dalhousie University, Halifax, Nova Scotia, Canada (piotr@cs.dal.ca).

Hod Lipson is an Associate Professor in the school of Mechanical and Aerospace Engineering and the school of Computing and Information Science at Cornell University, Ithaca, NY, USA (hod.lipson@cornell.edu).

Trent McConaghy is Chief Scientific Officer at Solido Design Automation Inc., Canada, and recently completed his PhD at ESAT-MICAS, Katholieke Universiteit Leuven, Belgium (trent_mcconaghy@yahoo.com).

Jason H. Moore is the Frank Lane Research Scholar in Computational Genetics and Associate Professor of Genetics at Dartmouth Medical School, USA (Jason.H.Moore@Dartmouth.edu).

Tomoharu Nagao is a Professor of the Faculty of Environment and Information Sciences at Yokohama National University, Japan (nagao@ynu.ac.jp).

Una-May O'Reilly is a Principal Research Scientist in the Computer Science and Artificial Intelligence Laboratory at Massachusetts Institute of Technology, USA (unamay@csail.mit.edu).

Riccardo Poli is a Professor of Computer Science in the School of Computer Science and Electronic Engineering at the University of Essex, UK (rpoli@essex.ac.uk).

Rick Riolo is Director of the Computer Lab and Associate Research Scientist in the Center for the Study of Complex Systems at the University of Michigan, USA (rlriolo@umich.edu).

Brian J. Ross is a Professor of Computer Science at Brock University, St. Catharines, ON, Canada (bross@brocku.ca).

Michael Schmidt is a graduate student in computational biology at Cornell University, Ithaca, NY, USA (mds47@cornell.edu).

Shinichi Shirakawa is a Reseacher of the Graduate School of Environment and Information Sciences at Yokohama National University and a Research Fellow of the Japan Society for the Promotion of Science (shirakawa@nlab.sogo1.ynu.ac.jp).

Guido F. Smits is a Research and Development Leader in the New Products Group within the Core R&D Organization of the Dow Chemical Company, Belgium (gfsmits@dow.com).

Ekaterina Vladislavleva is a Lecturer in the Department of Mathematics and Computer Science at the University of Antwerp, Belgium (katya@vanillamodeling.com).

Garnett Wilson is a postdoctoral fellow in the Department of Computer Science at Memorial University of Newfoundland, St. John's, NL, Canada (gwilson@cs.mun.ca).

Preface

The work described in this book was first presented at the Seventh Workshop on Genetic Programming, Theory and Practice, organized by the Center for the Study of Complex Systems at the University of Michigan, Ann Arbor, 14-16 May 2009. The goal of this workshop series is to promote the exchange of research results and ideas between those who focus on Genetic Programming (GP) theory and those who focus on the application of GP to various real-world problems. In order to facilitate these interactions, the number of talks and participants was small and the time for discussion was large. Further, participants were asked to review each other's chapters *before* the workshop. Those reviewer comments, as well as discussion at the workshop, are reflected in the chapters presented in this book. Additional information about the workshop, addendums to chapters, and a site for continuing discussions by participants and by others can be found at http://cscs.umich.edu/gptp-workshops/gptp2009 .

We thank all the workshop participants for making the workshop an exciting and productive three days. In particular we thank the authors, without whose hard work and creative talents, neither the workshop nor the book would be possible. We also thank our keynote speaker Margaret J. Eppstein, Associate Professor in Computer Science and Director of the Complex Systems Center at the University of Vermont. Maggie's talk inspired a great deal of discussion among the participants throughout the workshop.

The workshop received support from these sources:

- The Center for the Study of Complex Systems (CSCS);

- John Koza, Third Millennium Venture Capital Limited;

- Michael Korns, Freeman Investment Management;

- Ying Becker, State Street Global Advisors, Boston, MA;

- Mark Kotanchek, Evolved Analytics;

- Jason Moore, Computational Genetics Laboratory at Dartmouth College;

- Conor Ryan, Biocomputing and Developmental Systems Group, Computer Science and Information Systems, University of Limerick; and

- William and Barbara Tozier, Vague Innovation LLC.

We thank all of our sponsors for their kind and generous support for the workshop and GP research in general.

A number of people made key contributions to running the workshop and assisting the attendees while they were in Ann Arbor. Foremost among them was Howard Oishi, who makes GPTP workshops run smoothly with his diligent efforts before, during and after the workshop itself. During the workshop Bill Worzel moderated some of the sessions. After the workshop, many people provided invaluable assistance in producing this book. Special thanks go to Patrick Hooper, Sarah Cherng and Laura Tomassi, who did a wonderful job working with the authors, editors and publishers to get the book completed very quickly. Thanks to William Tozier for assisting in copy-editing many of the chapters. Jennifer Maurer and Melissa Fearon provided invaluable editorial efforts, from the initial plans for the book through its final publication. Thanks also to Deborah Doherty of Springer for helping with various technical publishing issues. Finally, we thank Carl Simon, Director of CSCS, for his support for this endeavor from its very inception.

RICK RIOLO, UNA-MAY O'REILLY AND TRENT MCCONAGHY

Foreword

Genetic programming (GP) has emerged as an important computational methodology for solving complex problems in a diversity of disciplines. The recent success of GP can be attributed to the highly innovative computer scientists that have developed and extended the approach over the last 20 years and the numerous investigators and analysts that have been on the front line of applying these algorithms to difficult problems in their specific domains. This is all supported by a vibrant and highly collaborative research community that includes numerous GP conferences and workshops, numerous GP journals and book series and a wealth of open-source software and internet-based resources. The continued growth of this community speaks to the impact of GP and its important place in the future of computation and analysis.

An important challenge for any discipline is to foster close relationships and collaborations between those that develop computational theory and those that practice the art of computation. The annual Genetic Programming Theory and Practice (GPTP) Workshop organized by the Center for the Study of Complex Systems at the University of Michigan in Ann Arbor was first organized and held in 2003 to specifically bring theorists and practitioners together to communicate and collaborate in an effort to transform GP from an innovative algorithm to a general computational strategy for solving complex problems. The positive impact of this workshop on those that attend has been substantial. There are several reasons for this. First and foremost, there is an openness and general sense of collegiality that is lacking at many other scientific venues. The attendees are genuinely interested in sharing their cutting edge ideas for group discussion. This selflessness combined with enthusiastic discussion and participation creates an environment that significantly fosters innovation. Second, there is an incredible sense of memory from past GPTP workshops. Attendees take what they have learned from previous years and integrate the new ideas into their work. This cascading of ideas from year to year provides a rare opportunity to synthesize innovation. Third, each of the attendees is truly interested in solving complex problems in their respective domains. This is important because the investigators are open to any idea that helps solve the problem at hand. The lack of dogmatism and openness to change is refreshing and has made this workshop a huge success.

This was my fourth year at GPTP and each year has been a tremendous learning experience. Perhaps the single most eye-opening GPTP event was learning that Michael Korns of Korns Associates was successfully using GP to make real life financial investment decisions. This to me is the ultimate endorsement for the use of GP for solving problems such as security analysis and stock ranking. There was a sense at GPTP this year that GP has turned the corner from an innovative algorithm used only by computer scientists to a truly useful discovery tool used by many. In fact, William Tozier made the prediction that 2010 marks the beginning of a GP bubble characterized by an exponential shift from art to craft. That is, within the next few years we will increasingly see GP being used by domain-specific experts such as bioinformaticists, economists, engineers and meteorologists to solve hard problems. If this is true, the next 10 years of GPTP will be more important than ever.

I encourage you to read and digest each of the chapters in this volume and those from all the previous volumes. I promise you will come away with a notebook full of new ideas for using GP to solve your domain-specific problem.

Jason H. Moore, Ph.D.
Frank Lane Research Scholar in Computational Genetics
Professor of Genetics and Community and Family Medicine
Dartmouth Medical School, Lebanon, NH, USA
July, 2009

Chapter 1

GPTP 2009: AN EXAMPLE OF EVOLVABILITY

Una-May O'Reilly[1], Trent McConaghy[2] and Rick Riolo[3]

[1]*Computer Science and Artificial Intelligence Laboratory, Massachusetts Institute of Technology;* [2]*Solido Design Automation Inc., Canada;* [3]*Center for Study of Complex Systems, University of Michigan.*

Abstract

This introductory chapter gives a brief description of genetic programming (GP); summarizes current GP algorithm aims, issues, and progress; and finally reviews the contributions of this volume, which were presented at the GP Theory and Practice (GPTP) 2009 workshop.

This year marks a transition wherein the aims of GP algorithms – reasonable *resource* usage, high quality *results*, and *reliable* convergence – are being consistently realized on an impressive variety of "real-world" *applications* by skilled practitioners in the field. These aims have been realized due to GP researchers' growing collective understanding of the nature of GP problems which require search across spaces which are massive, multi-modal, and with poor locality, and how that relates to long-discussed GP issues such as bloat and premature convergence. New ways to use and extend GP for improved computational resource usage, quality of results, and reliability are appearing and gaining momentum. These include: reduced resource usage via rationally designed search spaces and fitness functions for specific applications such as induction of implicit functions or modeling stochastic processes arising from bio-networks; improved quality of results by explicitly targeting the interpretability or trustworthiness of the final results; and heightened reliability via consistently introducing new genetic material in a structured manner or via coevolution and teaming. These new developments highlight that GP's challenges have changed from simply "making it work" on smaller problems, to consistently and rapidly getting high-quality results on large real-world problems. GPTP 2009 was a forum to advance GP's state of the art and its contributions demonstrate how these aims can be met on a variety of difficult problems.

R. Riolo et al. (eds.), *Genetic Programming Theory and Practice VII,*
Genetic and Evolutionary Computation, DOI 10.1007/978-1-4419-1626-6_1,
© Springer Science + Business Media, LLC 2010

1

1.   The Workshop

In the beautiful, springtime charm of Ann Arbor, the seventh annual Genetic Programming Theory and Practice (GPTP) workshop was held at the University of Michigan campus from May 14-16, 2009.

We are grateful to all sponsors and acknowledge the importance of their contributions to such an intellectually productive and regular event. The workshop is generously founded and sponsored by the University of Michigan Center for the Study of Complex Systems (CSCS) and receives further funding from the following people and organizations: Michael Korns of Freeman Investment Management, Ying Becker of State Street Global Advisors, John Koza of Third Millenium, Bill and Barbara Tozier of Vague Innovation, Mark Kotanchek of Evolved Analytics, Jason Moore of the Computational Genetics Laboratory of Dartmouth College and Conor Ryan of the Biocomputing and Developmental Systems Group of the University of Limerick.

To make the results of the workshop useful to even a relative novice in the field of GP, we start the chapter with a brief overview of genetic programming (GP). Sections 3 and 4 describe current GP challenges and progress in GP. Sections 5 and 6 then organize and summarize the contributions of chapters in this volume from two perspectives: according to how contributed empirical research is informing GP practice, then according to the domains of application in which success through best practices has been reported. We conclude with a discussion of observations that emerged from the workshop and potential avenues of future work.

2.   A Brief Introduction to Genetic Programming

Genetic programming (GP) is a search and optimization technique for executable expressions that is modeled on natural evolution. Natural evolution is a powerful process that can be described by a few central, general mechanisms; for an introduction, see (Futuyma, 2009). A population is composed of organisms which can be distinguished in terms of how fit they are with respect to their environment. Over time, members of the population breed in frequency proportional to their fitness. The new offspring inherit the combined genetic material of their parents with some random variation, and may replace existing members of the population. The entire process is iterative, adaptive and open ended. GP and other evolutionary algorithms typically realize this central description of evolution, albeit in somewhat abstract forms. GP is a set of algorithms that mimic of survival of the fittest, genetic inheritance and variation, and that iterate over a "parent"population, selectively "breeding" them and replacing them with offspring.

Though in general evolution does not have a problem solving goal, GP is nonetheless used to solve problems arising in diverse domains ranging from engineering to art. This is accomplished by casting the organism in the population as a candidate program-like solution to the chosen problem. The organism is represented as a computationally executable expression (aka structure), which is considered its genome. When the expression is executed on some supplied set of inputs, it generates an output (and possibly some intermediate results). This execution behavior is akin to the natural phenotype. By comparing the expression's output to target output, a measure of the solution's quality is obtained. This is used as the "fitness" of an expression. The fact that the candidate solutions are computationally executable structures (expressions), not binary or continuous coded values which are elements of a solution, is what distinguishes GP from other evolutionary algorithms (O'Reilly and Angeline, 1997). GP expressions include LISP functions (Koza, 1992; Wu and Banzhaf, 1998), stack or register-based programs (Kantschik and Banzhaf, 2002; Spector and Robinson, 2002), graphs (Miller and Harding, 2008; Mattiussi and Floreano, 2007; Poli, 1997), programs derived from grammars (Ryan et al., 2002; Whigham, 1995; Gruau, 1993), and generative representations which evolve the grammar itself (Hemberg, 2001; Hornby and Pollack, 2002; O'Reilly and Hemberg, 2007). Key steps in applying GP to a specific problem collectively define its search space: the problem's candidate solutions are designed by choosing a representation; variation operators (mutation and crossover) are selected (or specialized); and a fitness function (objectives and constraints) which expresses the relative merits of partial and complete solutions is formulated.

3. Genetic Programming Challenges

Current challenges for GP include economizing on GP *resource* usage, ensuring better quality *results*, extracting more *reliable* convergence, or applying GP to a challenging *problem domain*.

Economic Resource Usage includes shorter runtime, reduced usage of processor(s), and reduced memory and disk usage. Achieving it has traditionally been a major issue for GP. A key reason is that GP search spaces are astronomically large, multi-modal, and have poor locality. Poor locality means that a small change in the individual's genotype often leads to large changes in the fitness, introducing additional difficulty into the search effort. For example, the GP "crossover" operation of swapping the subtrees of two parents might change the comparison of two elements from a "less than" relationship to an "equal to" relationship. This usually gives dramatically different behavior and fitness. To handle such challenging search spaces, significant exploration is needed (e.g. large population sizes). This entails intensive processing and memory needs. Exacerbating the problem, fitness evaluations (objectives and constraints) of real-world problems tend to be expensive. Finally, because GP expressions have variable length, there is a tendency for them to "bloat"— to grow rapidly without a corresponding increase in performance. Bloat can be a significant drain on available memory and CPU resources.

Ensuring Quality Results. The key question is: "can a GP result *be used* in the target application?" This *usability* criteria may be more difficult to attain than evident at first glance because the result may need to be human-interpretable, trustworthy, or predictive on dramatically different inputs—and attaining such qualities can be challenging. Ensuring quality results has always been perceived as an issue, but the goal is becoming more prominent as GP is being applied to more real world problems. Practitioners, not GP, are responsible for deploying a GP result in their application domain. This means that practitioners (and potentially their clients) must trust the results sufficiently to be comfortable using them. Human-interpretability (readability) of the result is a key factor in trust. This can be an issue when deployment of the result is expensive or risky, such as analog circuit design (McConaghy and Gielen, 2005); when customers' understanding of the solution is crucial such as portfolio strategies (Becker et al., 2007); when the result must be inspected or approved; or to gain acceptance of GP methodology, e.g. for use of symbolic regression for modeling industrial processes (Kordon et al., 2005).

Reliable convergence means that the GP run can be trusted to return reasonable results, without the practitioner having to worry about premature convergence or whether algorithm parameters like population size were set correctly. GP can fail to capably identify sub-solutions or partially correct solutions and thus be unable to successfully promote, combine and reuse them to generate good solutions with effective structure. The default approach has been to use the largest population size possible, subject to time and resource constraints. However, this invariably implies high resource usage, and still gives no guarantee of hitting useful results even if such results exist.

Problem domains present both opportunities and challenges for GP. Due to its evolution of executable expressions, GP has a far broader set of problem domain opportunities than other EAs and optimization approaches. But expression spaces are non-trivial to search across and selecting the expression primitives is non-trivial. GP representation and variation operator designs must generate syntactically valid expressions. But that's the easy part! The design must be done thoughtfully. Poor choices will lead to high resource usage and poor quality results. Thoughtfully designed representations and operators can lead to orders of magnitude difference in speed or quality; e.g. as shown in (Poli and Page, 2000; McConaghy et al., 2007).

4.   Progress in Genetic Programming

The field of GP is making progress in addressing the challenges described in the last section. Resource usage has been decreased by improved algorithm design, improved design of representation and operators in specific domains. Its impact has been lessened by Moore's Law and increasing availability of parallel computational approaches, meaning that computational resources become exponentially cheaper over time. Results quality has improved for the same reasons, and due to a new emphasis by GP practioners on getting interpretable or trustworthy results. Reliability has been improved via algorithm techniques that support continuous evolutionary improvement in a systematic or structured fashion. For example, by using hierarchical fair competition (HFC) and Age-Layered Population Structure (ALPS) (Hu et al., 2003; Hornby, 2006), the practitioner no longer has to "hope" that the algorithm isn't stuck. Finally, practice in thoughtful design of expression representation and genetic operators, for general and specific problem domains, has led to GP systems achieving human-competitive performance. In the 2008 ACM SIGEVO annual Genetic and Evolutionary Computation Conference (GECCO) Humies competition GP was used to generate a novel synthetic RTL benchmark circuit (Pecenka et al., 2008) and to evolve terms with special properties for a large finite algebra (Spector et al., 2008). GP has been adopted for industrial scale modeling, data analysis , design and discovery (Kotanchek et al., 2007; Terry et al., 2006). In GPTP, we have seen applications ranging from finance to biology to antennae: (Kim et al., 2008; Korns, 2007; Driscoll et al., 2003; Lohn et al., 2005).

Despite these achievements, GP's computer-based evolution does not demonstrate the potential associated with natural evolution, nor does it always satisfactorily solve important problems we might hope to use it on. Even when using best-practice approaches to manage challenges in resources, results, and reliability, the computational load may still be too excessive and the final results may be inadequate. To achieve success in a difficult problem domain takes a great deal of human effort toward thoughtful design of representations and operators.

In the two sections that follow we provide two perspectives on the GPTP workshop's intellectual contributions and on the trends we observed with respect to resource economization, results quality and reliable convergence. First, we review how the empirical research contributions have informed GP practice. Second, we review how GP has achieved successful application by the employment of "best practice" approaches.

5.   Empirical Research Informing Practice

The intent of GPTP has been to bring together practitioners and theorists in order to unify the challenges practitioners face with the questions theorists study.

As well, GPTP provides a focused group setting where practitioners describe to theorists their problems, their GP system, and the issues they have encountered. This helps the theorists to better appreciate the nature of a problem, examine the practical outcome of an approach and, with immediacy, suggest how and why something is happening and what could be done about it. With the theorists present, there is an opportunity for practitioners to ask them whether their theoretical findings are illustrated in some aspect of the practioners' implementations, and whether a theoretical result can shed light on a problem they face.

One of the trends our readers might notice this year is fewer "conventional" theory submissions. Conventional GP theory is difficult by nature of GP's variable length genome representation, executable phenotype character, and stochasticity. It does not proceed as quickly in terms of novelty and major impact as practice.

This year marks contributions that inform practice, yet are not strictly pen-and-paper theorems and calculations. With Chapter 6 as an example, test problems are chosen to appropriately challenge a proposed technique, and the analysis provides an understanding of how it works. GPTP workshop participants have embraced this sort of study because it focuses on one issue while elegantly eliminating unrelated complexity and confounding factors. The theory is in the form of techniques that are measurably better, more transparently analyzed and better explained and deduced. This kind of result promotes a general (applicable across GP problem domains) best-practice approach and has occurred in approaches to designing representations, operators or fitness functions, or approaches to enhanced reliability, quality of results, and resource usage. Development of a best-practice approach is arguably "empirical research" theory.

The contributions of this volume can be organized accordingly:

- One best-practice approach to enhanced reliability and results quality is to reduce and modulate selection pressure on a specific cohort of the population. Modulation could be applied to new genetic material, to genetic material that is not the norm, or to expressions that trade off strict functionality with solution complexity. One specific technique which is gaining common use is Age-Layered Population Structure (ALPS) (Hornby, 2006). It provides a structured way for new genetic material to continually enter the population, allowing new individuals time to improve before they have to compete against older, more fit individuals. Because this approach is capable and also makes a run's success less sensitive to population size, the number of research groups adopting ALPS or similar mechanisms is growing (Hu et al., 2003; McConaghy et al., 2007; Patel and Clack, 2007; Sun et al., 2007; Willis et al., 2008; Korns and Nunez, 2008; Kotanchek et al., 2008; Slany, 2009). In Chapter 6, Hornby presents the steady-state variant of the ALPS.

- With respect to best practices in design of GP fitness functions, there are four papers which describe how fitness function design was the key to make each respective problem tractable for GP. In Chapter 4, Kotanchek *et al.* describe the "Data Balancing " technique, which, among other benefits, can reduce the cost of symbolic regression fitness functions by reducing the training data to a smaller yet representative set. In Chapter 10, Ross and Imada describe multi-objective techniques that can exploit feature tests which provide different dynamical-system descriptions of stochastic, noisy time series. In Chapter 5, Schmidt and Lipson describe fitness functions that provide GP with sufficient selectivity to evolve implicit functions. In Chapter 9, Citi *et al.* describe a mapping from genotype to fitness function for Electroencephalography (EEG) signal classification.

- With respect to best practices in representation and operator design on specific problems, there are four papers. In Chapter 3, Doucette *et al.* describe how to decompose a high-dimensional classification problem into subproblems that can be solved by a *team* of GP individuals. In Chapter 7, McConaghy *et al.* describe a technique to transform a high-dimensional symbolic regression problem into a 1-dimensional problem. This dramatically simplifies the problem that GP has to solve. In Chapter 11, Shirakawa and Nagao describe a simple, easy-to-apply representation for evolving register-based software programs, a general-purpose problem-solving method. In Chapter 13, Korns describes an operator to create a conditional expression of two subtrees in a behavior preserving fashion which enhances locality, and he also describes operators to locally explore symbolic regression functional spaces.

- With respect to best practices in *general* design of representations and operators, there are three papers. In Chapter 2, Greene *et al.* apply a GP system with a hierarchical organization of search operator control: evolving a single scalar for mutation probability at the top level, and at successively lower levels, evolving more fine-grained control down to the level where individuals themselves are manipulated. In Chapter 8, Wilson and Banzhaf apply the "PAM DGP" approach which adapts the mapping from genotype to phenotype *during* evolution. In Chapter 12, Bongard describes a "functional crossover" operator which aims to enhance the locality of search by restricting allowable subtree swaps to subtrees with similar output ranges.

6. GPTP 2009: Application Successes Via Best Practices

As discussed earlier, progress in the field of GP can be characterized by GP successes in attacking challenging, industrial-strength, human-competitive problem domains. In attacking such problems and sharing their experiences at forums like GPTP, the best practices emerging from the successes are propagated and improved, leading to further successes in a variety of domains. This section organizes the papers in the volume according to problem domain. The problem domain groupings are: GP as a "discovery engine", time-domain modeling, high-dimensional symbolic regression and classification, financial applications, and design of graph-based structures. In this book, each domain is represented by multiple papers.

GP as a Discovery Engine

The fact that GP can return an *interpretable* expression has been recognized as important for a long time (Koza, 1992), due to its implications for scientific discovery and engineering analysis (Keijzer, 2002). This volume marks two important steps towards broad use of GP: (1) capturing a new, broad class of functional forms which underpin many types of scientific theories, and (2) an easy-to-use GP system with novel data analysis capabilities, built directly into a world-standard mathematical package.

In Chapter 5, Schmidt and Lipson describe how many types of scientific problems have an *implicit* functional form: the functions are not merely a mapping from input variables to output variables, but instead a system of equations describes relationships among variables. For example, $x^2 + y^2 = z^2$ describes the equation for a circle; there is no single output variable. The challenge in discovering such functional forms is that a traditional least-squares comparison between target values and actual values is not meaningful, because the true problem involves capturing a surface (manifold) embedded within a multi-dimensional space. Simplistic fitness functions do not provide enough differentiation among candidate functions, making it hard for GP to find good initial designs and even harder to refine designs. To solve the problem, the authors propose the use of local finite-element analysis to measure gradients in the manifold, and then apply a least-squares error measure to differences in gradients. The authors demonstrate how the approach can successfully capture the dynamics in classical pendulum physics models, as well as capturing dynamics of more complex pendulum models for which closed-form equations describing dynamics are unknown.

In Chapter 4, Kotanchek *et al.* describe the use of a highly visual, easy-to-use GP symbolic regression system that is embedded in Mathematica. The visual, exploratory nature of the system leads to a truly iterative, interactive means to use GP to explore data in real time. The paper describes techniques to detect outliers in either a data-based or model-based fashion, measure relative importance among variables, detect regions in an input-output mapping space which are over- or under-represented by the training data at hand and rank the importance of each datapoint. They also describe a "Data Balancing" technique which is a key tool for many of these techniques.

Time-Domain Modeling

This year GPTP had three papers addressing three very different problems related to time-series signals: EEG time series classification, modeling stochastic reaction processes, and time series with many state variables.

In Chapter 9, Citi *et al.* classify time domain Electroencephalography (EEG) signals with the aim of improving brain-computer interfaces (BCIs). The approach focuses on Event-Related Potentials (ERPs) which are well-defined events within EEG signals. EEG signals during an ERP have characteristic waveforms that provide the possibility of accurate classification. While ERPs have been explored extensively, an issue is the large number of human-in-the-loop training trials. In past work Citi *et al.* have partly alleviated this using a simple binning technique but this moved the issue to selection of the bin properties themselves. In this volume they use GP to evolve probabilistic membership functions for the bins which yields promising improvement in performance.

GP is well suited to learning models that synthesize reaction processes because a language from the domain and domain dependent operations on the data can be transfered quite directly to the GP function and terminal set. This is the case with pi-calculus and process algebra structures that model reactions of bio-networks. However when the reaction process is stochastic, rather than deterministic, a challenge arises in specifying fitness objectives. Just using the error between model prediction and real data fails to account for the statistical features in the time series that arise from stochastic timing and variance. In Chapter 10, Ross and Imada discuss and evaluate how different statistical feature tests can be used simultaneously via multi-objective GP.

In Chapter 12, building on past work, Bongard applies GP to reverse engineering a broad set of dynamical systems. Because the systems are deterministic, and known in advance, Bongard's measure of success is whether GP can successfully recapture the original differential equations. While the focus of the paper is a novel crossover operator, the paper reconfirms that GP is consistently effective at capturing the system dynamics for a variety of problems.

High-Dimensional Symbolic Regression and Classification

GP modeling approaches have typically attacked problems in the range of 1 to roughly 20 dimensions. But it is well known that the nature of a problem dramatically shifts past 20 dimensions, because every training data point is effectively "very far away" from every other datapoint (Hastie et al., 2001). Problems with 100, 1000, or 10,000 input dimensions have very different properties. In this book, we have three diverse problems with high-dimensional inputs: high-dimensional classifier design, high-dimensional regressor design and identification of key input variable interactions (i.e., epistasis).

In Chapter 2, Greene *et al.* tackle what they deem a "needle in a haystack" problem: 10,000+ input variables but only a few have an effect, and the variable interactions have more effect than single-variable effects. The combination of high dimensionality and epistasis makes the problem tough. The application is for DNA analysis, to identify which sequence variations predict disease risk in human populations. The authors approach the problem via a GP system with hierarchical operator control, and demonstrate that GP is indeed able to extract expressions of great use to geneticists.

In supervised problems, where a model has to be learned from a class of exemplars with a domain of attributes, GP has been successfully used to find a single binary classifier that automatically identifies the relevant subset of attributes. However, for domains of large numbers of attributes, it is more natural to consider grouping the exemplars and learning a set of cooperative classifiers that function in a non-overlapping way over the subgroups. Different (and overlapping) sets of attributes are appropriate to each classifier. In Chapter 3, Doucette *et al.* show how to extend GP so it can accomplish this kind of classification without requiring any preliminary *ad hoc* intervention to group the exemplars or attributes. Furthermore, the resulting classifier set is a product of a single GP run. This is more efficient than using multiple runs to incrementally learn binary classifiers for multiple classes.

In Chapter 7, McConaghy *et al.* describe a class of regression problems where the input variables cannot be heavily pruned to a few key variables, because most variables have some effect. This class of problems includes modeling the effect of manufacturing variation in analog electronic circuits. The paper shows that traditional GP approaches fail badly on such a problem, along with many other well-known regression and data-mining techniques. It then proposes a "latent variable" solution, in which the input vector is transformed to a scalar via a linear transformation, then the scalar is passed through a nonlinear GP expression to get the output. The process is repeated on the residuals. The challenge is in determining the linear transformation vectors, and the final expression; the result is demonstrated to have effective prediction on unseen inputs.

Financial Applications

GPTP has regularly reported contributions from the domain of finance (Zhou, 2003; Yu et al., 2004; Caplan and Becker, 2004; Becker et al., 2006; Korns, 2006; Becker et al., 2007; Korns, 2007; Chen et al., 2008; Korns and Nunez, 2008; Kim et al., 2008). This year marks two new papers advancing the state of the art of GP application in the area of finance.

Over a number of years, a large-scale, industrial-strength, symbolic regression-classification GP system used for trading models developed by Investment Science Corporation has been revised, extended and improved. It combines standard genetic programming with abstract expression grammars, particle swarm optimization, differential evolution, context aware crossover and age-layered populations. Chief designer, Michael Korns, now of Freeman Investment Management, has stated that its design and analysis has been guided by insights gained from theoretical findings presented at GPTP. He also credits observations and analyses arising during cross-connecting discussions by participants. Korn's contribution this year, in Chapter 13, targets techniques for improving symbolic regression in cases where the target expression contains conditionals. The system is enhanced with pessimal vertical slicing, splicing of uncorrelated champions via abstract conditional expressions, and abstract mutation and crossover.

GPTP also welcomes a new team working on financial modeling. In Chapter 8, co-authors Wilson and Banzhaf consider day trading where a hold, buy or sell decision is made for each security on a daily basis. Predictions of returns are based on the recent past. The system addressing the problem is a developmental co-evolutionary genetic programming approach called PAM DGP. It was demonstrably better than with standard linear genetic programming in terms of profitable buys, but not necessarily protective sells, in particular stock price trend scenarios.

Design of Graph-Based Structures

In Chapter 11, Shirakawa and Nagao propose a method called Graph Structured Program Evolution (GRAPE). GRAPE expressions are graphs capable of expressing conditional branches and loops, which can be executed in a register-based computational machine. Graphs are complemented with a data set for each of the multiple data types GRAPE supports. The genotype is a linear string of integers. GRAPE is evaluated on problems emblematic of iterative and conditional requirements: factorial, exponentiation, and list sorting. While it can solve these instances, challenges remain with the number of evaluations required and the complexity of the solutions.

In Chapter 6, Hornby describes the application of ALPS to two problems: evolving a NASA X-Band antenna, and evolving the structure of a table. The generative representation used for tables and antennae (GENRE) is general enough to handle graph-based structures. While the focus of the paper was ALPS itself, the improved quality of the results themselves is notable.

7.   Themes, Summary and Looking Forward

The consensus among the participants this year was that genetic programming has reached a watershed in terms of practicality for a well defined range of applications. With appropriate determination of algorithm techniques, representation, operators, and fitness function, GP has applicability to such challenging problems as scientific discovery and data modeling, time-domain modeling, high-dimensional symbolic regression and classification, financial applications, and design of graph-based structures. In this book, each domain is represented by two to three papers.

The participants expressed confidence, based on experience, that there are successful technical approaches that alleviate commonly occurring problems such as premature evolutionary convergence, bloat, and scalability. Employing these approaches has become "standard practice" among the participants, though they admittedly are experts. This convergence on approaches has arisen over the course of multiple annual GPTP meetings. Participants first proposed diverse solutions, some of which were stimulated by GP theory. Then, when brought into the GPTP forum, the solutions were collectively analyzed for key similarities, differences and capabilities. This enabled those present to arrive at an understanding of central principles and to unify their ideas into recognizable broader technical approaches with theoretical and empirical foundations. It is this process that has bolstered the participants' confidence in new techniques and from which best-practice approaches have emerged.

There will always be tradeoffs among results, resources, reliability and human up-front setup effort in designing representation, operators, and fitness functions. The workshop seems to herald a transition away from these largely-explored issues toward those that arise from using GP for other purposes. The new directions for GP that are exciting and present their unique challenges are, for example:

- What fundamental contributions will allow GP to be adopted into broader use beyond that of expert practitioners? For example, how can GP be scoped so that it becomes another standard, off-the-shelf method in the "toolboxes" of scientists and engineers around the world? Can GP follow in the same vein of linear programming? Can it follow the example of support vector machines and convex optimization methods? One challenge is in formulating GP so that it is easier to lay out a problem. Another is determining how, by default—without parameter tuning—GP can efficiently exploit specified resources to return results reliably.

- Success with GP often requires extensive human effort in capturing and embedding the domain knowledge. How can this up-front human effort be reduced while still achieving excellent results? Are there additional automatic ways to capture domain knowledge for input to GP systems?

How can a system of evolutionary modules interact to exploit domain knowledge?

- Scalability is always relative. GP has attacked fairly large problems, but how can GP be improved to solve problems that are substantially (10x, 100x, 10,000x or 1,000,000x) larger?

- How can the inherent distributed nature of GP be better and more easily exploited, especially in the current era of multicore CPUs, GPUs, and cloud computing? What are the implications of distribution in terms of algorithm dynamics and capabilities?

- How can GP be extended with more sophisticated evolutionary mechanisms such as co-evolution or speciation to improve its ability to generate solutions that exhibit complex properties such as module formation, module reuse and self-organization into hierarchies and high level systems?

- What other "uncrackable" problems await a creative GP approach?

These questions and their answers will provide the fodder for future GPTP workshops. We wish you many hours of stimulating reading of this volume's contributions.

References

Becker, Ying, Fei, Peng, and Lester, Anna M. (2006). Stock selection : An innovative application of genetic programming methodology. In Riolo, Rick L., Soule, Terence, and Worzel, Bill, editors, *Genetic Programming Theory and Practice IV*, volume 5 of *Genetic and Evolutionary Computation*, chapter 12, pages 315–334. Springer, Ann Arbor.

Becker, Ying L., Fox, Harold, and Fei, Peng (2007). An empirical study of multi-objective algorithms for stock ranking. In Riolo, Rick L., Soule, Terence, and Worzel, Bill, editors, *Genetic Programming Theory and Practice V*, Genetic and Evolutionary Computation, chapter 14, pages 241–262. Springer, Ann Arbor.

Caplan, Michael and Becker, Ying (2004). Lessons learned using genetic programming in a stock picking context. In O'Reilly, Una-May, Yu, Tina, Riolo, Rick L., and Worzel, Bill, editors, *Genetic Programming Theory and Practice II*, chapter 6, pages 87–102. Springer, Ann Arbor.

Chen, Shu-Heng, Zeng, Ren-Jie, and Yu, Tina (2008). Co-evolving trading strategies to analyze bounded rationality in double auction markets. In Riolo, Rick L., Soule, Terence, and Worzel, Bill, editors, *Genetic Programming Theory and Practice VI*, Genetic and Evolutionary Computation, chapter 13, pages 195–215. Springer, Ann Arbor.

Driscoll, Joseph A., Worzel, Bill, and MacLean, Duncan (2003). Classification of gene expression data with genetic programming. In Riolo, Rick L. and Worzel, Bill, editors, *Genetic Programming Theory and Practice*, chapter 3, pages 25–42. Kluwer.

Futuyma, Douglas (2009). *Evolution, Second Edition*. Sinauer Associates Inc.

Gruau, Frederic (1993). Cellular encoding as a graph grammar. *IEE Colloquium on Grammatical Inference: Theory, Applications and Alternatives*, (Digest No.092):17/1–10.

Hastie, Trevor, Tibshirani, Robert, Friedman, Jerome, and Franklin, James (2001). *The Elements of Statistical Learning*. Springer, New York, 2nd edition.

Hemberg, Martin (2001). GENR8 - A design tool for surface generation. Master's thesis, Department of Physical Resource Theory, Chalmers University, Sweden.

Hornby, Gregory S. (2006). ALPS: the age-layered population structure for reducing the problem of premature convergence. In Keijzer, Maarten, Cattolico, Mike, Arnold, Dirk, Babovic, Vladan, Blum, Christian, Bosman, Peter, Butz, Martin V., Coello Coello, Carlos, Dasgupta, Dipankar, Ficici, Sevan G., Foster, James, Hernandez-Aguirre, Arturo, Hornby, Greg, Lipson, Hod, McMinn, Phil, Moore, Jason, Raidl, Guenther, Rothlauf, Franz, Ryan, Conor, and Thierens, Dirk, editors, *GECCO 2006: Proceedings of the 8th annual conference on Genetic and evolutionary computation*, volume 1, pages 815–822, Seattle, Washington, USA. ACM Press.

Hornby, Gregory S. and Pollack, Jordan B. (2002). Creating high-level components with a generative representation for body-brain evolution. *Artificial Life*, 8(3):223–246.

Hu, Jianjun, Goodman, Erik D., and Seo, Kisung (2003). Continuous hierarchical fair competition model for sustainable innovation in genetic programming. In Riolo, Rick L. and Worzel, Bill, editors, *Genetic Programming Theory and Practice*, chapter 6, pages 81–98. Kluwer.

Kantschik, Wolfgang and Banzhaf, Wolfgang (2002). Linear-graph GP—A new GP structure. In Foster, James A., Lutton, Evelyne, Miller, Julian, Ryan, Conor, and Tettamanzi, Andrea G. B., editors, *Genetic Programming, Proceedings of the 5th European Conference, EuroGP 2002*, volume 2278 of *LNCS*, pages 83–92, Kinsale, Ireland. Springer-Verlag.

Keijzer, Maarten (2002). *Scientific Discovery using Genetic Programming*. PhD thesis, Danish Technical University, Lyngby, Denmark.

Kim, Minkyu, Becker, Ying L., Fei, Peng, and O'Reilly, Una-May (2008). Constrained genetic programming to minimize overfitting in stock selection. In Riolo, Rick L., Soule, Terence, and Worzel, Bill, editors, *Genetic Programming Theory and Practice VI*, Genetic and Evolutionary Computation, chapter 12, pages 179–195. Springer, Ann Arbor.

Kordon, Arthur, Castillo, Flor, Smits, Guido, and Kotanchek, Mark (2005). Application issues of genetic programming in industry. In Yu, Tina, Riolo, Rick L., and Worzel, Bill, editors, *Genetic Programming Theory and Practice III*, volume 9 of *Genetic Programming*, chapter 16, pages 241–258. Springer, Ann Arbor.

Korns, Michael F. (2006). Large-scale, time-constrained symbolic regression. In Riolo, Rick L., Soule, Terence, and Worzel, Bill, editors, *Genetic Programming Theory and Practice IV*, volume 5 of *Genetic and Evolutionary Computation*, chapter 16, pages –. Springer, Ann Arbor.

Korns, Michael F. (2007). Large-scale, time-constrained symbolic regression-classification. In Riolo, Rick L., Soule, Terence, and Worzel, Bill, editors, *Genetic Programming Theory and Practice V*, Genetic and Evolutionary Computation, chapter 4, pages 53–68. Springer, Ann Arbor.

Korns, Michael F. and Nunez, Loryfel (2008). Profiling symbolic regression-classification. In Riolo, Rick L., Soule, Terence, and Worzel, Bill, editors, *Genetic Programming Theory and Practice VI*, Genetic and Evolutionary Computation, chapter 14, pages 215–229. Springer, Ann Arbor.

Kotanchek, Mark, Smits, Guido, and Vladislavleva, Ekaterina (2007). Trustable symoblic regression models. In Riolo, Rick L., Soule, Terence, and Worzel, Bill, editors, *Genetic Programming Theory and Practice V*, Genetic and Evolutionary Computation, chapter 12, pages 203–222. Springer, Ann Arbor.

Kotanchek, Mark, Smits, Guido, and Vladislavleva, Ekaterina (2008). Exploiting trustable models via pareto GP for targeted data collection. In Riolo, Rick L., Soule, Terence, and Worzel, Bill, editors, *Genetic Programming Theory and Practice VI*, Genetic and Evolutionary Computation, chapter 10, pages 145–163. Springer, Ann Arbor.

Koza, John R. (1992). *Genetic Programming: On the Programming of Computers by Means of Natural Selection*. MIT Press, Cambridge, MA, USA.

Lohn, Jason D., Hornby, Gregory S., and Linden, Derek S. (2005). Rapid re-evolution of an X-band antenna for NASA's space technology 5 mission. In Yu, Tina, Riolo, Rick L., and Worzel, Bill, editors, *Genetic Programming Theory and Practice III*, volume 9 of *Genetic Programming*, chapter 5, pages 65–78. Springer, Ann Arbor.

Mattiussi, Claudio and Floreano, Dario (2007). Analog genetic encoding for the evolution of circuits and networks. *IEEE Transactions on Evolutionary Computation*, 11(5):596–607.

McConaghy, Trent and Gielen, Georges (2005). Genetic programming in industrial analog CAD: Applications and challenges. In Yu, Tina, Riolo, Rick L., and Worzel, Bill, editors, *Genetic Programming Theory and Practice III*, volume 9 of *Genetic Programming*, chapter 19, pages 291–306. Springer, Ann Arbor.

McConaghy, Trent, Palmers, Pieter, Gielen, Georges, and Steyaert, Michiel (2007). Genetic programming with reuse of known designs. In Riolo, Rick L., Soule, Terence, and Worzel, Bill, editors, *Genetic Programming Theory and Practice V*, Genetic and Evolutionary Computation, chapter 10, pages 161–186. Springer, Ann Arbor.

Miller, Julian Francis and Harding, Simon L. (2008). Cartesian genetic programming. In Ebner, Marc, Cattolico, Mike, van Hemert, Jano, Gustafson, Steven, Merkle, Laurence D., Moore, Frank W., Congdon, Clare Bates, Clack, Christopher D., Moore, Frank W., Rand, William, Ficici, Sevan G., Riolo, Rick, Bacardit, Jaume, Bernado-Mansilla, Ester, Butz, Martin V., Smith, Stephen L., Cagnoni, Stefano, Hauschild, Mark, Pelikan, Martin, and Sastry, Kumara, editors, *GECCO-2008 tutorials*, pages 2701–2726, Atlanta, GA, USA. ACM.

O'Reilly, Una-May and Angeline, Peter J. (1997). Trends in evolutionary methods for program induction. *Evolutionary Computation*, 5(2):v–ix.

O'Reilly, Una-May and Hemberg, Martin (2007). Integrating generative growth and evolutionary computation for form exploration. *Genetic Programming and Evolvable Machines*, 8(2):163–186. Special issue on developmental systems.

Patel, S. and Clack, C. D. (2007). ALPS evaluation in financial portfolio optimisation. In Srinivasan, Dipti and Wang, Lipo, editors, *2007 IEEE Congress on Evolutionary Computation*, pages 813–819, Singapore. IEEE Computational Intelligence Society, IEEE Press.

Pecenka, Tomas, Sekanina, Lukas, and Kotasek, Zdenek (2008). Evolution of synthetic rtl benchmark circuits with predeÞned testability. The 5th Annual (2008) ÒHUMIESÓ Awards.

Poli, Riccardo (1997). Evolution of graph-like programs with parallel distributed genetic programming. In Back, Thomas, editor, *Genetic Algorithms: Proceedings of the Seventh International Conference*, pages 346–353, Michigan State University, East Lansing, MI, USA. Morgan Kaufmann.

Poli, Riccardo and Page, Jonathan (2000). Solving high-order boolean parity problems with smooth uniform crossover, sub-machine code GP and demes. *Genetic Programming and Evolvable Machines*, 1(1/2):37–56.

Ryan, Conor, Nicolau, Miguel, and O'Neill, Michael (2002). Genetic algorithms using grammatical evolution. In Foster, James A., Lutton, Evelyne, Miller, Julian, Ryan, Conor, and Tettamanzi, Andrea G. B., editors, *Genetic Programming, Proceedings of the 5th European Conference, EuroGP 2002*, volume 2278 of *LNCS*, pages 278–287, Kinsale, Ireland. Springer-Verlag.

Slany, Karel (2009). Comparison of CGP and age-layered CGP performance in image operator evolution. In Vanneschi, Leonardo, Gustafson, Steven, Moraglio, Alberto, De Falco, Ivanoe, and Ebner, Marc, editors, *Proceedings of the 12th European Conference on Genetic Programming, EuroGP 2009*, volume 5481 of *LNCS*, pages 351–361, Tuebingen. Springer.

Spector, Lee, Clark, David M., Lindsay, Ian, Barr, Bradford, and Klein, Jon (2008). Genetic programming for finite algebras. In Keijzer, Maarten, Antoniol, Giuliano, Congdon, Clare Bates, Deb, Kalyanmoy, Doerr, Benjamin, Hansen, Nikolaus, Holmes, John H., Hornby, Gregory S., Howard, Daniel, Kennedy, James, Kumar, Sanjeev, Lobo, Fernando G., Miller, Julian Francis, Moore, Jason, Neumann, Frank, Pelikan, Martin, Pollack, Jordan, Sastry, Kumara, Stanley, Kenneth, Stoica, Adrian, Talbi, El-Ghazali, and Wegener, Ingo, editors, *GECCO '08: Proceedings of the 10th annual conference on Genetic and evolutionary computation*, pages 1291–1298, Atlanta, GA, USA. ACM.

Spector, Lee and Robinson, Alan (2002). Genetic programming and autoconstructive evolution with the push programming language. *Genetic Programming and Evolvable Machines*, 3(1):7–40.

Sun, Lei, Hines, Evor L., Green, Roger J., Leeson, Mark S., and Iliescu, D. Daciana (2007). Phase compensating dielectric lens design with genetic programming: Research articles. *International Journal of RF and Microwave Computer-Aided Engineering*, 17(5):493–504.

Terry, Michael A., Marcus, Jonathan, Farrell, Matthew, Aggarwal, Varun, and O'Reilly, Una-May (2006). GRACE: generative robust analog circuit exploration. In Rothlauf, Franz, Branke, Jurgen, Cagnoni, Stefano, Costa, Ernesto, Cotta, Carlos, Drechsler, Rolf, Lutton, Evelyne, Machado, Penousal, Moore, Jason H., Romero, Juan, Smith, George D., Squillero, Giovanni, and Takagi, Hideyuki, editors, *Applications of Evolutionary Computing, EvoWorkshops2006: EvoBIO, EvoCOMNET, EvoHOT, EvoIASP, EvoInteraction, EvoMUSART, EvoSTOC*, volume 3907 of *LNCS*, pages 332–343, Budapest. Springer Verlag.

Whigham, P. A. (1995). Grammatically-based genetic programming. In Rosca, Justinian P., editor, *Proceedings of the Workshop on Genetic Programming: From Theory to Real-World Applications*, pages 33–41, Tahoe City, California, USA.

Willis, Amy, Patel, Suneer, and Clack, Christopher D. (2008). GP age-layer and crossover effects in bid-offer spread prediction. In Keijzer, Maarten, Antoniol, Giuliano, Congdon, Clare Bates, Deb, Kalyanmoy, Doerr, Benjamin, Hansen, Nikolaus, Holmes, John H., Hornby, Gregory S., Howard, Daniel, Kennedy, James, Kumar, Sanjeev, Lobo, Fernando G., Miller, Julian Francis, Moore, Jason, Neumann, Frank, Pelikan, Martin, Pollack, Jordan, Sastry, Kumara, Stanley, Kenneth, Stoica, Adrian, Talbi, El-Ghazali, and Wegener, Ingo, editors, *GECCO '08: Proceedings of the 10th annual conference on Genetic and evolutionary computation*, pages 1665–1672, Atlanta, GA, USA. ACM.

Wu, Annie S. and Banzhaf, Wolfgang (1998). Introduction to the special issue: Variable-length representation and noncoding segments for evolutionary algorithms. *Evolutionary Computation*, 6(4):iii–vi.

Yu, Tina, Chen, Shu-Heng, and Kuo, Tzu-Wen (2004). Discovering financial technical trading rules using genetic programming with lambda abstraction. In O'Reilly, Una-May, Yu, Tina, Riolo, Rick L., and Worzel, Bill, editors, *Genetic Programming Theory and Practice II*, chapter 2, pages 11–30. Springer, Ann Arbor.

Zhou, Anjun (2003). Enhance emerging market stock selection. In Riolo, Rick L. and Worzel, Bill, editors, *Genetic Programming Theory and Practise*, chapter 18, pages 291–302. Kluwer.

Chapter 2

ENVIRONMENTAL SENSING OF EXPERT KNOWLEDGE IN A COMPUTATIONAL EVOLUTION SYSTEM FOR COMPLEX PROBLEM SOLVING IN HUMAN GENETICS

Casey S. Greene[1], Douglas P. Hill[1], Jason H. Moore[1]

[1] *Dartmouth College, One Medical Center Drive, HB7937, Lebanon, NH 03756 USA.*

Abstract   The relationship between interindividual variation in our genomes and variation in our susceptibility to common diseases is expected to be complex with multiple interacting genetic factors. A central goal of human genetics is to identify which DNA sequence variations predict disease risk in human populations. Our success in this endeavour will depend critically on the development and implementation of computational intelligence methods that are able to embrace, rather than ignore, the complexity of the genotype to phenotype relationship. To this end, we have developed a computational evolution system (CES) to discover genetic models of disease susceptibility involving complex relationships between DNA sequence variations. The CES approach is hierarchically organized and is capable of evolving operators of any arbitrary complexity. The ability to evolve operators distinguishes this approach from artificial evolution approaches using fixed operators such as mutation and recombination. Our previous studies have shown that a CES that can utilize expert knowledge about the problem in evolved operators significantly outperforms a CES unable to use this knowledge. This environmental sensing of external sources of biological or statistical knowledge is important when the search space is both rugged and large as in the genetic analysis of complex diseases. We show here that the CES is also capable of evolving operators which exploit one of several sources of expert knowledge to solve the problem. This is important for both the discovery of highly fit genetic models and because the particular source of expert knowledge used by evolved operators may provide additional information about the problem itself. This study brings us a step closer to a CES that can solve complex problems in human genetics in addition to discovering genetic models of disease.

Keywords: Genetic Epidemiology, Symbolic Discriminant Analysis, Epistasis

R. Riolo et al. (eds.), *Genetic Programming Theory and Practice VII*,
Genetic and Evolutionary Computation, DOI 10.1007/978-1-4419-1626-6_2,
© Springer Science + Business Media, LLC 2010

1.   Introduction

Computational Challenges in Human Genetics

Human genetics is quickly transitioning away from the study of single genes to evaluating the entire genome. This has been made possible by inexpensive new technologies for measuring 10^6 or more single nucleotide polymorphisms (SNPs) across the genome and emerging technologies that allow us to measure all 3×10^9 nucleotides. As this technological shift occurs, it is critical that the bioinformatics and data analysis approaches for sifting through these large volumes of data keep pace. The development of machine learning and data mining methods that are capable of identifying important patterns of genetic variations that are predictive of disease susceptibility will depend critically on the complexity of the mapping relationship between genotype and phenotype. For common human disease such as breast cancer and schizophrenia this mapping relationship is expected to be very complex with multiple interacting genetic and environmental factors (Moore, 2003; Moore and Williams, 2005; Thornton-Wells et al., 2004).

For the purposes of this paper we will focus exclusively on the SNP, which is a single nucleotide or point in the DNA sequence that differs among people. Most SNPs have two alleles (e.g. A or a) that combine in the diploid human genome in one of three possible genotypes (e.g. AA, Aa, aa). It is anticipated that at least one SNP occurs approximately every 100 nucleotides across the human genome making it the most common type of genetic variation. Some SNPs will be predictive of disease risk only in the context of other SNPs in the genome (Moore, 2003). This phenomenon has been referred to as epistasis for more than 100 years now (Bateson, 1909) and is the focus of the present study. The general challenge of modeling attribute interactions has been previously described (Freitas, 2001). The question we address is whether a computational evolution system is capable of identifying combinations of interacting SNPs when the fitness landscape is large and rugged. Our results reinforce the idea that expert knowledge is critical to solving these problems.

A Simple Example of the Concept Difficulty

Epistasis or gene-gene interaction can be defined as biological or statistical (Moore and Williams, 2005). Biological epistasis occurs at the cellular level when two or more biomolecules physically interact. In contrast, statistical epistasis occurs at the population level and is characterized by deviation from additivity in a linear mathematical model. Consider the following simple example of statistical epistasis in the form of a penetrance function. Penetrance is simply the probability (P) of disease (D) given a particular combination of genotypes (G) that was inherited (i.e. $P[D|G]$). A single genotype is deter-

Table 2-1. Penetrance values for genotypes from two SNPs.

	AA (0.25)	Aa (0.50)	aa (0.25)
BB (0.25)	0	1	0
Bb (0.50)	1	0	1
bb (0.25)	0	1	0

mined by one allele (i.e. a specific DNA sequence state) inherited from the mother and one allele inherited from the father. For most single nucleotide polymorphisms or SNPs, only two alleles (encoded by A or a) exist in the biological population. Therefore, because the order of the alleles is unimportant, a genotype can have one of three values: AA, Aa or aa. The model illustrated in Table 2-1 is an extreme example of epistasis. Let's assume that genotypes AA, aa, BB, and bb have population frequencies of 0.25 while genotypes Aa and Bb have frequencies of 0.5 (values in parentheses in Table 2-1). What makes this model interesting is that disease risk is dependent on the particular combination of genotypes inherited. Individuals have a very high risk of disease if they inherit Aa or Bb but not both (i.e. the Exclusive–OR function). The penetrance for each individual genotype in this model is 0.5 and is computed by summing the products of the genotype frequencies and penetrance values. Thus, in this model there is no difference in disease risk for each single genotype as specified by the single-genotype penetrance values. This model was first described by Li and Reich (Li and Reich, 2000). Heritability, or the size of the genetic effect, is a function of these penetrance values. In this model, the heritability is 1.0, the maximum possible, because the probability of disease is completely determined by the genotypes at these two DNA sequence variations. All the heritability in this model is due to epistasis. As Freitas reviews, this general class of problems has high concept difficulty (Freitas, 2002).

Artificial and Computational Evolution

Numerous machine learning and data mining methods have been developed and applied to the detection of gene-gene interactions in population-based studies of human disease. These include, for example, traditional methods such as neural networks (Lucek and Ott, 1997) and novel methods such as multifactor dimensionality reduction (Ritchie et al., 2001). Evolutionary computing methods such as genetic programming (GP) have been applied to both attribute selection and model discovery in the domain of human genetics. For example, Ritchie et al (Ritchie et al., 2003) used GP to optimize both the weights and the architecture of a neural network for modeling the relationship between genotype and phenotype in the presence of gene-gene interactions. More recently, GP has been successfully used for both attribute selection (Moore and White,

2006a; Moore and White, 2007a; Moore, 2007; Greene et al., 2007) and genetic model discovery (Moore et al., 2007).

Genetic programming is an automated computational discovery tool that is inspired by Darwinian evolution and natural selection (Banzhaf et al., 1998a; Koza, 1992; Koza, 1994; Koza et al., 1999; Koza et al., 2003; Langdon, 1998; Langdon and Poli, 2002). The goal of GP is to evolve computer programs to solve problems. This is accomplished by first generating random computer programs composed of the building blocks needed to solve or approximate a solution. Each randomly generated program is evaluated and the good programs are selected and recombined to form new computer programs. This process of selection based on fitness and recombination to generate variability is repeated until a best program or set of programs is identified.

Genetic programming and its many variations have been applied successfully to a wide range of different problems including data mining and knowledge discovery (e.g. (Freitas, 2002)) and bioinformatics (e.g. (Fogel and Corne, 2003)). Despite the many successes, there are a large number of challenges that GP practitioners and theorists must address before this general computational discovery tool becomes one of several tools that a modern problem solver calls upon (Yu et al., 2006). Spector, as part of an essay regarding the roles of theory and practice in genetic programming, discusses the push towards biology by GP practitioners (Spector, 2003). Banzhaf et al. propose that overly simplistic and abstracted artificial evolution (AE) methods such as GP need to be transformed into computational evolution (CE) systems that more closely resemble the complexity of real biological and evolutionary systems (Banzhaf et al., 2006). Evolution by natural selection solves problems by building complexity. We are thus interested in testing the working hypothesis that a GP-based genetic analysis system will find better solutions faster if it is implemented as a CE system that can evolve a variety of complex operators that in turn generate variability in solutions. This is in contrast to an AE system that uses a fixed set of operators.

Research Questions Addressed and Overview

We have previously developed a prototype CE system and have shown that it is capable of evolving complex operators for problem solving in human genetics (Moore et al., 2008b). We have also previously extended and evaluated this new open-ended computational evolution system for the detection and characterization of epistasis or gene-gene interactions that are associated with risk of human disease (Moore et al., 2008a). New features in this previous study included simpler operator building blocks, list-based solutions with stack-based evaluation and an attribute archive that provides the system with a feedback loop between the population of solutions and the solution operators. These recently added features are consistent with the idea of transforming an AE system to a CE system. This study showed that a CE system that could exploit expert knowledge performed better than a system that could not. This provides the basis for the present study that addresses the question of whether the CE system is capable of identifying and exploiting a good source of expert knowledge from among several other randomly generated sources.

2.   A Computational Evolution System

Our primary goal was to develop, extend and evaluate a computational evolution system that is capable of open-ended evolution for bioinformatics problem-solving in the domain of human genetics. Figure 2-1 gives a graphical overview of our hierarchically-organized and spatially-extended GP system that is capable of open-ended computational evolution. At the bottom layer of this hierarchy is a grid of solutions. At the second layer of the hierarchy is a grid of operators of any size and complexity that are capable of modifying the solutions (i.e. solution operators). At the third layer is a grid of mutation operators that are capable of modifying the solution operators. At the highest level of the hierarchy is the mutation frequency that determines the rate at which operators are mutated. An attribute archive provides a feedback loop between the solutions and the solution operators. One or more sources of expert knowledge is also provided to the system for environmental sensing. The details of the experimental design used to evaluate this system are described in Section 3.

Problem Solutions: Their Representation, Fitness Evaluation and Reproduction

The goal of a classifier is to accept as input two or more discrete attributes (i.e. SNPs) and produce a discrete output that can be used to assign class (i.e. healthy or sick). Here, we used symbolic discriminant analysis or SDA as our classifier. The SDA method (Moore et al., 2002) has been described previously for this problem domain (Moore et al., 2008b; Moore et al., 2007; Moore and White, 2007a). SDA models consist of a set of attributes and constants as input and a set of mathematical functions that produce for each instance in the data set a score called a symbolic discriminant score. Here, our SDA function set was $+, -, *, /, \%, <, <=, >, >=, ==, ! =$ where the $\%$ operator is a mod operation and $/$ is a protected division. The SDA models are represented as a list of expressions here instead of as expression trees as has been used in the past to facilitate stack-based evaluation of the classifiers and to facilitate their representation in text files. This is similar to the GP implementation using arrays and stack as described by Keith and Martin (Keith and Martin, 1994), Perkis (Perkis, 1994), and Banzaf et al. (Banzhaf et al., 1998b).

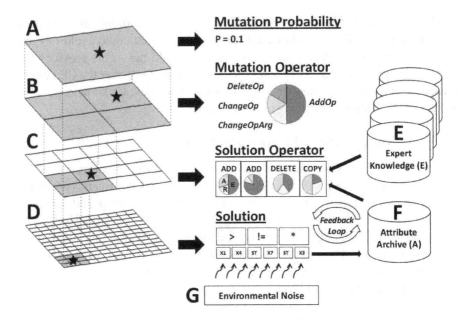

Figure 2-1. Visual overview of our computational evolution system for discovering symbolic discriminant functions that differentiate disease subjects from healthy subjects using information about single nucleotide polymorphisms (SNPs). The hierarchical structure is shown on the left while some specific examples at each level are shown in the middle. At the lowest level (D) is a grid of solutions. Each solution consists of a list of functions and their arguments (e.g. X1 is an attribute) that are evaluated using a stack (denoted by ST in the solution). The next level up (C) is a grid of solution operators that each consists of some combination of the ADD, DELETE and COPY functions each with their respective set of probabilities that define whether expert knowledge (E) or the archive (F, denoted by A in the probability pie) are used instead of a random generator (denoted by R in the probability pie). The attribute archive (F) is derived from the frequency with which each attribute occurs among solutions in the population. Finally, environmental noise (G) perturbs the data in small ways to prevent over fitting. The top two levels of the hierarchy (A and B) exist to generate variability in the operators that modify the solutions. This system allows operators of arbitrary complexity to modify solutions. Note that we used 18×18 grids of 324 solutions in the present study. A 12×12 grid is shown here as an example.

Classification of instances into one of the two classes requires a decision rule that is based on the symbolic discriminant score. Thus, for any given symbolic discriminant score (S_{ij}) in the ith class and for the jth instance, a decision rule can be formed such that if $S_{ij} > S_o$ then assign the instance to one class and if $S_{ij} <= S_o$ then assign the observation to the other class. When the prior probability that an instance belongs to one class is equal to the probability that it belongs to the other class, S_o can be defined as the arithmetic mean of the median symbolic discriminant scores from each of the two classes. This is the classification rule we used in the present study and is consistent with previous work in this domain (Moore et al., 2008b; Moore et al., 2007; Moore and White, 2007a). Using this decision rule, the classification accuracy for a particular discriminant function can be estimated from the observed data. Here, accuracy is defined as (TP + TN)/(TP + TN + FP + FN) where TP are true positives (TP), TN are true negatives, FP are false positives, and FN are false negatives. We used accuracy as the fitness measure for SDA solutions as has been described previously but lightly weight it such that for solutions with equivalent accuracy, ones with shorter genome sizes are preferable (Moore et al., 2008b; Moore et al., 2007; Moore and White, 2007a).

All SDA solutions in a population are organized on a toroidal grid with specific X and Y coordinates (see example in Figure 2-1). As such, they resemble previous work on cellular genetic programming (Folino et al., 1999). In the present study we used a grid size of 18×18. Reproduction of solutions in the population is handled in a spatial manner. Each solution is considered for reproduction in the context of its Moore neighborhood using an elitist strategy. That is, each solution in question will compete with its eight neighbors and be replaced in the next generation by the neighbor with the highest fitness. This combines ideas of tournament selection that is common in GP with a set of solutions on a grid. Variability in solutions is generated using hierarchically organized operators. This is described below.

Operators for Computational Evolution: Generating Solution Variability

Traditional artificial evolution approaches such as GP use a fixed set of operators that include mutation and recombination, for example. The goal of developing a computational evolution system was to provide building blocks (i.e. simple functions) for operators that could be combined to create new operators. We started with the following three basic operator building blocks. The first operator building block, ADD, adds a new function and its arguments to the list of functions and arguments that comprise a solution. The second operator building block, DELETE, deletes a function from the list of functions. The third operator, COPY, copies one function from the list of functions in the Moore neighborhood. These operators can combine in any number and order to generate solution operators of arbitrary complexity. The mutation operators described below increase or decrease the size and content of the solution operators.

Each of the operator building blocks has a vector of three probabilities associated with it. The first number specifies the probability that the function that is added, deleted or copied to a solution is determined stochastically. The second specifies the probability that the function that is added, deleted or copied to a solution is determined according to an archive of attributes that is ranked according to the frequency that they occur in the population of solutions (see below). The third specifies the probability that the function that is added, deleted or copied to a solution is determined according to ReliefF scores for the attributes (see below). The ability to use expert knowledge (i.e. environmental sensing) is important in this domain. For example, pre-processed ReliefF scores have been shown to improve the performance of GP as a wrapper in this domain when used in a multiobjective fitness function (Moore and White, 2007a), when used to guide recombination (Moore and White, 2006a) and when used to guide mutation (Greene et al., 2007). This is consistent with Goldberg's ideas about exploiting good building blocks in competent genetic algorithms (Goldberg, 2002) and provides a source of complexity as recommended by Banzhaf et al. (Banzhaf et al., 2006). For example, the use of the archive creates a feedback loop between the solutions and the solution operators. In the present study we evaluated whether this system is able to identify a good source of expert knowledge from among five candidates. Here, each building block had six probabilities associated with it, one for each of the five sources of expert knowledge and one for the stochastic element. We did not use the archive in this study given the focus was on understanding the role of multiple sources of expert knowledge.

As with the solutions, each operator is organized on a toroidal grid with a specific X and Y coordinate. We assigned each operator to a set of solutions. This allows for averaging an operator's positive or negative effects on multiple solutions. In this study, we assigned each operator to a 3×3 grid of nine solutions. Thus, the population of solution operators is organized in a 6×6 grid when an 18×18 grid is used for the solutions and 12×12 when a 36×36 grid is used for the solutions. The assignment of fitness to solution operators is a variant of Edmond's Meta-GP framework (Edmonds, 1998; Edmonds, 2001). To assign fitness to an operator, we first identify the two solutions under the operator's control that show the most positive change in fitness, on the basis that an operator is more fit if it greatly increases fitness in a few solutions, even if it reduces fitness in many cases. We average these changes in fitness and this becomes the fitness of the operator. If the operator has not been modified in this generation, we smooth its fitness by adding half of the previous generation's fitness and multiplying by two thirds, so the fitness scale is comparable between new and unchanged operators.

Mutation of Operators for Computational Evolution: Generating Operator Variability

An important goal for the computational evolution system is the ability to generate variability in the operators that modify solutions. To accomplish this goal we previously developed an additional level in the hierarchy (Figure 2-1) with mutation operators that specifically alter the operators described above. We defined four different fixed mutation operators that are each assigned to a 2×2 grid of solution operators. Solution operators can be modified in the following four ways. First, an operator can have a specific operator building block deleted (DeleteOperator). Second, an operator can have a specific operator building block added (AddOperator). Third, an operator can have a specific operator building block changed (ChangeOperator). Finally, an operator can have its probabilities changed (ChangeOperatorArguments). In this study, we initialized the probabilities with which each the these mutation operators are used to 0.25. These are randomly regenerated at a frequency equal to the overall mutation probability (see below) and their fitness is determined by the change in fitness of the solution operators that they act on.

Mutation Frequency

The top level of the computational evolution system hierarchy (see Figure 2-1) is the mutation frequency that controls the probability that one of the four mutation sets in the next level down will mutate a given solution operator two levels down. In the present study we fixed this to 0.1. In the future this will be an evolvable parameter. This frequency does not control the frequency with which a solution operator modifies a solution. That is controlled by the operator when it specifies which solution(s) it will modify.

Environmental Sensing Using an Archive

Previous studies have demonstrated the utility of archiving GP results for reuse (Vladislavleva et al., 2007). We have previously implemented an archive that ranks the attributes by the frequency with which they appear in solutions from the population. These are ranked by their frequency and then used by the ADD, DELETE and COPY operators to decide what gets added, deleted or copied. We have previously used a cumulative archive that updates the previous results each generation. The archive is an important part of the complexity of the CE system because it provides a feedback loop between the solutions and the solution operators. The archive was not used in the present study to allow us to focus on the use of multiple source of expert knowledge.

Environmental Sensing Using Expert Knowledge

As mentioned above, the use of expert knowledge is important for the application of GP strategies to solving complex problems in human genetics. Here, we used pre-processed ReliefF scores for all of the attributes in the dataset as a source of statistical knowledge for the analysis. Kira and Rendell developed the Relief algorithm that is capable of detecting attribute dependencies (Kira and Rendell, 1992). Relief estimates the quality of attributes through a type of nearest neighbor algorithm that selects neighbors (instances) from the same class and from the different class based on the vector of values across attributes. Weights (W) or quality estimates for each attribute (A) are estimated based on whether the nearest neighbor (nearest hit, H) of a randomly selected instance (R) from the same class and the nearest neighbor from the other class (nearest miss, M) have the same or different values. This process of adjusting weights is repeated for m instances. The algorithm produces weights for each attribute ranging from -1 (worst) to +1 (best). Kononenko improved upon Relief by choosing n nearest neighbors instead of just one (Kononenko, 1994). This new ReliefF algorithm has been shown to be more robust to noisy attributes and is widely used in data mining applications. We have developed a modified ReliefF algorithm for the domain of human genetics called Tuned ReliefF (TuRF). We have previously shown that TuRF is significantly better than ReliefF in this domain (Moore and White, 2007b). The TuRF algorithm systematically removes attributes that have low quality estimates so that the ReliefF values if the remaining attributes can be re-estimated. We applied TuRF as described by Moore and White (Moore and White, 2007b) to the data set analyzed and provided the results to the CE system as expert knowledge that can then used by the ADD, DELETE and COPY operators to decide what gets added, deleted or copied (Moore et al., 2008a). We also provided four random permutations of the TuRF knowledge as additional null sources of knowledge to assess whether the CE system could identify and exploit the correct source.

Implementation

The computational evolution system described above was programmed entirely in C++. A single run of the system with a population of 324 solutions on a 18×18 grid for 1000 generations took approximately 15 minutes on a 3.0 GHz AMD Opteron processor. Multiple runs for the experiments described below were carried out in parallel using 100 or more processors.

3.   Experimental Design and Data Analysis

Our goal was to provide an evaluation of the CE system described above using a repeated measures experimental design. The central question addressed in this study is whether the CE system has the ability to identify and exploit the correct source of expert knowledge out of a total of five. Here, the probability of a given operator such as ADD using any given source of knowledge is initialized randomly for the first generation. The probability associated with each source of knowledge can change over time based on its fitness reward that is assessed by the fitness change in the solutions that operator operates on.

Here, we ran the CE system for a total of 1000 generations with a solution grid size of 18×18. A total of 100 runs each with different random seeds

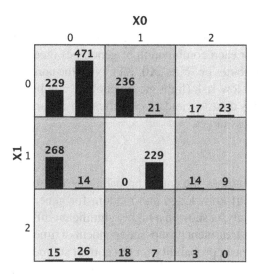

Figure 2-2. Distribution of healthy controls (left bars) and diseased cases (right bars) for each combination of genotypes (coded 0, 1 and 2) for the two functional attributes or SNPs (X0 and X1). Note the nonlinear pattern of high-risk (dark grey) and low-risk (light grey) genotype combinations that is indicative of a nonlinear interaction.

were performed on the simulated data described below. For each of 100 runs we recorded the average probability for each source of knowledge at generation zero and 1000. We used a repeated measures analysis of variance (RMANOVA) to test three hypotheses about the results. First, we tested the null hypothesis that the mean probabilities are the same for each source of expert knowledge (i.e. the treatment effect). Second, we tested the null hypothesis that the vector or profile of mean probabilities across generations zero and 1000 are flat for each source of expert knowledge (i.e. the time effect). Third, we tested the null hypothesis that the mean probabilities don't change across generations in a manner that is dependent on the particular source of knowledge (i.e. treatment by time interaction). Treatment, time and treatment by time effects were considered statistically significant at the 0.05 level. Following the RMANOVA analysis we performed a post-hoc analysis of the time effect within each treatment using a paired t-test. Specifically, we tested the null hypothesis that difference in means between generation zero and generation 1000 is zero within each source of expert knowledge or the random element. Specific contrasts were considered statistically significant at the 0.008 level. The is a Bonferroni-corrected level of significance that accounts for the multiple statistical tests that were performed across contrasts.

We used a simulated data set consisting of 1000 total attributes (SNPs) and 1600 instances (800 cases and 800 controls). Two of the 1000 SNPs are associated with disease class through a nonlinear interaction as described in the

introduction. This dataset has been previously described (Velez et al., 2007).
Figure 2-2 illustrates the distribution of healthy controls (left bars) and diseased
cases (right bars) for each combination of genotypes (coded 0, 1 and 2) for the
three functional attributes or SNPs (X0, X1). Note the nonlinear pattern of high-
risk (dark grey) and low-risk (light grey) genotype combinations. The optimal
classification of this dataset yields a classification accuracy of approximately
0.8. This is the fitness target.

4.   Results

Figure 2-3 summarizes the mean probabilities for selecting attributes for
each source of expert knowledge and random for generation zero and 1000.
The RMANOVA analysis showed a highly significant difference in mean probabilities between the treatment groups independent of time ($P < 0.001$). Figure
2-3 shows that the mean probability for the correct source of expert knowledge
is higher than the others. We also found no overall time or generation effect
independent of knowledge source ($P > 0.1$). This is consistent with what
we see in Figure 2-3. On average there is no generation effect. Finally, the
RMANOVA indicated a highly significant source of knowledge by generation
interaction ($P < 0.001$). Figure 2-3 illustrates this very clearly with the mean

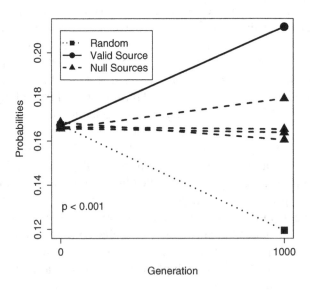

Figure 2-3. The mean probabilities of operators using expert knowledge increases from the
beginning to the end of the run. The probabilities of operators acting randomly decreases. The
probabilities of the null sources do not significantly change.

probability increasing from generation zero to 1000 for the correct source of expert knowledge while staying the same for other null sources of knowledge and decreasing with the random element. The different slopes of these lines accounts for the statistically significant interaction. We used a paired t-test with correction for multiple testing to carry out a post-hoc analysis to verify that the probabilities for the correct source of expert knowledge do in fact increase. We found that statistically significant evidence to reject the null hypothesis that the difference in mean probabilities for generation zero and 1000 are zero ($P \leq 0.001$). This same null hypothesis for each of the null sources of knowledge were not rejected ($P > 0.1$). Interestingly, the probabilities for the random element significantly decrease ($P < 0.001$). These results provide significant evidence in support of our working hypothesis that the CE system is capable of identifying and exploiting an important source of expert knowledge in the context of multiple other null sources.

Figure 2-4 illustrates the results from a single run of the CE system for 1000 generations. Plotted in this figure is the maximum fitness (classifier accuracy) for each generation. Note the first major increase in fitness is associated with the best model obtaining the correct two attributes while the second major increase

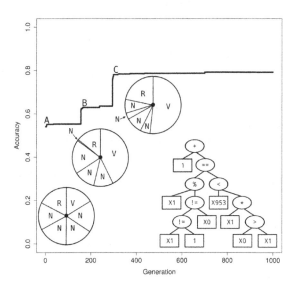

Figure 2-4. The line shows the fitness of the best solution from generation 1 to 1000. The pies, in ascending order, show the average probabilities associated with the different sources of expert knowledge at the initial generation (Point A) as well as generations 165 (Point B) and 310 (Point C). The probabilities are shown for Random (R), the four null sources (N) and the valid source of knowledge (V). The tree representation of the final solution is shown in the bottom right.

is associated with obtaining a set of functions that approximates the optimal solution to the problem. Also shown in Figure 2-4 are the average probabilities tied to the operator that operated on the best solution. Note that in generation zero the probabilities start out approximately equal. By the first increase in fitness the probability of picking attributes based on the good source of expert knowledge has increased to approximately 0.5. This illustrates the ability of the CE system to identify and exploit a particular source of knowledge. The solution shown in Figure 2-4 illustrates an example solution to the problem that was discovered by the CE system. The CE system was able to discover an optimal or near optimal solution to this problem in each of the 100 runs.

5.   Discussion and Conclusions

Human genetics is transitioning away from the study of single genes to the study of the entire genome as a risk factor for common human diseases (Moore, 2009). This means we need to prepare the next generation of computational intelligence approaches that are able to model multiple interacting genetic risk factors simultaneously in data derived from large epidemiological and genetic studies. We present here a computational evolution (CE) approach to this problem that builds on the successes and failures of artificial evolution (e.g. genetic programming) to provide a comprehensive framework for genetic analysis. We have previously shown that adding complexity to these algorithms improves their ability to identify complex genetic models (Moore et al., 2008b; Moore et al., 2008a). This is consistent with our previous work showing how expert knowledge can greatly improve the performance of these algorithms (Moore and White, 2007a; Moore and White, 2006b; Greene et al., 2007). The goal of this study was to determine whether a CE system could learn to recognize and exploit a good source of expert knowledge from among several different options. Our results demonstrate that the CE system does indeed learn to use a valid source of expert knowledge to discover optimal solutions in this domain.

The ability of the system to identify and exploit a particular source of expert knowledge to solve a complex problem is important. However, equally exciting is the possibility of inferring from the behavior of the evolved system what source(s) of expert knowledge seems to be important. The results summarized in Figure 2-3 show the change in probabilities for each source of knowledge shift from being approximately equal to favoring one particular source of knowledge. This is important because that source of knowledge may tell us something about the problem itself. For example, let's assume that each source of knowledge was biological in nature representing perhaps biochemical pathways, gene ontology, chromosomal location, protein-protein interactions and prior knowledge derived from microarray experiments. Preferential use of microarray knowledge may tell us that the DNA sequence variations in the best model might have something to do with gene expression. This in turn provide an important basis for interpreting the model and understanding why it is important. One ultimate goal of these studies is to understand why particular genetic factors increase or decrease risk. A biological understanding may play an important role in developing interventions and treatments for the disease. The present study opens the door to using multiple sources of biological and statistical knowledge for solving real world genetic analysis problems.

An important future goal will be to explore how multiple sources of knowledge might be used together. Could the CE system learn to use two or three sources of knowledge that each provide complementary information? How will we need to modify the operators to effectively use joint information? How will the sources of expert knowledge interact with the archive? This last point will be particularly interesting to explore. We turned the archive off in the present study so as not to confound the question being addressed about multiple sources of expert knowledge. However, a logical next step will be to turn this back on to determine whether there is a benefit to having both working together. It is reasonable to assume that the expert knowledge will be important early in the process when it is important to find the functional attributes. Once they are found and rewarded these important building blocks will spread throughout the population and then become part of the archive. The relative weighting of the attributes in the archive could be greater than that provided by the expert knowledge. If this is the case, one might predict that archive would take over and become more important than the source of expert knowledge. These are all interesting new directions to pursue. These questions and others will need to be addressed before this system is ready for the routine analysis of real data.

Acknowledgment

This work was supported by National Institutes of Health (USA) grants LM009012 and AI59694. We thank the attendees of the 2008 Genetic Programming Theory and Practice (GPTP) Workshop for their insightful ideas about computational evolution.

References

Banzhaf, W., Beslon, G., Christensen, S., Foster, J. A., Kepes, F., Lefort, V., Miller, J., Radman, M., and Ramsden, J. J. (2006). From artificial evolution to computational evolution: a research agenda. *Nature Reviews Genetics*, 7:729–735.

Banzhaf, Wolfgang, Nordin, Peter, Keller, Robert E., and Francone, Frank D. (1998a). *Genetic Programming – An Introduction; On the Automatic Evolution of Computer Programs and its Applications*. Morgan Kaufmann, San Francisco, CA, USA.

Banzhaf, Wolfgang, Poli, Riccardo, Schoenauer, Marc, and Fogarty, Terence C., editors (1998b). *Genetic Programming*, volume 1391 of *LNCS*, Paris. Springer-Verlag.

Bateson, W. (1909). *Mendel's Principles of Heredity*. Cambridge University Press, Cambridge.

Edmonds, Bruce (1998). Meta-genetic programming: Co-evolving the operators of variation. CPM Report 98-32, Centre for Policy Modelling, Manchester Metropolitan University, UK, Aytoun St., Manchester, M1 3GH. UK.

Edmonds, Bruce (2001). Meta-genetic programming: Co-evolving the operators of variation. *Elektrik*, 9(1):13–29. Turkish Journal Electrical Engineering and Computer Sciences.

Fogel, G.B. and Corne, D.W. (2003). *Evolutionary Computation in Bioinformatics*. Morgan Kaufmann Publishers.

Folino, Gianluigi, Pizzuti, Clara, and Spezzano, Giandomenico (1999). A cellular genetic programming approach to classification. In Banzhaf, Wolfgang, Daida, Jason, Eiben, Agoston E., Garzon, Max H., Honavar, Vasant, Jakiela, Mark, and Smith, Robert E., editors, *Proceedings of the Genetic and Evolutionary Computation Conference*, volume 2, pages 1015–1020, Orlando, Florida, USA. Morgan Kaufmann.

Freitas, A. (2001). Understanding the crucial role of attribute interactions. *Artificial Intelligence Review*, 16:177–199.

Freitas, A. (2002). *Data Mining and Knowledge Discovery with Evolutionary Algorithms*. Springer.

Goldberg, D. E. (2002). *The Design of Innovation*. Kluwer.

Greene, C. S., White, B. C., and Moore, J. H. (2007). An expert knowledge-guided mutation operator for genome-wide genetic analysis using genetic programming. *Lecture Notes in Bioinformatics*, 4774:30–40.

Keith, M. J. and Martin, M. C. (1994). *Advances in Genetic Programming*. MIT Press.

Kira, K. and Rendell, L. A. (1992). A practical approach to feature selection. *In: Machine Learning: Proceedings of the AAAI'92*.

Kononenko, I. (1994). Estimating attributes: Analysis and extension of relief. *Machine Learning: ECML-94*, pages 171–182.

Koza, John R. (1992). *Genetic Programming: On the Programming of Computers by Means of Natural Selection*. MIT Press, Cambridge, MA, USA.

Koza, John R. (1994). *Genetic Programming II: Automatic Discovery of Reusable Programs*. MIT Press, Cambridge Massachusetts.

Koza, John R., Andre, David, Bennett III, Forrest H, and Keane, Martin (1999). *Genetic Programming 3: Darwinian Invention and Problem Solving*. Morgan Kaufman.

Koza, John R., Keane, Martin A., Streeter, Matthew J., Mydlowec, William, Yu, Jessen, and Lanza, Guido (2003). *Genetic Programming IV: Routine Human-Competitive Machine Intelligence*. Kluwer Academic Publishers.

Langdon, W. B. and Poli, Riccardo (2002). *Foundations of Genetic Programming*. Springer-Verlag.

Langdon, William B. (1998). *Genetic Programming and Data Structures: Genetic Programming + Data Structures = Automatic Programming!*, volume 1 of *Genetic Programming*. Kluwer, Boston.

Li, W. and Reich, J. (2000). A complete enumeration and classification of two-locus disease models. *Human Heredity*, 50:334–49.

Lucek, P.R. and Ott, J. (1997). Neural network analysis of complex traits. *Genetic Epidemiology*, 14(6):1101–1106.

Moore, J. H. (2003). The ubiquitous nature of epistasis in determining susceptibility to common human diseases. *Human Heredity*, 56:73–82.

Moore, J. H. (2007). Genome-wide analysis of epistasis using multifactor dimensionality reduction: feature selection and construction in the domain of human genetics. In *Knowledge Discovery and Data Mining: Challenges and Realities with Real World Data*. IGI.

Moore, J. H. and White, B. C. (2006a). Exploiting expert knowledge in genetic programming for genome-wide genetic analysis. *Lecture Notes in Computer Science*, 4193:969–977.

Moore, J. H. and White, B. C. (2007a). Genome-wide genetic analysis using genetic programming: The critical need for expert knowledge. In Riolo, Rick L., Soule, Terence, and Worzel, Bill, editors, *Genetic Programming Theory and Practice IV*, Genetic and Evolutionary Computation. Springer.

Moore, J. H. and White, B. C. (2007b). Tuning relieff for genome-wide genetic analysis. *Lecture Notes in Computer Science*, 4447:166–175.

Moore, J. H. and Williams, S. W. (2005). Traversing the conceptual divide between biological and statistical epistasis: Systems biology and a more modern synthesis. *BioEssays*, 27:637–46.

Moore, Jason H., Greene, Casey S., Andrews, Peter C., and White, Bill C. (2008a). Does complexity matter? artificial evolution, computational evolution and the genetic analysis of epistasis in common human diseases. In Riolo, Rick L., Soule, Terence, and Worzel, Bill, editors, *Genetic Programming Theory and Practice VI*, Genetic and Evolutionary Computation, chapter 9, pages 125–145. Springer, Ann Arbor.

Moore, Jason H. and White, Bill C. (2006b). Exploiting expert knowledge in genetic programming for genome-wide genetic analysis. In Runarsson, Thomas Philip, Beyer, Hans-Georg, Burke, Edmund, Merelo-Guervos, Juan J., Whitley, L. Darrell, and Yao, Xin, editors, *Parallel Problem Solving from Nature - PPSN IX*, volume 4193 of *LNCS*, pages 969–977, Reykjavik, Iceland. Springer-Verlag.

Moore, J.H. (2009). From genotypes to genometypes: putting the genome back in genome-wide association studies. *Eur J Hum Genet.*

Moore, J.H., Andrews, P.C., Barney, N., and White, B.C. (2008b). Development and evaluation of an open-ended computational evolution system for the genetic analysis of susceptibility to common human diseases. *Lecture Notes in Computer Science*, 4973:129–140.

Moore, J.H, Barney, N., Tsai, C.T, Chiang, F.T, Gui, J., and White, B.C (2007). Symbolic modeling of epistasis. *Human Heridity*, 63(2):120–133.

Moore, J.H, Parker, J.S., Olsen, N.J, and Aune, T. (2002). Symbolic discriminant analysis of microarray data in autoimmune disease. *Genetic Epidemiology*, 23:57–69.

Perkis, Tim (1994). Stack-based genetic programming. In *Proceedings of the 1994 IEEE World Congress on Computational Intelligence*, volume 1, pages 148–153, Orlando, Florida, USA. IEEE Press.

Ritchie, M. D., Hahn, L. W., and Moore, J. H. (2003). Power of multifactor dimensionality reduction for detecting gene-gene interactions in the presence of genotyping error, phenocopy, and genetic heterogeneity. *Genetic Epidemiology*, 24:150–157.

Ritchie, M. D., Hahn, L. W., Roodi, N., Bailey, L. R., Dupont, W. D., Parl, F. F., and Moore, J. H. (2001). Multifactor dimensionality reduction reveals high-order interactions among estrogen metabolism genes in sporadic breast cancer. *American Journal of Human Genetics*, 69:138–147.

Spector, Lee (2003). An essay concerning human understanding of genetic programming. In Riolo, Rick L. and Worzel, Bill, editors, *Genetic Programming Theory and Practice*, chapter 2, pages 11–24. Kluwer.

Thornton-Wells, T. A., Moore, J. H., and Haines, J. L. (2004). Genetics, statistics and human disease: Analytical retooling for complexity. *Trends in Genetics*, 20:640–7.

Velez, D.R., White, B.C., Motsinger, A.A., Bush, W.S., Ritchie, M.D., Williams, S.M., and Moore, J.H. (2007). A balanced accuracy function for epistasis modeling in imbalanced datasets using multifactor dimensionality reduction. *Genetic Epidemiology*, 31(4).

Vladislavleva, Ekaterina, Smits, Guido, and Kotanchek, Mark (2007). Soft evolution of robust regression models. In Riolo, Rick L., Soule, Terence, and Worzel, Bill, editors, *Genetic Programming Theory and Practice V*, Genetic and Evolutionary Computation, chapter 2, pages 13–32. Springer, Ann Arbor.

Yu, T., Riolo, R., and Worzel, B. (Eds.) (2006). *Genetic Programming Theory and Practice III*. Springer.

Chapter 3

EVOLVING COEVOLUTIONARY CLASSIFIERS UNDER LARGE ATTRIBUTE SPACES

John Doucette[1], Peter Lichodzijewski[1] and Malcolm Heywood[1]

[1]*Faculty of Computer Science, Dalhousie University, 6050 University Av., Halifax, NS, B3H 1W5. Canada.*

Abstract   Model-building under the supervised learning domain potentially face a dual learning problem of identifying both the parameters of the model and the subset of (domain) attributes necessary to support the model, thus using an embedded as opposed to wrapper or filter based design. Genetic Programming (GP) has always addressed this dual problem, however, further implicit assumptions are made which potentially increase the complexity of the resulting solutions. In this work we are specifically interested in the case of classification under very large attribute spaces. As such it might be expected that multiple independent/ overlapping attribute subspaces support the mapping to class labels; whereas GP approaches to classification generally assume a single binary classifier per class, forcing the model to provide a solution in terms of a single attribute subspace and single mapping to class labels. Supporting the more general goal is considered as a requirement for identifying a 'team' of classifiers with *non-overlapping* classifier behaviors, in which each classifier responds to different subsets of exemplars. Moreover, the subsets of attributes associated with each team member might utilize a unique 'subspace' of attributes. This work investigates the utility of coevolutionary model building for the case of classification problems with attribute vectors consisting of 650 to 100,000 dimensions. The resulting team based coevolutionary evolutionary method – Symbiotic Bid-based (SBB) GP – is compared to alternative embedded classifier approaches of C4.5 and Maximum Entropy Classification (MaxEnt). SSB solutions demonstrate up to an order of magnitude lower attribute count relative to C4.5 and up to two orders of magnitude lower attribute count than MaxEnt while retaining comparable or better classification performance. Moreover, relative to the attribute count of individual models participating within a team, no more than six attributes are ever utilized; adding a further level of simplicity to the resulting solutions.

Keywords: Problem Decomposition, Bid-based Cooperative Behaviors, Symbiotic Coevolution, Subspace Classifier, Large Attribute Spaces.

R. Riolo et al. (eds.), *Genetic Programming Theory and Practice VII*,
Genetic and Evolutionary Computation, DOI 10.1007/978-1-4419-1626-6_3,
© Springer Science + Business Media, LLC 2010

37

1.   Introduction

Team or ensemble based frameworks for machine learning may be used to provide explicit support for the 'divide and conquer' metaphor of problem decomposition. Thus under a classification problem domain, rather than assuming a single model-based classifier[1] per class, the process of credit assignment is able to actively decompose the problem as originally posed. The resulting solution engages multiple classifiers to provide the same class label, but in the case of this work we do so while seeking an explicitly *non-overlapping* interaction between classifiers. Such a non-overlapping behavioral requirement implies that the team of classifiers associated with the same class respond to different partitions of the exemplars comprising the class in question.[2] Thus, under such an approach, the overall solution is potentially much simpler than assuming a single classifier per class. For the purposes of this work the simple solution property has at least two specific properties: (1) the complexity of individual classifiers associated with the same class is less than that when a priori forcing a *single* classifier to represent *each class*, and; (2) the attributes/ features[3] indexed by a team member need only be a subset of the total attributes utilized under the single classifier per class approach. The net result is that the transparency of a solution increases relative to non-team based classifiers and a wider acceptance of machine learning solutions might be expected in general.

Recent advances to team based evolutionary model building appear to represent a particularly appropriate approach for realizing both of the above simplification properties simultaneously. To date, however, there has been little effort to investigate the utility of such models to problem domains with hundreds to hundreds of thousands of attributes. With these goals in mind, we begin by reviewing advances in team-based evolutionary model building under the classification domain (Section 2). Section 3 summarizes the properties of the Symbiotic Bid-Based (SBB) model of coevolutionary machine learning as employed in this study. The evaluation methodology is established in Section 4, where this includes the details of data sets employed and a summary of two alternative classification methodologies that also support the embedded identification of attribute sets (C4.5 and Maximum Entropy Classification). Results of the empirical benchmarking study follow in Section 5, with conclusions and future work in Section 6.

---

[1]By 'model-based' representation we imply that individuals are required to discover a mapping from the original attribute space to the output space.

[2]Hereafter 'team' and 'ensemble' will be used interchangeably with the non-overlapping behavioral constraint implicit.

[3]The term 'attribute' and 'feature' have became interchangeable in the general literature; although in some works 'feature space' is distinct from the original attribute vector associated with the application domain. In the following we will associate a 'feature count' with all zero argument terms included in a solution, thus including attributes explicitly included in the classifier as a subset.

2.   Related Work

When faced with a data set composed of a large potential number of attributes one of two methods are generally employed: filter or embedded (Lal et al., 2006). Filter methods divide the overall task into two *independent* steps, attribute subset identification and then classification; a process that potentially makes the overall task computationally faster at the potential expense of overall accuracy. Conversely, the embedded approach takes the view that by performing *both* tasks in one step, as part of a single *integrated* process of learning, the subset of attributes most appropriate for the model of classification can be explicitly identified. A third approach – wrapper methods – use the classification model to iteratively evaluate suggested attribute subsets, but without integrating the two steps within a single learning algorithm; thus any classification algorithm would suffice for evaluation of the suggested attribute subset. However, such wrapper methods do not appear to work as well in practice.

Whether one of the two former methods is pursued over the other is often based on additional factors such as the ultimate cost of model building or the availability of expert knowledge appropriate for reducing the size of the attribute space. Moreover, some models of classification have a bias towards including all attributes and then simplifying (e.g., neural networks and SVM models); whereas other models of machine learning begin with a bias towards including a low number of attributes and incrementally include more until an 'optimal' classification performance is achieved (e.g. decision tree induction and evolutionary methods of model building).

Our work naturally assumes an embedded approach under the hypothesis that evolutionary methods for constructing models of classification provide a suitable basis for incremental attribute identification. Indeed, previous works have demonstrated that both Genetic Algorithms (GA) and Genetic Programming (GP) are appropriate for attribute subset identification/ attribute creation (Krawiec, 2002), (Smith and Bull, 2005), (Zhang and Rockett, 2006). In each case evaluation was limited to problem domains with tens of attributes. However, such approaches to classification still fall short of the overall objective pursued in this work as the solution takes the form of a single classifier per class. That is to say, solutions fail to support transparency under the aforementioned two properties of: (1) team-based classifier decomposition through non-overlapping behaviors, and; (2) the identification of (potentially) independent attribute subsets by each team member. More recently, GP was used as a pairwise attribute selector in combination with statistical feature selection and a linearly weighted bi-objective fitness function for wrapper based attribute selection under a Bayes model of classification and dimensionality in the order of thousands of attributes (More and White, 2007). The work reported here concentrates on the single step embedded approach to classification–attribute selection.

In order to support problem decomposition under evolutionary methods various metaphors have been investigated, including learning classifier systems (Bernado-Mansilla and Garrell-Guiu, 2003), cooperative coevolution (Potter and de Jong, 2000), GP teaming (Brameier and Banzhaf, 2001), (Thomason and Soule, 2007), and various evolutionary approaches for building ensembles (Jin, 2006). Some of the generic difficulties faced in attempting to compose such models under the supervised learning domain of classification include: establishing how many classifiers to include per class; defining an appropriate credit assignment policy; deciding how to combine multiple individuals once identified; and simultaneously scaling the model for efficient evolution over large data sets. Specifically, the generic model of cooperative coevolution established by Potter and de Jong assigns an independent population per 'team member' (Potter and de Jong, 2000). Thus, *a priori* knowledge is necessary in order to specify the number of individuals required to participate in the class-wise decomposition. The same constraint has limited teaming metaphors under GP (Brameier and Banzhaf, 2001), (Thomason and Soule, 2007). In the case of evolutionary ensemble methods a common requirement is to hold multiple independent runs to produce each member of the ensemble, where this often implies suitable computational support, especially when scaling to large data sets (Folino et al., 2006). Moreover, the generic ensemble learning approach does not guarantee that the resulting learners will have non-overlapping behaviors (Imamura et al., 2003), (Thomason and Soule, 2007). Indeed, in order to guarantee diversity in the ensemble, techniques such as strongly typed GP (Kumar et al., 2008), local membership functions (McIntyre and Heywood, 2008), or negative correlation (Chandra et al., 2006) have been proposed; all under the context of Multi-objective fitness formulations.

With the above discussion in mind, our approach to evolving a team of learners under the classification domain will assume the Symbiotic Bid-based (SBB) framework for model building under discrete domains (Lichodzijewski and Heywood, 2008b). Such an approach provides problem decomposition without pre-specifying the nature of the decomposition (c.f. the number of cooperating learners per class) and scales to large data sets care of a competitive coevolutionary mechanism. Section 3 will summarize the characteristics of the SBB learning algorithm.

3.   Symbiotic Bid-Based framework

Motivation and Methodology

The framework typically assumed for applying model based cases of evolution – such as Genetic Programming (GP) – to the supervised learning domain of classification requires an individual to map exemplars from an attribute space to a class label space. An individual's program expresses the mapping. However, this is not the case under the bid-based GP framework (Lichodzijewski and Heywood, 2008a). Instead the task is divided into two components: (1) deciding *which* exemplars to label, or the *bid*, and (2) suggesting class label, or the *action*. In the case of the individual's action, the assumption is made that an individual will always be associated with the same action (class label). Thus at initialization, a problem with C classes results in $\frac{PopSize}{C}$ individuals in the population being pre-assigned to each class. The assignment is defined by assigning a scalar a to each individual at initialization. Scalars are selected with uniform probability over the interval $\{1, ..., C\}$. The actions are *not adapted* during evolution. Conversely, the task of deciding which subset of exemplars to label is expressed in terms of a bid. The individual with maximum (winning) bid suggests their pre-assigned action as the class label. Individuals suggesting an action a that matches the exemplar class label are rewarded, whereas individuals winning the bid, but not providing a class matching action are penalized.

The most recent form of the bid-based framework – hereafter Symbiotic Bid-based (SBB) – makes extensive use of coevolution (Lichodzijewski and Heywood, 2008b), with a total of three populations involved: a population of points, a population of learners, and a population of teams (Figure 3-1). Specifically, individuals comprising a team are specified by the team population, thus establishing a symbiotic relationship with the learner population. Only the subset of individuals indexed by an individual in the team population compete to bid against each other on training exemplars. The use of a symbiotic relation between teams and learners makes the credit assignment process more transparent than in the case of a population wide competition between bids (as used in the earlier variant of the model (Lichodzijewski and Heywood, 2008a)). Thus, variation operators may now be defined for independently investigating team composition (team population) and bidding strategy (learner population). The third population provides the mechanism for scaling evolution to large data sets. In particular the interaction between team and point population is formulated in terms of a competitive coevolutionary relation (de Jong, 2007). As such, the point population indexes a subset of the training data set under an active learning model (i.e. the subset indexed varies as classifier performance improves). Biases are enforced to ensure equal sampling of each class, irrespective of their original exemplar class distribution (Doucette and Heywood, 2008). The concept of Pareto competitive coevolution is used to retain points of most relevance to the competitive coevolution of teams.

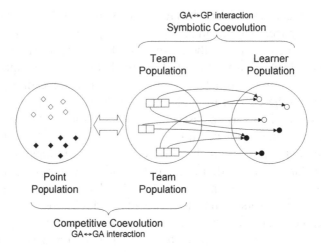

Figure 3-1. Architecture of Symbiotic Bid-based GP. Black/ white diamonds denote exemplars from different classes; Black/ white circles denote programs with different actions.

SBB Algorithm

The SBB model of evolution generates $P_{gap}\%$ new exemplar indexes in the point population and $M_{gap}\%$ new teams in the team population at each generation. Specifically, individuals in the point population take the form of indexes to the training data and are generated stochastically (subject to the aforementioned class balancing heuristic). New teams are created through variation operators applied to the current team population. Fitness evaluation evaluates all teams against all points with $(1 - P_{gap})\%$ points and $(1 - M_{gap})\%$ teams appearing in the next generation. Pareto competitive coevolution ranks the performance of teams in terms of a vector of outcomes, thus the Pareto non-dominated teams are ranked the highest (de Jong, 2007). Likewise, the points supporting the identification of non-dominated individuals (distinctions) are also retained. In addition, use is made of competitive fitness sharing in order to bias survival in favor of teams that exhibit uniqueness in the non-dominated set (Pareto front).

Evaluation of team m_i on a training exemplar defined by point population member p_k results in the construction of an outcome matrix $G(m_i, p_k)$ in which unity implies a correctly classified exemplar, and zero an incorrectly classified exemplar. The ensuing distinction matrix details the pairwise outcome of each team over all exemplars sampled by the point population, or,

$$\begin{cases} 1 & \text{if } G(m_i, p_k) > G(m_j, p_k) \\ 0 & \text{otherwise} \end{cases} \tag{3.1}$$

where unity implies that point p_k 'distinguishes' between team m_i and m_j. The ensuing Pareto competitive coevolutionary process identifies the non-dominated teams and points supporting their identification.

Denoting the non-dominated and dominated points as $F(P)$ and $D(P)$ respectively, the SBB framework notes that as long as $F(P)$ contains less than $(1 - P_{gap})\%$ points, all the points from $F(P)$ are copied into the next generation. On the other hand, if $F(P)$ contains more points than are allowed to survive, then the following fitness sharing heuristic is imposed to rank the collection of non-dominated points (Rosin and Belew, 1997),

$$\sum_i \frac{d_k[i]}{1 + N_i} \qquad (3.2)$$

where $d_k[i]$ is the ith entry of the distinction vector for p_k; and N_i is the sum of the i th entries over the distinction vectors across all points in $F(P)$ i.e., the number of points making the same distinction. Thus, points making the same distinction are weighted less than points making unique distinctions.

An analogous process is repeated for the case of team selection, with $(1 - M_{gap})\%$ individuals copied into the next generation. Naturally, under the condition where the (team) non-dominated set exceeds this fraction, the fitness sharing ranking employs $F(M)$ and $D(M)$ in place of $F(P)$ and $D(P)$ respectively. The resulting process of fitness sharing under a Pareto model of has been shown to be effective at promoting solutions in which multiple models cooperate to decompose the original $|C|$ class problem into a set of non-overlapping behaviors (Lichodzijewski and Heywood, 2008a), (Lichodzijewski and Heywood, 2008b).

Finally, the learner population of individuals expressing specific bidding strategies employs a linear representation. Bid values are standardized to the unit interval through the use of a sigmoid function, or $bid(y) = (1 + \exp -y)^{-1}$, where y is the real valued result of program execution on the current exemplar. Variation operators take the form of instruction add, delete, swap and mutate; applied with independent likelihoods, under a uniform probability of selection. When an individual is no longer indexed by the team population it becomes extinct and deleted from the learner population. Conversely, during evaluation of the team population, exactly $M_{gap}\%$ children are created pairwise care of team based crossover. Learners that are common to both child teams are considered to be the candidates for retention. Learners not common to the child teams are subject to stochastic deletion or modification; with corresponding tests for deletion/ insertion at the learner population. The instruction set follows from that assumed in (Lichodzijewski and Heywood, 2008b) and consists of eight opcodes ($\{cos, exp, log, +, \times, -, \div, \%\}$) operating on up to 8 registers, as per a linear GP representation.

Table 3-1. Data set properties.

Data set	Exemplar Count train (test)	Feature Count
Handwritten character recognition		
Multifeature	1,510 (490)	649
Gisette	6,000 (1,000)	5,000
Document Classification: Bag-of-words		
NIPS	7,000 (3,500)	12,419
Enron	7,000 (3,500)	28,102
NY Times	7,000 (3,500)	102,660

4.   Evaluation Methodology

The Evaluation Methodology is first considered from two perspectives, the selection of data sets appropriate for performing the comparison, and identification of alternative models for establishing a realistic baseline of performance. Parameterization of the SBB model is briefly discussed and the metrics deployed for evaluating performance post training are presented.

Data Sets

Data sets with large attribute spaces are frequently encountered under the context of document analysis (information retrieval), speech recognition, bioinformatics, and image processing. In this work, we make use of data sets from the domains of document analysis and image processing. In the case of the image processing domain, the 'Multifeature' and 'Gisette' data sets were employed (Asuncion and Newman, 2008), where both pertain to the recognition of handwritten digits (Table 3-1) and used 'as is' with no pre-processing applied. The Multifeature data set is a 10 class problem with each class equally represented; whereas Gisette is a binary classification problem in which 55% (45%) of the exemplars are in-class (out-class). Moreover, Gisette has the additional property that half of the attributes (2,500) are 'probes,' thus redundant from the perspective of building an appropriate classification model.

In the case of the document analysis domain, three binary classification problems were composed from the UCI Bag-of-words data set (Asuncion and Newman, 2008). The data set is comprised from a series of distinct document repositories. The repository content are unlabeled; however, it is known from which repository a document is sourced. Thus we first combine the common words from the NIPS, Enron and New York Times (NYT) repositories; whereas the three binary classification problems entail distinguishing documents in the

NIPS/ Enron/ NYT repository from the combination of all three. In each case document files were normalized with respect to the target class. Thus under the goal of distinguishing the Enron repository from NIPS and NYT, only words appearing in the Enron vocabulary were used to build the corresponding bag-of-words across all three document repositories. The resulting documents were labeled as in-class if they came from the set of documents that originated the vocabulary or out-class otherwise. This resulted in the largest attribute spaces deployed during the ensuing performance evaluation (see Table 3-1). Class representation was also generally unbalanced with in-class representation at 14, 29 and 43 percent respectively for NIPS, Enron and NYT.

Comparator Models of Classification

In establishing a set of baseline classifiers we considered two alternative examples of models that operate under an explicitly embedded paradigm and are widely utilized under large attribute space domains: decision tree induction and Maximum Entropy Classifiers (MaxEnt). Both models make use of entropy frameworks for model building. However, decision tree induction – C4.5 – naturally assumes a greedy incremental non-linear model building methodology. As such this gives the model the explicit ability to trade off model complexity/ feature count with classification performance. Conversely, MaxEnt classifiers are based on a linear model and might therefore be expected to utilize many more attributes relative to non-linear models such as C4.5 or SBB. However, they have repeatedly been shown to be very accurate under domains with high feature counts, even relative to methods incorporating SVM models of classification (Haffner, 2006). Indeed, both SVM and MaxEnt are large margin classifiers, with the SVM approach formulated for exemplar optimization and MaxEnt formulated for attribute selection (Haffner, 2006).

Finally, in both cases we also consider the impact of model pruning on the classification performance of the resulting models, with the goal of establishing to what degree the baseline models can approach the feature counts returned under SBB solutions. In the following subsections we provide background on the parameterization/ modifications necessary prior to benchmarking and a summary of the C4.5 and MaxEnt approaches.

C4.5 Decision Tree Induction. C4.5 is a widely used model for the construction of decision trees under a recursive algorithm in which attributes are incrementally added to the model care of their respective maximum normalized information gain relative to class label (Quinlan, 1993). The deployment used here is essentially the original code from Quinlan with modifications to support wider ranges of (confidence value) pruning than would normally be the case. In order to support efficient operation under the larger data sets, modification was necessary of the code in order to accept implicit data formats. Naturally, extensive evaluation was performed to verify that results remained consistent with the original version under smaller attribute dimensions. Such formats are widely used in text classification domains where they provide a significant reduction on memory requirements under sparse data sets.

Maximum Entropy Classifier.   MaxEnt methods are either based on a conditional distribution, $P(y|x)$, (Nigam et al., 1999) or a joint distribution, $P(y, x)$, (Haffner, 2006). Moreover, MaxEnt models' each class independently, thus the conditional probability of a binary problem becomes,

$$P(y = +1|x) = \frac{\exp(y(w^+)^T x)}{Z(x)} \tag{3.3}$$

for the in-class exemplars, and,

$$P(y = -1|x) = \frac{\exp(y(w^-)^T x)}{Z(x)} \tag{3.4}$$

for the out-class exemplars. However, $Z(x) = \exp(y(w^+)^T x) + \exp(y(w^-)^T x)$, thus a conditional MaxEnt classifier reduces to a logistic classifier i.e., a sigmoid function applied to the linear combination of weights $w = (w^+) + (w^-)$, with an exponentially weighted error term,

$$E_{\log}(y_i w^T x_i) = \log(1 + \exp(-2y_i w^T x_i)) \tag{3.5}$$

This is the most common formulation and will be employed here. In addition, the frequently employed l_2 Gaussian regularization factor for reducing the likelihood of overfitting will be assumed (Nigam et al., 1999), (Haffner, 2006), (Lal et al., 2006).

The foregoing description establishes the basis for the definition of the error term, but says nothing about the scheme employed for adapting the free parameters, w. One of the very nice properties of MaxEnt methods is that the constrained multi-objective formulation results in a single unimodal objective search space (Nigam et al., 1999). As such, gradient based optimization routines are sufficient. However, it is still important to address stability issues (c.f. sparse training data) and direct inversion of the Hessian matrix is generally not possible. In this work, we make use of a recent Conjugate Gradient (binary) and BFGS (multi-class) implementation, or MegaM, (Daumè III, 2004) – rather than the originally widely employed Improved Iterative Scaling (IIS) routine (Nigam et al., 1999) – where MegaM provides a considerable speedup over the IIS methodology.

Finally, we note that pruning was applied post training through the application of a simple thresholding scheme in which attributes with free parameters below the threshold were ignored. Such a simplistic scheme was deemed sufficient for

Table 3-2. Parameterization of the Symbiotic Bid-Based model.

Parameter	Value
Team/ Point population	90
Point replacement (P_{gap})	1 / 3
Team replacement (M_{gap})	2 / 3
Max. Team size	100
Prob. Team add/ remove/ swap	0.1
Prob. Learner add remove/ swap/ mutate	0.1
Max. Generations	30,000
Number of Trials	40

qualifying to what degree the resulting linear model was reliant on the overall composition of the attribute space (as opposed to the potential ability of a non-linear model to compose features from a smaller subset of the total attribute space).

SBB Configuration

Relative to the original SBB configuration the most significant modification necessary to undertake this work was to: (1) provide support for implicit data formats, and; (2) extend the range of attributes learners may index from 64 to over 100,000. Parameterization of the model essentially follows that of the original work (Lichodzijewski and Heywood, 2008b), but with larger team sizes appearing here, and is summarized in Table 3-2. A distribution of the source code and data is available (http://www.cs.dal.ca/~mheywood/Code/SBB/).

Post Training Performance Metrics

Post training performance will be assessed from the perspective of classification and feature count. In the case of classification performance we make use of detection (sensitivity) as measured class-wise, resulting in a multi-class measure of detection. Thus, defining the class specific detection rate as $DR(i) = \frac{tp(i)}{tp(i)+fn(i)}$ where *tp(i)* and *fn(i)* are the true positive and false negative counts under class $i \in \{1, ..., C\}$, leads to the following definition for class-wise detection,

$$CW\text{-}detection = \frac{DR(1) + \cdots + DR(C)}{C} \tag{3.6}$$

Such a measure is independent of the distribution of exemplars per class. Thus under an imbalanced binary data set in which 95% (5%) of the exemplars

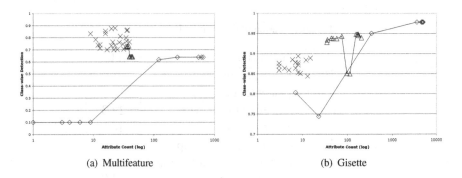

(a) Multifeature   (b) Gisette

Figure 3-2. Class-wide detection (Y axis) versus complexity (log of Attribute count, X axis) on the Character Recognition data sets. Feature counts are 649 (Multifeature) and 5,000 (Gisette). × denote solutions from SBB; △ denote solutions from C4.5; and ◊ denote solutions from MaxEnt.

were out-class (in-class) a degenerate classifier might label all exemplars as the out-class and achieve an accuracy of 95%; whereas the CW-detection metric would return a value of 50% or more generally $\frac{1}{C}$. Feature count will be measured in terms of the number of zero argument terms included in the model i.e., the number of constants and unique domain attributes actually utilized.

5.   Benchmarking Results

Benchmarking results will be summarized in terms of 2-D scatter plots of CW-detection versus Feature count. SBB solutions are plotted per run; C4.5 and MaxEnt solutions are plotted for increasing levels of pruning (c.f. the pruning threshold of C4.5 and the post training thresholding of the model free parameters in the case of MaxEnt). As such the C4.5 and MaxEnt results are likely to span from complex but most accurate, to the simplest achievable but (relatively speaking) least accurate. This is further emphasized by linking the points formed by pruning C4.5 and MaxEnt solutions to provide a corresponding performance curve. Points which tend to the top left of a curve will naturally dominate the performance of other points in a manner similar to that used to interpret ROC curves. However, the interaction between CW-detection and attribute count will not necessarily result in a monotonic curve. Finally, SBB solutions will naturally result in a distribution of points, due to the multiple stochastic sources of variation implicit in GP; thus the *training* partition is used to identify the top 50 percent of solutions for which test evaluation is performed.

Character Recognition data sets

Figure 3-2 characterizes performance of the three classifiers under the two Character Recognition data sets considered in this study (Multifeature and

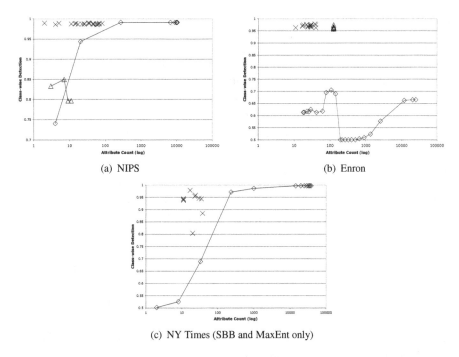

(a) NIPS   (b) Enron

(c) NY Times (SBB and MaxEnt only)

Figure 3-3. Class-wide detection (Y axis) versus complexity (log of Attribute count, X axis) on the Bag-of-words data sets. Feature counts are 12,419 (NIPS), 28,102 (Enron) and 102,660 (NY Times). × denote solutions from SBB; △ denote solutions from C4.5; and ◊ denote solutions from MaxEnt.

Gisette). In the case of the smaller attribute space of the Multifeature data set SBB solutions appear to be stronger in terms of both simplicity and classification performance with the equivalent of up to nine of ten classes correctly classified while using 10 to 70 of the 649 attributes. C4.5 and MaxEnt managed to classify the equivalent of 6 to 7 of the classes, with MaxEnt degenerate under the higher levels of pruning. Moreover, outside of the degenerate solutions (i.e., CW-detection of 0.1) there is a clear ordering of model feature count from SBB (simplest) to C4.5 to MaxEnt (largest feature utilization). This pattern is also reflected under Gisette, with the inclusion of additional attributes improving CW-detection from 90% (SBB) to 95% (C4.5) to 98% (MaxEnt). The penalty paid for the increased classification performance appears in terms of attribute count, where MaxEnt generally utilizes thousands of attributes whereas SBB generally uses no more then 15. We also note that all but the larger MaxEnt models managed to index less than half of the attributes under Gisette; where half of the attributes are known to be redundant/ duplicate probes although the exact identity of the probes remains concealed (Asuncion and Newman, 2008).

Bag-of-words data set

Figure 3-3 characterizes performance under the NIPS, Enron and NY Times (NYT) domains from the UCI 'Bag-of-words' data set; as formulated in terms of three independent binary classification problems. In the case of NYT, results are expressed in terms of MaxEnt and SBB alone; C4.5 requiring more memory capacity than was available under the 2GB RAM limit imposed by the computing platform. In this case the simple SBB models are generally able to reach the classification performance identified under MaxEnt. Indeed, they are within 1% of MaxEnt under NIPS, about 25% more accurate under Enron and within 5 to 2% of MaxEnt under NYT while utilizing 15 to 90 out of a possible 12,419 (NIPS), 28,102 (Enron) or 102,660 (NYT) attributes. Moreover, at each level of model feature count identified by SBB, the SBB models dominated the corresponding MaxEnt solution. C4.5 found solutions with the same attribute counts as SBB under NIPS, but were about 15% less accurate; whereas under Enron C4.5 were as accurate, but only by including 50 more attributes than SBB.

In the case of MaxEnt one characteristic of interest was the pair of peaks appearing under the Enron category. Rather than pruning resulting in a monotonic decline in performance (as in all previous cases) a series of two monotonic performance profiles are identified. Moreover, it is the curve from the more complex MaxEnt model which begins at a lower level of classification performance and decays to degenerate solutions; whereas the second MaxEnt peak identified solutions that were simpler and avoided degenerate solutions.

SBB team properties

Figure 3-4 summarizes complexity across the SBB teams as a whole. Gisette appears to require the lowest team complexity, although some of this characteristic is undoubtedly due to the problem with the smallest attribute count (Multi-feature) also being a ten class problem; thus requiring a greater diversity in model behavior. The three larger 'bag-of-words' data sets did establish some correlation between total attributes indexed over the entire team and attribute count of the original problem domain, Figure 3-4. However, individual models participating in the team generally indexed no more than in the case of Multi-feature or Gisette (see Figure 3-5).

Figure 3-5 summaries complexity as measured per individual. It is apparent that the total number of unique attributes indexed by individual team members is very low, or typically less than 4 attributes. This makes for very simple rules that are able to act independently from each other; as opposed to C4.5 which builds a single monolithic solution from a hierarchy of decisions, thus building up to quite complex rules as the tree depth increases. Indeed, the simplest SBB rules tend to be of the form "if attribute X appears in document, it is about

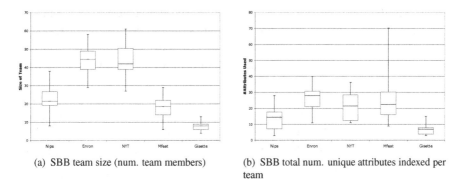

(a) SBB team size (num. team members)　　(b) SBB total num. unique attributes indexed per team

Figure 3-4. Summary of SBB Team complexity on each data set.

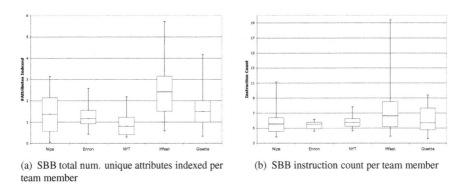

(a) SBB total num. unique attributes indexed per team member

(b) SBB instruction count per team member

Figure 3-5. Summary of SBB team member (learner) complexity on each data set. Box boundaries denote 1st, 2nd (median) and 3rd quartiles. Whiskers denote max and min.

topic Y". In the case of several data sets we note that some individuals are returned that do not index any attributes. In these cases, the team member is bidding a constant value, leaving the bids from the alternate action (class) and/ or same action (class) to provide the counter balancing bid strategy. Finally, we note that relative simplicity in terms of attribute count is not being traded for greater model complexity. Specifically, after removal of structural introns, team members generally consisted of between 4 to 9 instructions, thus, not detracting from the overall simplicity of SBB solutions—see Figure 3-5 (b).

6.　Conclusions

A case is made for the utility of evolutionary model based teaming (or ensembles) under classification problems described over large attribute spaces. The initial hypothesis was that when teams are explicitly designed to seek non-overlapping behaviors, assuming an evolutionary bias to model building would enable the resulting teams to provide very simple solutions without compromising classification performance. Benchmarking conducted under data sets selected from the domains of character recognition and document retrieval (as represented under a bag-of-words vector space model) appears to support this hypothesis. In particular the SBB paradigm of evolutionary teaming/ ensemble generation tends to be more effective at balancing classification performance versus feature count. Conversely, the domain standard of MaxEnt Classification can be counted on to maximize classification performance at the expense of attributes indexed, whereas the C4.5 model of classification appears to build models with an intermediate level of complexity and classification performance.

Key properties from SBB supporting this result take at least three forms: (1) Active learning – evolving solutions directly over the entire training partition would represent a prohibitively expensive computational overhead. In this work a Pareto competitive coevolutionary approach was assumed although alternatives such as host-parasite models or stochastic sampling would also be appropriate. (2) Cooperative problem decomposition – a wide range of ensemble methods exist, however, most do not support non-overlapping models of problem decomposition. Instead widespread use is made of post training voting schemes. This results in multiple models responding to each exemplar and clarity of the solution is lost (c.f. a weak learner metaphor). The SBB algorithm specifically addresses this problem by using fitness sharing to discount the Pareto evaluation before ranking solutions. A learning bias supporting the reward of teams consisting of non-overlapping bidding strategies is therefore established. (3) Clear paths of credit assignment – unlike the traditional process of classification through mapping exemplars to a class membership value, the SBB approach explicitly separates the generally combined tasks of "what to do" (action) and "when to do it" (bid). Moreover, this is reinforced by assuming a symbiotic model which explicitly separates the tasks of optimizing team membership and evolving bidding policy. Without such a separation the bidding competition responsible for establishing cooperative team behavior would have to take place across an entire population, thus each time children are created the current team interaction would face disruption.

Natural extensions of the current study might consider the case of biomedical data sets (More and White, 2007) or investigate the impact of attribute support on the relative cost of model complexity, where this appears to be of particular importance to non-linear classifiers such as the SVM (Doucette et al., 2009). More generally, we are also interested in the utility of the SBB framework to problem domains with temporal discounting (reinforcement learning). Such a context might also benefit from the ability to pose solutions in terms of teams, as indicated by ongoing research in multi-agent systems in general.

Acknowledgments

This work was conducted while John Doucette held an NSERC USRA summer scholarship and Peter Lichodzijewski held a Precarn Graduate Scholarship and a Killam Postgraduate Scholarship. Malcolm Heywood would like to thank research grants from NSERC, MITACS, and CFI and industrial sponsorship from SwissCom Innovations SA. and TARA Inc.

References

Asuncion, A. and Newman, D. J. (2008). UCI Repository of Machine Learning Databases [http://www.ics.uci.edu/~mlearn/mlrepository.html]. Irvine, CA: University of California, Dept. of Information and Comp. Science.

Bernado-Mansilla, E. and Garrell-Guiu, J.M. (2003). Accuracy-based learning classifier systems: Models, analysis and applications to classification tasks. *Evolutionary Computation*, 11:209–238.

Brameier, M. and Banzhaf, W. (2001). Evolving teams of predictors with linear Genetic Programming. *Genetic Programming and Evolvable Machines*, 2(4):381–407.

Chandra, A., Chen, H., and Yao, X. (2006). *Trade-off between diversity and accuracy in ensemble generation*, chapter 19, pages 429–464. In ((Jin, 2006)).

Daumè III, Hal (2004). Notes on CG and LM-BFGS optimization of logistic regression. Paper and code available at http://www.cs.utah.edu/~hal/megam.

de Jong, E.D. (2007). A monotonic archive for pareto-coevolution. *Evolutionary Computation*, 15(1):61–93.

Doucette, J. and Heywood, M.I. (2008). GP Classification under Imbalanced Data Sets: Active Sub-sampling and AUC Approximation. In *European Conference on Genetic Programming*, volume 4971 of *Lecture Notes in Computer Science*, pages 266–277.

Doucette, J., McIntyre, A.R., Lichodzijewski, P., and Heywood, M. I. (2009). Problem decomposition under large feature spaces using a coevolutionary memetic algorithm. *Manuscript under review*.

Folino, G., Pizzuti, C., and Spezzano, G. (2006). GP ensembles for large-scale data classification. *IEEE Transactions on Evolutionary Computation*, 10(5):604–616.

Haffner, P. (2006). Scaling large margin classifiers for spoken language understanding. *Speech Communication*, 48:239–261.

Imamura, K., Soule, T., Heckendorn, R. B., and Foster, J. A. (2003). Behavioral diversity and a probabilistically optimal GP ensemble. *Genetic Programming and Evolvable Machines*, 4(3):235–253.

Jin, Y., editor (2006). *Multi-Objective Machine Learning*, volume 16 of *Studies in Computational Intelligence*. Springer-Verlag.

Krawiec, K. (2002). Genetic Programming-based Construction of Features for Machine Learning and Knowledge Discovery tasks. *Genetic Programming and Evolvable Machines*, 3(4):329–343.

Kumar, R., Joshi, A.H., Banka, K.K., and Rockett, P.I. (2008). Evolution of hyperheuristics for the biobjective 0/1 knapsack problem by multiobjective Genetic Programming. In *Proceedings of the Genetic and Evolutionary Computation Conference*, pages 1227–1234.

Lal, T. N., Chapelle, O., Weston, J., and Elisseeff, A. (2006). Embedded methods. In Guyon, I., Gunn, S., Nikravesh, M., and Zadeh, L.A., editors, *Feature Extraction: Foundations and Applications*, pages 137–165. Springer Verlag.

Lichodzijewski, P. and Heywood, M. I. (2008a). Coevolutionary bid-based Genetic Programming for problem decomposition in classification. *Genetic Programming and Evolvable Machines*, 9(4):331–365.

Lichodzijewski, P. and Heywood, M.I. (2008b). Managing team-based problem solving with Symbiotic Bid-based Genetic Programming. In *Proceedings of the Genetic and Evolutionary Computation Conference*, pages 363–370.

McIntyre, A.R. and Heywood, M.I. (2008). Cooperative problem decomposition in Pareto competitive classifier models of coevolution. In *European Conference on Genetic Programming*, volume 4971 of *Lecture Notes in Computer Science*, pages 289–300.

More, J. H. and White, B. C. (2007). Genome-wide genetic analysis using genetic programming. In Riolo, R., Soule, T., and Worzel, B., editors, *Genetic Programming Theory and Practice IV*, pages 11–28. Springer Verlag.

Nigam, K., Lafferty, J., and McCallum, A. (1999). Using Maximum Entropy for Text Classification. In *Workshop on Machine Learning for Information Filtering (IJCAI)*, pages 61–67.

Potter, M. and de Jong, K. (2000). Cooperative coevolution: An architecture for evolving coadapted subcomponents. *Evolutionary Computation*, 8(1):1–29.

Quinlan, Ross J. (1993). *C4.5: Programs for Machine Learning*. Morgan Kaufmann.

Rosin, C. D. and Belew, R. K. (1997). New methods for competitive coevolution. *Evolutionary Compuatation*, 5:1–29.

Smith, M.G. and Bull, L. (2005). Genetic Programming with a Genetic Algorithm for Feature Construction and Selection. *Genetic Programming and Evolvable Machines*, 6(3):265–281.

Thomason, R. and Soule, T. (2007). Novel ways of improving cooperation and performance in Ensemble Classifiers. In *Proceedings of the Genetic and Evolutionary Computation Conference*, pages 1708–1715.

Zhang, Y. and Rockett, P.I. (2006). *Feature extraction using multi-objective genetic programming*, chapter 4, pages 75–99. In ((Jin, 2006)).

Chapter 4

SYMBOLIC REGRESSION VIA GENETIC PROGRAMMING AS A DISCOVERY ENGINE: INSIGHTS ON OUTLIERS AND PROTOTYPES

Mark E. Kotanchek[1], Ekaterina Y. Vladislavleva[2] and Guido F. Smits[3]

[1]*Evolved Analytics L.L.C, Midland, MI, U.S.A.;* [2]*University of Antwerpen, Antwerpen, Belgium;* [3]*Dow Benelux B.V., Terneuzen, the Netherlands.*

Abstract

In this chapter we illustrate a framework based on symbolic regression to generate and sharpen the questions about the nature of the underlying system and provide additional context and understanding based on multi-variate numeric data.

We emphasize the necessity to perform data modeling in a global approach, iteratively applying data analysis and adaptation, model building, and problem reduction procedures. We illustrate it for the problem of detecting outliers and extracting significant features from the CountryData [1] – a data set of economic, political, social and geographic data collected. We present two complementary ways of extracting outliers from the data -the content-based and the model-based approach. The content-based approach studies the geometrical structure of the multi-variate data, and uses data-balancing algorithms to sort the data records in the order of decreasing typicalness, and identify the outliers as the least typical records before the modeling is applied to a data set. The model-based outlier detection approach uses symbolic regression via Pareto genetic programming (GP) to identify records which are systematically under- or over-predicted by diverse ensembles of (thousands of) global non-linear symbolic regression models.

Both approaches applied to the CountryData produce insights into outlier vs. prototypes division among world countries and about driving economic properties predicting gross domestic product (GDP) per capita.

Keywords: symbolic regression, data modeling, system identification, research assistant, discovery engine, outlier detection, outliers, prototypes, data balancing

[1] http://reference.wolfram.com/mathematica/ref/CountryData.html

R. Riolo et al. (eds.), *Genetic Programming Theory and Practice VII*,
Genetic and Evolutionary Computation, DOI 10.1007/978-1-4419-1626-6_4,
© Springer Science + Business Media, LLC 2010

1.   Introduction

The purpose of models is not to fit the data but to sharpen the questions.
–Samuel Karlin

Reality has a way of destroying beautiful theory. Thus, even though data modelers might construct beautiful algorithms, if the data does not agree with the implicit principles in that construct (e.g., system linearity, variable independence, variable significance, Gaussian additive noise) the house-of-cards comes tumbling down when it intersects with reality.

Pursuing data modeling as a main research direction, we have been building a framework based on symbolic regression to develop models which generate and sharpen the questions about what constitutes the underlying data-generating system. A useful framework helps us to understand what we know and do not know based on the data presented to us. We can begin to understand which data variables (or features, or attributes) are important and which are not, or whether we are missing some essential variables, because a reasonable prediction accuracy cannot be achieved. A good framework helps us to detect that some regions of the data space are either under- or over-represented.

Knowledge about these areas is essential for understanding the data. Data samples in over-represented areas can be flagged as prototypes, and possibly pruned for balancing the information content of samples over the data space. Samples in under-represented areas should be marked as outliers. They either represent measurement or computation errors, and should be removed from the modeling process, or on the contrary contain important nuggets of information about the system. In both cases the outliers are special, need to be treated with care during data interpretation and modeling, and always require human insight for the final verdict.

In this chapter we illustrate two sides of a holistic approach for understanding a multi-variate dataset from real-life - a collection of economic, political and geographic attributes gathered for 109 world countries. To understand and interpret the CountryData we present two approaches for outlier detection before and after the model development stage. The first is a content-based approach, which checks the spatial structure of the data. The second is a model-based approach. It uses symbolic regression to check the relationships among the attributes, and to extract the driving attributes for prediction of a characteristic economical feature of a country - the gross domestic product (GDP) per capita[2]. We apply two approaches to identify the special "outlier" countries:

- the countries, which are special, because they are spatially remote from the prototypic countries, and therefore are located in the under-

---

[2]Gross domestic product per capita is the value of all final goods and services produced within a nation in a given year divided by the average population for the same year.

represented regions of the data space, and therefore require special treatment during modeling, analysis, measurement justification, etc. (content-based approach); and

- the countries, which are special because they possess an extraordinary GDPperCapita (extraordinary with respect to predictions of various ensembles of diverse symbolic regression models).

The first approach originates in our research on data balancing. It uses heuristic algorithms for weighting multi-variate input and input-output data, and for ordering the data in the order of decreasing importance - from outliers to prototypes (see (Vladislavleva, 2008)).

The second approach is model-based. It uses symbolic regression via genetic programming to generate ensembles of diverse regression models, which predict GDPperCapita attribute on the CountryData, and suggests outliers as points which consistently produce bad predictions on selected model ensembles.

Both approaches propose an interesting division of countries into "outliers" and "prototypes" without using any expert knowledge or interpretation of the CountryData. We believe that the hypothesis-generating aspect of symbolic regression enhanced with the insights from data balancing is essential for understanding multi-variate numeric data and data-generating system. It is also unique compared with other modeling methods, due to the transparency of explicit symbolic regression models.[3]

2.   CountryData

The CountryData of Wolfram Research is a comprehensive collection of economic, geographic, social, and political data (224 attributes in total) over 237 world countries (taken from several credible sources like Encyclopaedia Britannica, United Nations Department of Economic and Social Affairs, United Nations Statistics Division, World Health Organization, and many others, see http://reference.wolfram.com/mathematica/note/CountryData- Source-Information.html). We selected this data set because many attributes are highly correlated, so classic modeling methods alternative to symbolic regression would not be applicable; the dataset is of high dimensionality and heavily under-sampled (number of countries is approximately equal to the number of attributes); an average reader is aware of the economic positions of richest, poorest, and rapidly developing countries, which makes it easier to relate to the CountryData and interpret modeling results.

---

[3] The only other method with comparable power for discovery and insights is linear regression, but only in a situation where the underlying model structure is known, which is not the case in many real-life systems.

Our implementation of symbolic regression requires the data samples to be numeric, finite, and complete (no missing records), so we had to remove some countries and some attributes from the analysis, and were left with a list of 132 countries, and 128 attributes for them, including the GDPperCapita.

A challenge in our analysis is to reveal the relationship of the GDPper-Capita of a country with other economic attributes, and to identify outlier countries with extraordinary GDPperCapita. To increase the chances of finding non-obvious relationships, we also excluded the attributes, which are explicitly related to GDP (we strive for insights, rather then for trivial relationships of the type GDPperCapita=GDP/TotalPopulation). All attributes other than GDPperCapita, containing the word GDP, or ValueAdded in their name were removed from the data set, e.g. AgriculturalValueAdded, ConstructionValueAdded, GDP, GDPAtParity, GDPPerCapita, GDPRealGrowth, IndustrialValueAdded, ManufacturingValueAdded, MiscellaneousValueAdded, NationalIncome, TradeValueAdded, TransportationValueAdded, ValueAdded.

The remaining attributes for the analysis are:

CountryIndex, AdultPopulation, Airports, AMRadioStations, AnnualBirths, AnnualDeaths, ArableLand-Area, ArableLandFraction, Area, BirthRateFraction, BoundaryLength, CallingCode, CellularPhones, Child-Population, CoastlineLength, CropsLandArea, CropsLandFraction, DeathRateFraction, EconomicAid, ElderlyPopulation, ElectricityConsumption, ElectricityExports, ElectricityImports, ElectricityProduction, ExchangeRate, ExportValue, ExternalDebt, FemaleAdultPopulation, FemaleChildPopulation, FemaleElderlyPopulation, FemaleInfantMortalityFraction, FemaleLifeExpectancy, FemaleLiteracyFraction, FemaleMedianAge, FemalePopulation, FixedInvestment, FMRadioStations, GovernmentConsumption, GovernmentExpenditures, GovernmentReceipts, GovernmentSurplus, GrossInvestment, HighestElevation, HouseholdConsumption, ImportValue, InfantMortalityFraction, InflationRate, InternetHosts, InternetUsers, InventoryChange, IrrigatedLandArea, IrrigatedLandFraction, LaborForce, LandArea, LifeExpectancy, LiteracyFraction, LowestElevation, MaleAdultPopulation, MaleChildPopulation, MaleElderlyPopulation, MaleInfantMortalityFraction, MaleLifeExpectancy, MaleLiteracyFraction, MaleMedianAge, MalePopulation, MedianAge, MigrationRateFraction, MilitaryAgeMales, MilitaryExpenditureFraction, MilitaryFitMales, NaturalGasConsumption, NaturalGasExports, NaturalGasImports, NaturalGasProduction, NaturalGasReserves, OilConsumption, OilExports, OilImports, OilProduction, PavedAirports, PavedRoadLength, PhoneLines, Population, PopulationGrowth, PriceIndex, RadioStations, RoadLength, ShortWaveRadioStations, TelevisionStations, TotalConsumption, TotalFertilityRate, UnemploymentFraction, UNNumber, WaterArea, ExpenditureFractions● { ExportValue, FixedInvestment, GovernmentConsumption, GrossInvestment, HouseholdConsumption, ImportValue, InventoryChange }, TotalConsumption, PavedAirportLengths ● { 3000To- 5000Feet, 5000To8000Feet, 8000To10000Feet, Over10000Feet, Total, Under3000Feet }.

This chapter focuses on outlier detection, so our goal in the analysis of the CountryData is to extract the countries out of 132 available, which are special, i.e. they deviate from the prototypic countries with 'normal' economic indicators. We are striving to develop a research assisting framework for data analysis, and thus our 'outlier' detecting techniques should suggest 'outlier' candidates to the domain expert, but should not use any expert knowledge during the identification process. The expert is the one to decide what to do with suggested outliers, and he or she is the one to gain additional insights from these. The data analysis system is just an enabling technology that triggers the expert to ask a new question, and learn something new about the data-generating system.

3.   Data balancing as an insightful pre-processing step and content-based outlier detection

Data weighting for detecting under-represented regions of the data space

Pre-processing and scrutinizing data is a crucial first step of the learning process. Constructing bivariate plots of all variable pairs and computing a correlation matrix of data can sometimes reveal strong linear dependencies among variables of interest. This can allow breaking the data down into sets of smaller dimensionality, which are easier to explore visually, and to reveal outliers. However, when the data is of high dimensionality and very sparse (we have 132 records and 128 variables in the CountryData), visual exploration of bivariate plots of data for potential outliers is, first, time-consuming, and, second, risky in terms of being deceptive.

In this section we describe a more structured and automated approach of exploring the geometric structure of data. It does not make any assumptions about the underlying relationships among data variables, and identifies the records, which are spatially remote from other records in the data space. We refer to it as data balancing, since the approach belongs to a suite of techniques for analysis, adaptation and modeling of imbalanced data, see (Vladislavleva, 2008).

In (Vladislavleva, 2008) several algorithms for weighting and balancing multi-variate input- and input-output data are presented. Data weighting assigns weights to data records, and the weight is interpreted as a measure of relative importance (information content) of that data record. Information content is connected to the sparsity of the neighborhood of a data sample. It can reflect the proximity of a sample to its k nearest or nearest-in-the-input space neighbors, the surrounding of a sample by k nearest or nearest-in-the-input-space neighbors, or the local deviation from a hyper-plane approximating k nearest-in-the input space neighbors. The first two weights are introduced in (Harmeling et al., 2006) for unlabeled data, and are further extended to include input-response data and use a particular fractional distance metric.

Due to space limitations of this chapter we will give the definition for one weighting functional only - the surrounding weight.

By input-output data we mean a set $\mathcal{M} = \{M_1, \ldots, M_N\}$ of N points in a $(d+1)$-dimensional space $\mathbb{R}^{d+1}$. Point M_i has coordinates $(x_1^i, x_2^i, \ldots, x_d^i, y^i) \in \mathbb{R}^{d+1}$, $i = \overline{1, N}$, with y^i corresponding to the response value at the input point $P_i = (x_1^i, x_2^i, \ldots, x_d^i) \in X \subset \mathbb{R}^d$. We say that the input-output point M_i represents the input point P_i, since the projection of M_i

on the input space $X \subset \mathbb{R}^d$ is exactly P_i. The set of all input points is denoted as $\mathcal{P}$, the vector of outputs as $Y = (y^1, \ldots, y^N)^T$.

By $\{n_1(P_i, \mathcal{P}), n_2(P_i, \mathcal{P}), \ldots, n_k(P_i, \mathcal{P})\} \in \mathcal{P}$ we denote k nearest neighbors of the point $P_i \in \mathcal{P}$ in metric L_2 or $L_{1/d}$.

For unlabeled data the surrounding weight is defined as the length of the sum of vectors connecting a sample with its k nearest neighbors (averaged over k):

$$\sigma(i, \mathcal{P}, k) = \left\| \frac{1}{k} \sum_{j=1}^{k} (P_i - n_j(P_i, \mathcal{P})) \right\|, \tag{4.1}$$

where the $n_j(P_i, \mathcal{P})$ is the j-th nearest neighbor of the point P_i from the set $\mathcal{P}$ in the norm $\| \cdot \|_{1/d}$ or $\| \cdot \|_2$.

For labeled data, the surrounding weight is defined as the length of the sum of vectors connecting a sample with its k nearest-in-the-input space neighbors:

$$\sigma(i, \mathcal{M}, \mathcal{P}, k) = \left\| \frac{1}{k} \sum_{j=1}^{k} (M_i - \bar{n}_j(M_i, \mathcal{M}, \mathcal{P})) \right\|, \tag{4.2}$$

where $\bar{n}_j(M_i, \mathcal{M}, \mathcal{P})$ is the j-th nearest-in-the-input-space neighbor of point M_i in the set $\mathcal{M}$. This means that the projection of $\bar{n}_j(M_i, \mathcal{M}, \mathcal{P})$ onto the input space X is $n_j(P_i, \mathcal{P})$.

The neighborhood definition changes to reflect the fact that labeled data is assumed to belong to the response-surface, and in the input-output data space the notion of closeness to the closest neighbors can be deceiving (points, which are the closest in the input-response space may not be the closest on the response surface).

Data balancing for construction of smaller subsets with similar information content

The neighborhood size k dictates the scale in the perception of the data - small neighborhood size suggests local analysis of data, while big neighborhood size implies a global view on data. High weights, computed for the neighborhood size of $k = 1$, reflect the local importance of the points. They identify points, which are remote even from their nearest, or nearest-in-the-input-space neighbors. Such points are located in remote clusters of size one, and can therefore be interpreted as 'outliers'.

This approach of identifying remote clusters of points as outliers stops working if the size of the clusters is bigger than the neighborhood size k used in the weight computation.

For example, the points which are located in remote clusters of size $k+1$, will all have small weights computed for the neighborhood k, because they are close

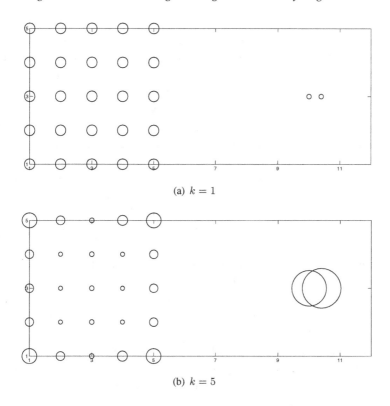

(a) $k = 1$

(b) $k = 5$

Figure 4-1. Straightforward weight computation in one pass cannot discover remote clusters of data if the neighborhood size is smaller than the size of the cluster.

to its k neighbors in the cluster. Small weights do not indicate the remoteness of such a cluster relative to the entire data set. To discover that the cluster is remote, we would need to compute weights of points with neighborhoods larger than the cluster size.

In Figure 4-1 we illustrate the problem of detecting remote data clusters with one-pass weighting. Figure 4-1 shows the unlabeled data set of 27 points, two of which are located in a sparse region of data space. In Figure 4-1(a) we indicate the surrounding weights of 27 points computed with 1 nearest neighbor (weights correspond to the radii of the circles with centers in data points). The weights of the remote points are very small in this case relative to the weights of other points in the data set. A simple observation of the sorted weights profile does not provide insights into the fact that the two points are outliers.

In Figure 4-1(b) we show the surrounding weights computed with the neighborhood size of $k = 5$. Since the k is greater than the size of the remote cluster - the large weights of the points in the cluster do reflect the discrepancy in the spatial location of cluster points relative to other points in the data set.

To still be able to identify the records belonging to regions which are globally remote from prototypic samples, but locally densely populated, we use an algorithm which iteratively eliminates records with the smallest weight from the data set, and recomputes the weights for points which had the eliminated record among the k nearest, or nearest-in-the-input-space neighbors. This procedure, called a Simple Multi-dimensional Iterative Technique for Sub-sampling (SMITS), gradually prunes the data set starting from the most densely populated regions, removes records with the smallest obtained weight from the data set, and ranks these points by the order, in which they are eliminated. After the record is eliminated from the data set, the weights of the points that had the eliminated point among k nearest or nearest-in-the-input-space neighbors must be re-evaluated at each iteration step. At the end of the elimination procedure only k points remain in the data set, and those points are randomly ranked by indexes $N - k + 1, \ldots, N$.

We interpret the elimination rank as a measure of the global relative importance of a data point. Points, which are representatives of the dense clusters will be eliminated the last. The weights of these points gradually increase as their neighbors get eliminated. At the moment when a point gets eliminated (which happens if the current weight of this point is the smallest among all points left) - the weight of the point represents the cumulative weight of the cluster, in which the point was originally located. For this reason archiving the weights of eliminated points at each elimination step - will get us the ordering of data records from prototypes (located in well- or over-represented regions) to the "back-bone" points (forming a space-filling support structure of the data set).

The geometrical outliers, or representatives of clusters of outliers (as in the example with three points) will never be eliminated before the prototypic points which have a smaller weight. Therefore the outliers, or representatives of the clusters of outliers will stay in the data set till the last stage of the elimination process.[4]

The SMITS procedure defines an order of the data records, which can be used to partition the data set into nested subsets of increasing size (when the eliminated records are added one by one to a subset of k records). If during the elimination process we archive a weight of each eliminated point, we can compute the cumulative sum of these weights for each elimination step in the order opposite to the order of elimination. If the weights are normalized by the total sum of the weights of the data set they will sum up to the number of records N. After normalization the resulting cumulative sum of eliminated

---

[4]The elimination stops when there are k records left n the data set, since the surrounding weight weight relative to k nearest or nearest-in-the-input space neighbors will not be defined for less than k records.

weights can be interpreted as a cumulative information content of the data set ranked with the SMITS procedure.

We illustrate the procedures of data weighting and cumulative information content calculation on the CountryData.

Scaling the CountryData

If all attributes are equally important for the modeler, we suggest scaling the data to a standard range before weighting and balancing it. But rather than scaling the ranges of all attributes to a particular range, e.g. $[0, 1]$, we advise mapping the 10th and 90th percentiles of the attribute ranges to the ends of the selected interval. This decreases the sensitivity of the scaled results to outliers in the records.

Insights for CountryData

Weighting the data: Since we are interested in the outlier-countries with atypical GDPperCapita we turn our data into input-response data, with 108 input attributes, and one response attribute - GDPperCapita. We weigh the data with the surrounding weight and one nearest-in-the-input-space neighbor. By definition of the surrounding weight, the countries located in the very sparse regions of the data space will get the highest surrounding weights. In Figure 4-2 we plot the sorted surrounding weights computed for one neighbor (the nearest neighbors are determined in the input space, and distances are computed in the 109 dimensional input-output space). The weights are normalized, so they sum up to the number of countries. From the plot we can infer that the weights of five countries are radically different from the rest. These countries with corresponding single-pass weights are UnitedStates (weight 18.1), Russia (weight 7.7), Canada (weight 6.2), India (weight 5.9), and China (weight 5.9). Other countries all have weights smaller than 3.6 (the weight of Japan), and can be considered as prototypes, since they are located in the better proximity to their nearest-in-the-input space neighbors[5].

Since the Euclidean distance $L_2(p, q) = \left(\sum_{j=1}^{d}(p_i - q_i)^2\right)^{1/2}$, $p, q \in \mathbf{R}^d$ was shown to fail in giving a meaningful notion of proximity in a high-dimensional space, we suggest using a fractional distance metric $L_{1/d}$ in a d-dimensional space, when d is large:

$$dist_{1/d}(\mathbf{u}, \mathbf{v}) = \left(\sum_{i=1}^{d}|u^i - v^i|^{1/d}\right)^d,$$

---

[5]The results of the weighting are almost the same in this example compared with weighting of CountryData without specifying GDPperCapita as a response variable. Only the rankings of 7 countries in the mid-weights range change slightly for a different definition of nearest neighbors.

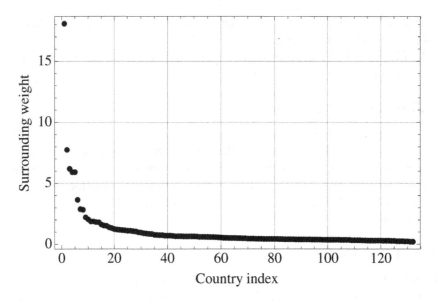

Figure 4-2. Exploration of the weights of data records gives insights into the remote outlier records located in sparse under-represented regions of the data space.

$$L_{1/d} : \|\mathbf{u}\|_{1/d} = \left(\sum_{i=1}^{d} |u^i|^{1/d} \right)^d .$$

A fractional distance metric in a space of high dimensionality can scale better, see (Aggarwal et al., 2001). See (Francois et al., 2007) for the detailed discussion on the relevance of using fractional distances with respect to the distance concentration phenomenon.

Balancing the data: Now we apply a balancing heuristic (the SMITS algorithm) to order the CountryData with GDPperCapita as a response variable in the order of decreasing importance. We again use one nearest-in-the input space neighbor, and two distance measures.

In Figure 4-3 we plot the cumulative information contents (CIC) of the CountryData ranked with surrounding weight via the SMITS procedure using two distance metrics. A value on a curve at point m is by definition a cumulative elimination weight of the first m samples in the balanced subset. It can be interpreted as a fraction of the information about the data contained in the first m samples of the ranked data set, $m = 1 : N$.

We can observe that the shape of the cumulative information content and also the SMITS-based ranking of countries changes, if the distance metric changes. From the plot 4-3(b) we can observe that the first nine to ten countries in the CountryData subset, balanced with the fractional distance metric, are representing 80% of the information content (i.e. have the cumulative elimination

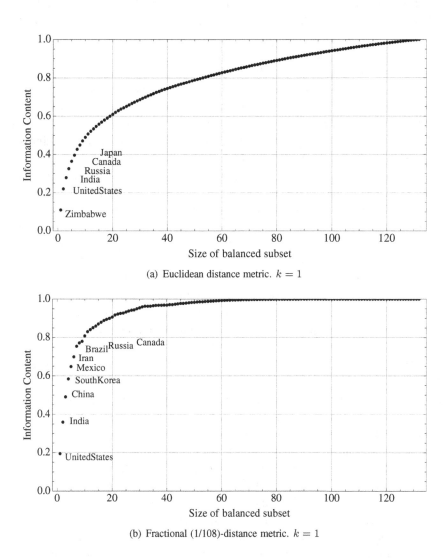

(a) Euclidean distance metric. $k = 1$

(b) Fractional (1/108)-distance metric. $k = 1$

Figure 4-3. Cumulative information content of the balanced data set can indicate compressibility of the set, and the fractions of outliers and prototypes.

weight of 0.8). The back-bone countries, i.e. outliers and the most representative prototypes are contained in this subset of countries. The difference between the elimination weight of a country and its actual weight (computed with the one-pass procedure) provides insight into the likelihood of a country to be an outlier. Since the elimination weight of the country can be interpreted as a cumulative weight of a cluster that the country is representing, the small difference in the elimination and one-pass weight indicates that the country represents a cluster of size one (i.e. is very likely to be an outlier). A big difference in the elimination weight and the one-pass weight indicates that the country is a representative of a big cluster, and cannot be viewed as a special data point.

So, the data balancing with euclidean distance and neighborhood of $k = 1$ produces the ranking of countries with the following elimination weights[6]: Zimbabwe (14.1), UnitedStates (14.1), India (7.7), Russia (6.2), Canada (5.6), Japan (4.2), China (4.1), UnitedKingdom (3.1), Brazil (2.8), Italy (2.4), Indonesia (2.2), and other countries, whose elimination weights quickly decrease below 2. Observing the differences we can hypothesize, that the seven to ten countries represent data clusters, which are likely to be outliers.

The data balancing with a fractional $L_1/109$ distance and $k = 1$ produces the following elimination weights: UnitedStates (38.3), India (38.3), China (12.9), SouthKorea (3.9), Mexico (6.1), Iran (5.4), Brazil (5.3), Russia (4.4), Canada (2.9), and other countries, whose weights quickly decrease in values below 2.

We provide the interested reader with the rankings of the subset of 30 countries obtained with weighting and balancing with different distance metrics in Table 4-1.

Identifying outliers among attributes by balancing the transposed data matrix: We note that the data balancing algorithm can also be applied to identify the 'back-bone' attributes of the data set. By applying the SMITS algorithm to the transposed data matrix of the CountryData, and treating attributes as records - we can get interesting insights into attributes, which are representative of the entire set of 109 attributes. By using a fractional distance metric $L_{1/132}$ and balancing the transposed data matrix (of the size 109×132) with SMITS for the neighborhood size of $k = 1$ we obtain a content-based ranking of attributes and their elimination weights. Because of space limitations we cannot give a full ranking of attributes, but would like to share the top ones with the reader. The *blind* data balancing algorithm applied to the scaled (transposed) data matrix (without any *a priori* information about the importance, or preferences for any attributes) discovers the following top four attributes for the CountryData: GDPPerCapita, ExpenditureFractions–>TotalConsumption, CallingCode, and MaleLiteracyFraction!

---

[6]For comparison purposes all elimination weights are normalized to sum up to the total number of records (132 in this case).

Table 4-1. Content-based rankings of 30 countries of the CountryData for $k = 1$. The first column represents the ranking obtained by sorting the one-pass surrounding weights computed with Euclidean distance. The second and the third columns represent ranking obtained with data balancing via SMITS algorithm with Euclidean distance and fractional $1/109$-distance respectively. Observe that changing the distance generates different 'back-bone' countries as representatives of the dense clusters of countries.

Country	Weight rank	SMITS **Euclidean**	SMITS **Fractional**
UnitedStates	1	2	1
Russia	2	4	8
Canada	3	5	9
India	4	3	7
China	5	7	3
Japan	6	6	29
Brazil	7	9	7
UnitedKingdom	8	8	40
Indonesia	9	11	57
Germany	10	12	65
Italy	11	10	12
France	12	29	14
Iran	13	22	6
Qatar	14	14	67
SaudiArabia	15	15	79
Australia	16	20	64
Lesotho	17	16	110
Mexico	18	25	5
Turkmenistan	19	27	34
Vietnam	20	13	33
Norway	21	18	24
Nigeria	22	20	72
Bangladesh	23	32	10
Spain	24	24	28
Paraguay	25	26	19
Peru	26	21	31
Algeria	27	31	25
Philippines	28	28	37
Turkey	29	23	53
SouthKorea	30	36	4

In the next section we use symbolic regression to discover relationships of the GDPperCapita with other attributes of the CountryData. After creating hundreds of explicit regression models we define outliers as countries, whose GDPperCapita is consistently under or over-predicted by the constructed models.

4.   Symbolic regression and model-based outlier detection

Symbolic regression as a modeling engine

Symbolic regression via genetic programming (GP) is a non-parametric non-linear regression technique that looks for an appropriate model structure and model parameters (as opposed to classic regression that assumes a certain model structure and estimates the optimal parameters). Symbolic regression is an attractive modeling engine because it mitigates the need to make a cascade of simplifying assumptions about the system and, instead, allows the data to define the appropriate model forms (provided it is used with intelligent and rigorous complexity control!). We use a particular flavour of genetic programming, with a multi-objective selection operator, which favors high prediction accuracy and low model complexity in models during the selection process. Propagation rights are distributed among individuals satisfying some conditions on Pareto-optimality in the objective space of accuracy vs. complexity. We refer to this methodology as to symbolic regression via Pareto genetic programming (Pareto GP), see (Smits and Kotanchek, 2004),(Kotanchek et al., 2006).

The strongest capabilities of modeling with symbolic regression via Pareto GP (and with other GP flavors with incorporated complexity control, fitness inheritance for successful variables, ensemble-based predictions) are:

- automatic (and robust) selection of significant variables related to a response variable (see e.g. (Smits et al., 2005));

- automatic generation of diverse model structures describing the relationship between the response and significant input variables;

- automatic generation of ensembles of diverse prediction models (all of which are global learners, but are constrained to be diverse with respect to complexity and uncorrelated w.r.t. prediction error), see (Kotanchek et al., 2007);

- automatic "outlier" identification (where outliers are defined as samples, which persistently imply worse prediction errors compared with the average (or prototypic) data samples on selected ensembles of diverse regression models).

With symbolic regression we can discover simplifying variable transformations, that make subsequent modeling cycles more efficient, accurate, and easier to interpret and might potentially reveal something about the underlying physical system. With symbolic regression via Pareto GP we can identify optimal trade-offs between competing modeling structures. We can begin to understand what dimensionality of the space is sufficient to describe the system. We can exploit the multitude of solutions of competing accuracy and complexities generated by symbolic regression to our advantage: ensembles of diverse models can always be used to generate an estimate of prediction trustworthiness that guides the user in his exploration of the new areas of the data space.

The hypothesis generating aspects of symbolic regression embedded into a global data modeling framework turn it into a valuable research assistant. Rather than eliminating the modeler from the modeling cycle, it frees more thinking time for a modeler, triggers new ideas and reveals the flaws in existing levels of understanding.

Model ensembles and suggested "outliers" on CountryData

We executed 150 independent runs of 10 minutes each for modeling GDP-perCapita via other 108 attributes of the CountryData. All runs used the default settings Pareto GP evolutionary strategy - two-objective selection with archiving, 300 population individuals, 100 archive members, 95%crossover, 5% mutation rates, and standard basis functions - multiplication, subtraction, product, division, inverse, negation, square root, and square (maximal arity of non-unary operators limited to 4). Objective functions for pareto-based model selection were normalized sum of squared errors (scaled to the interval $[0, 1]$, with zero corresponding to no error) and expressional complexity, computed as the total sum of nodes in all subtrees of a model tree. In both objectives smaller values are preferred.

Variable Selection

The GP runs generated more than 18000 regression models. We selected 3914 'interesting' models with expressional complexity of at most 150, and normalized prediction error of at most 0.3. These models were inspected for variable presence to identify the driving attributes related to the GDP-perCapita. We plot the variable presence map in Figure 4-4. The following (correlated) attributes were present in the 3914 interesting models: Total-Consumption (in 86% models), FixedInvestment (68%), GovernmentReceipts (59%), Population (45%), GrossInvestment (42%), AdultPopulation (28%), FemalePopulation (21%), HouseholdConsumption (21%), FemaleAdultPopulation (20%), GovernmentSurplus(16%), GovernmentConsumption (12%), ExportValue (12%), ImportValue(8%), GovernmentExpenditures (6%). It is interesting to observe that the Population-related variable is clearly a driving attribute for predicting the GDPperCapita, and attributes of consumption, investment, import, and export have a stronger relation to GDPperCapita (according to symbolic regression results) than NaturalGasProduction, or Road-Length, etc. The attributes, which are not listed above appeared in less than 5% of interesting models.

Ensemble construction and outlier identification

We pruned the set of interesting models further to automatically select 927 candidate models, from which an ensemble of 17 diverse accurate and parsimonious models was created. In the left plot of Figure 4-5 we plot the prediction of this ensemble. Based on deviation of predictions of ensemble models, we define a measure of ensemble disagreement for each point of the data space,

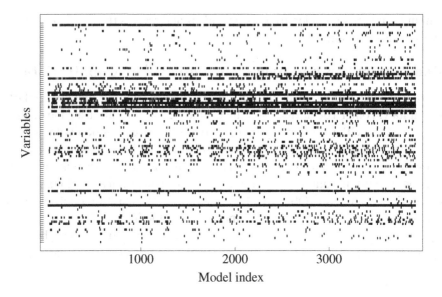

Figure 4-4. Symbolic regression can be used to discover significant attributes related to GDP-perCapita in a robust and reproducible fashion.

where the prediction is computed. In this way solutions of symbolic regression become trustworthy - with each prediction a confidence interval is supplied, see (Kotanchek et al., 2007) for more details. As soon as an ensemble is created, we can analyze data records with respect to systematic errors in predictions of ensemble models. Records, which are consistently under- or over-predicted by an ensemble are candidates for outliers. The top 19 countries deviating from ensemble predictions are shown in the right of Figure 4-5. Relative to the constructed models such countries as CaymanIslands, Greece, Iceland, Spain, Bahamas, and Estonia are underperforming, and should have shown a higher GDPperCapita than actual. The countries like Singapore, Switzerland, Qatar, Ireland, Bermuda, Japan, Bahrain, and others are on the contrary over-performing, which might imply that some other hidden attributes not included in our current list are contributing to an increased GDPperCapita. This in itself is an interesting and very relevant result of this type of data analysis using symbolic regression.

In such an interpretation the outliers are defined as records which disagree with produced models. Such an approach is viable only if produced models are reliable, and provide plausible descriptions of the system or process. This requires a domain expert to take decisions about reliability of produced models. There are, however, two factors, which contribute to justification of the approach and to convincing the expert to exploit symbolic regression as a research assistant:

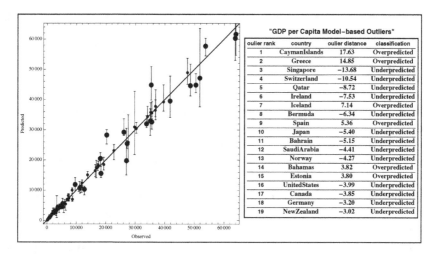

"GDP per Capita Model–based Outliers"			
oulier rank	country	outlier distance	classification
1	CaymanIslands	17.63	Overpredicted
2	Greece	14.85	Overpredicted
3	Singapore	−13.68	Underpredicted
4	Switzerland	−10.54	Underpredicted
5	Qatar	−8.72	Underpredicted
6	Ireland	−7.53	Underpredicted
7	Iceland	7.14	Overpredicted
8	Bermuda	−6.34	Underpredicted
9	Spain	5.36	Overpredicted
10	Japan	−5.40	Underpredicted
11	Bahrain	−5.15	Underpredicted
12	SaudiArabia	−4.41	Underpredicted
13	Norway	−4.27	Underpredicted
14	Bahamas	3.82	Overpredicted
15	Estonia	3.80	Overpredicted
16	UnitedStates	−3.99	Underpredicted
17	Canada	−3.85	Underpredicted
18	Germany	−3.20	Underpredicted
19	NewZealand	−3.02	Underpredicted

Figure 4-5. Ensembles of symbolic regression models can be used to discover records, which systematically disagree with predictions of individual ensemble models.

- The fact that thousands of diverse regression models are created during the modeling process without external assumptions about the model structure implies, the models in the ensemble have maximal predictive power and the highest reliability warranted by the data.

- The fact that the ensemble of multiple symbolic regression models is used to decide whether a record is an outlier or not makes this approach robust (the more models from a reliable and diverse collection identify a record as an outlier, the more likely this is actually true).

5. Conclusions and Recommendations

Outlier detection for nonlinear systems with lots of input variables is hard to achieve using conventional methods, and is dangerous to perform if samples are defined as outliers with respect to a model, and the model is "guessed" incorrectly. An outlier is either the most important nugget in the data set or something which should be removed from the modeling process to avoid distorting the results. Interpretation of an outlier always requires human insight of a domain expert.

We have shown two approaches for (automatic) outlier detection both before and after the model development process. It is automatic in a sense that no assumptions or guesses are made about the model or about the trustworthiness of the data records up until the final stage, where the outliers are identified. At that point the user or the modeler need to make a decision about an outlier's destiny - it is a "jewel or junk". We believe that both approaches are viable and need to be used in combination to fully exploit the power of symbolic regression as a discovery engine.

References

Aggarwal, Charu C., Hinneburg, Alexander, and Keim, Daniel A. (2001). On the surprising behavior of distance metrics in high dimensional space. *Lecture Notes in Computer Science*, 1973:420–434.

Francois, Damien, Wertz, Vincent, and Verleysen, Michel (2007). The concentration of fractional distances. *IEEE Trans. on Knowledge and Data Engineering*, 19(7):873–886.

Harmeling, Stefan, Dornhege, Guido, Tax, David, Meinecke, Frank, and Muller, Klaus-Robert (2006). From outliers to prototypes: Ordering data. *Neurocomputing*, 69(13-15):1608–1618.

Kotanchek, Mark, Smits, Guido, and Vladislavleva, Ekaterina (2006). Pursuing the pareto paradigm tournaments, algorithm variations & ordinal optimization. In Riolo, Rick L., Soule, Terence, and Worzel, Bill, editors, *Genetic Programming Theory and Practice IV*, volume 5 of *Genetic and Evolutionary Computation*, chapter 12, pages 167–186. Springer, Ann Arbor.

Kotanchek, Mark, Smits, Guido, and Vladislavleva, Ekaterina (2007). Trustable symbolic regression models. In Riolo, Rick L., Soule, Terence, and Worzel, Bill, editors, *Genetic Programming Theory and Practice V*, Genetic and Evolutionary Computation, chapter 12, pages 203–222. Springer, Ann Arbor.

Smits, Guido, Kordon, Arthur, Vladislavleva, Katherine, Jordaan, Elsa, and Kotanchek, Mark (2005). Variable selection in industrial datasets using pareto genetic programming. In Yu, Tina, Riolo, Rick L., and Worzel, Bill, editors, *Genetic Programming Theory and Practice III*, volume 9 of *Genetic Programming*, chapter 6, pages 79–92. Springer, Ann Arbor.

Smits, Guido and Kotanchek, Mark (2004). Pareto-front exploitation in symbolic regression. In O'Reilly, Una-May, Yu, Tina, Riolo, Rick L., and Worzel, Bill, editors, *Genetic Programming Theory and Practice II*, chapter 17, pages 283–299. Springer, Ann Arbor.

Vladislavleva, Ekaterina (2008). *Model-based Problem Solving through Symbolic Regression via Pareto Genetic Programming*. PhD thesis, Tilburg University, Tilburg, the Netherlands.

Chapter 5

SYMBOLIC REGRESSION OF IMPLICIT EQUATIONS

Michael Schmidt[1] and Hod Lipson[2,3]

[1] *Computational Biology, Cornell University, Ithaca, NY 14853, USA;* [2] *School of Mechanical and Aerospace Engineering, Cornell University, Ithaca NY 14853, USA;* [3] *Computing and Information Science, Cornell University, Ithaca, NY 14853, USA.*

Abstract   Traditional Symbolic Regression applications are a form of supervised learning, where a label y is provided for every $\vec{x}$ and an explicit symbolic relationship of the form $y = f(\vec{x})$ is sought. This chapter explores the use of symbolic regression to perform unsupervised learning by searching for implicit relationships of the form $f(\vec{x}, y) = 0$. Implicit relationships are more general and more expressive than explicit equations in that they can also represent closed surfaces, as well as continuous and discontinuous multi-dimensional manifolds. However, searching these types of equations is particularly challenging because an error metric is difficult to define. We studied several direct and indirect techniques, and present a successful method based on implicit derivatives. Our experiments identified implicit relationships found in a variety of datasets, such as equations of circles, elliptic curves, spheres, equations of motion, and energy manifolds.

Keywords: Symbolic Regression, Implicit Equations, Unsupervised Learning

1.   Introduction

Symbolic regression (Koza, 1992) is a method for searching the space of mathematical expressions, while minimizing various error metrics. Unlike traditional linear and nonlinear regression methods that fit parameters to an equation of a given form, symbolic regression searches both the parameters and the form of equations simultaneously. This process automatically forms mathematical equations that are amenable to human interpretation and help explicate observed phenomena. This paper focuses on the symbolic regression of functions in implicit form.

R. Riolo et al. (eds.), *Genetic Programming Theory and Practice VII*,
Genetic and Evolutionary Computation, DOI 10.1007/978-1-4419-1626-6_5,
© Springer Science + Business Media, LLC 2010

An implicit equation represents a mathematical relationship where the dependent variable is not given explicitly. For example, an implicit function could be given in the form $f(\vec{x}, y) = 0$, whereas an explicit function would be given in the form $y = f(\vec{x})$. Implicit equations can be more expressive and are often used to concisely define complex surfaces or functions with multiple outputs. Consider, for example, the equation of a circle: It could be represented implicitly as $x^2 + y^2 - r^2 = 0$, explicitly using a multi-output square root function as $y = \pm\sqrt{r^2 - x^2}$, or as a parametric equation of the form $x = cos(t)$, $y = sin(t)$, $t = 0..2\pi$. Our goal is to automatically infer implicit equations to model experimental data.

Regressing implicit relationships can be thought of as a form of unsupervised learning. Traditional Symbolic Regression applications are a form of supervised learning, where a label y is provided for every input vector $\vec{x}$ and a symbolic relationship of the form $y = f(\vec{x})$ is sought. When seeking an implicit relationship of the form $f(\vec{x}, y) = 0$, we are looking for any pattern that uniquely identifies the points in the dataset, and excludes all other points in space.

Like clustering methods and other data mining approaches (McConaghy et al., 2008), unsupervised learning has the potential to find unexpected relationships in the data (De Falco et al., 2002; Mackin and Tazaki, 2000; Hetland and Saetrom, 2005). For example, unsupervised learning can create a model from positive examples only, and then use that model to detect outliers that do not belong to the original set. This is important in many practical applications where negative examples are difficult or costly to come by. For example, when training a system to monitor a jet engine, a learning algorithm will typically

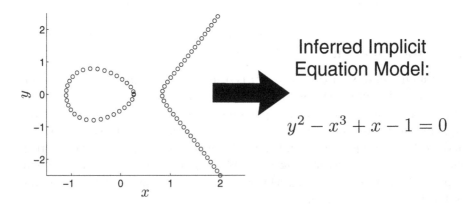

Figure 5-1. Many datasets exist that do not have explicit dependent variables, such as an elliptic curve shown here. Instead, this type of data must be modeled with an implicit equation. We explore using symbolic regression to infer these types of models.

be trained using sensor data from intact operation only, but will be required to alert an operator if abnormal sensor data is detected.

Implicit equations can also provide deeper insight into the mechanism underlying an observed phenomenon by identifying conservations. For example, when observing a pendulum, an explicit equation can be used to fit the data and thus predict the pendulum's future state based on its current and past states. In contrast, searching for implicit relationships can lead to finding equations of invariants, such as conservation of energy or momentum (Schmidt and Lipson, 2009). These conservations can also be used to make predictions, but provide more insight into the underlying principles, beyond prediction.

While symbolic regression has been used to find explicit (Korns, 2006; Duffy and Engle-Warnick, 1999; Bautu et al., 2005) and differential equations (Bongard and Lipson, 2007), it is not immediately obvious how it could be used to search for implicit equations (Figure 5-1). Symbolic regression ordinarily models and predicts a specific signal or value. In implicit equations, the equation always evaluates to zero over the dataset.

A key challenge is that there are an infinite number of valid implicit equations for any given dataset. For example, $sin^2(x) + cos^2(x) - 1$ is exactly zero for all points in the dataset, but it is also exactly zero for all points not in the dataset. There are also an infinite number of relationships that are arbitrarily close to zero, such as $1/(1000 + x^2)$. In order to utilize symbolic regression, we need to devise a fitness function that avoids these trivial solutions.

We experimented with a number of fitness functions for searching invariant equations. We explored minimizing the variance of the function from zero over the dataset while penalizing trivial equations that are zero everywhere, and numerically solving the implicit equation and minimizing its distance to each data point. Due to the difficulty of trivial solutions and susceptibility to local optima, none of these direct methods worked well.

Based on these results, we looked for a different metric that would relate an implicit equation to the dataset. Rather than attempting to model the data points themselves or the zeros of the target function, we decided to look at the gradients of the data. We found that we could derive implicit derivatives of the data variables using an arbitrary implicit equation, and then compare the two. Instead of fitting data points directly, this approach fits line segments (partial derivatives) derived from the data to the line segments (implicit derivatives) of the implicit function.

To test this approach, we experimented on modeling a number of implicit systems – ranging from equations of circles to equations of motion. We found this to be a reliable method for all these systems, whereas the other methods failed to find even the equation of the circle with similar computational effort.

In the remaining sections, we describe the direct methods in more detail, our proposed fitness for arbitrary implicit equations, the experiments and results on modeling implicit systems, and finally, concluding remarks.

2.   The Implicit Equation Problem

The need to search for implicit equations arises when we do not know or do not have an explicit dependent variable in a dataset. Instead, we are given a large vector of data points and our goal is to find an equation that holds true for all of these points. For example, an equation that when solved numerically reproduces the points in the dataset.

An implicit equation has the form:

$$f(x, y, ...) = 0 \qquad\qquad (5.1)$$

where x, y, etc. are independent variables of the system. Implicit equations in this form may or may not have an explicit equation in general (it may not be possible to solve for any single variable). However, these equations can be solved numerically or graphically when the equation is known.

Our task is to identify expression $f(x, y, ...)$ that satisfies the Equation 5.1 uniquely for all points in the dataset.

3.   Direct Methods

Table 5-1. A summary of direct methods and their difficulties

Method	Difficulty
Equations that equal zero at all data points	Trivial solutions such as $0 = 0$, $x - x = 0$, etc
Equations that equal zero near data, but grow with distance	Places too many constraints on the resulting equations
Equations that equal zero but have non-zero derivative	Places too many constraints on the resulting equations
Equations that equal zero but not symbolically zero when simplified	Trivial solutions, just more complex zero identities such as $\cos^2 x^3 + \sin^2 x^3 - 1$
Equations that Equal zero, but nonzero at random point away from data	Trivial solutions such as $f(x) = 1/(100 + x)^2$, which is non-zero near $x = -100$
Numerically solve equation, measure distance from data points to closest zero	Difficult to evolve, many degenerate equations do not have solutions, and computationally expensive

Based on Equation 5.1, it might be tempting to search for equations that evaluate to zero for all data points in the dataset. A simple fitness function for this would be second moment or squared-error from zero. The problem with this naive method is quickly obvious however: evolution almost immediately converges to a trivial solution such as $x - x = 0$ or $x + 4.56 - yx/y$, etc. These trivial solutions are zero everywhere and are not particularly interesting or useful for analyzing the data.

We tried a slight modification of this method by adding a test for trivial solutions such as $0 = 0$. For each candidate equation, we would perform a quick symbolic simplification to see if the result reduces to zero. Unfortunately, the evolution always converged to more complex identities equal to zero than we could add to our simplification test. For example, $(x-1) - (x^2 - 2x + 1)/(x-1)$ and $-\sin^2(x) - \cos^2(x) + 1$, or more complex elaborations of zero identities.

A third method we tried was rewarding the function for being non-zero away from the points in the dataset. In this circumstance, evolution still converged on trivial solutions that were arbitrarily close to zero over most of the data, but still nonzero away from the data. For example, solutions such as $1/(1 + x^2)$, can become arbitrarily close implicit equations over the data, but are still trivial.

Finally, we decided to try numerically solving the candidate implicit equations and comparing with the data points. This method is extremely slow as the numerical solution requires an iterative procedure. It also has serious evolvability problems. Many candidate equations do not have implicit solutions (for example, $f(x) = 1/x^2$ never crosses zero) which makes finding the numerical solution non-convergent.

We modified this procedure slightly to find the local absolute valued minimum of a candidate equation around each point in the data set, summing the distance from the data points to their minima on the implicit function and the distance of the minima from zero. In the case that there is no local minimum for a data point, we capped the iterated procedure to a maximum distance.

This approach was able to identify implicit versions of simple lines, such as $x + y = 0$, and once found the correct implicit equations in the unit circle dataset (though these solutions were not repeatable). Unfortunately, all runs on more complex datasets, and most runs on the unit circle dataset, became trapped in local optima solutions. A common type of local optima evolved zeros around a part of the dataset (for example $1/(x+a) - b - y$ can model the left and bottom sides of a circle accurately), but rarely jumped to fit remaining data points.

While this final direct method may be a workable approach with more sophistication, it is far from elegant or efficient. Below, we describe a more direct and greatly more reliable and efficient fitness calculation for implicit equations.

4. The Implicit Derivatives Method

The difficulties of the direct methods (Table 5-1) suggest that comparing the zeros of the candidate implicit equation directly is insufficient to reliably find accurate and nontrivial models.

Rather than looking at the individual points, we decided to look at the local derivatives of these points. If the candidate implicit equation is modeling the points in a meaningful way, it should be able to predict relationships between derivatives of each variable. Importantly, we must also be able to measure such a relationship readily from the dataset.

For our method, we propose using the ratio of partial derivatives between pairs of variables (implicit derivatives). The idea is that dividing two partial derivatives of a candidate implicit equation $f(...) = 0$ cancels out the implicit $f(...)$ signal, leaving only the implied derivative between two variables of the system.

For example, in a two-dimensional dataset we could measure variables $x(t)$ and $y(t)$ over time. The system's implicit derivatives estimated from time-series data would then be $\Delta x/\Delta y = x'/y'$ and $\Delta y/\Delta x = y'/x'$, where x' and y' represent the time-derivatives of x and y. Similarly, given a candidate implicit equation $f(x, y)$, we can derive the same values through differentiation: $\delta x/\delta y = (\delta f/\delta y)/(\delta f/\delta x)$ and $\delta y/\delta x = (\delta f/\delta x)/(\delta f/\delta y)$. We can now compare $\Delta x/\Delta y$ values from the experimental data with $\delta x/\delta y$ values from a candidate implicit equation $f(x, y)$ to measure how well it predicts indirect relationships between variables of the system.

Finally, we can use this process in a fitness function for implicit equations. We simply measure the error on all implicit derivatives that we can derive from each candidate equation. In our experiments, we return the mean logarithmic error of these derivatives:

$$-\frac{1}{N} \sum_{i=1}^{N} log \left(1 + |\frac{\Delta x_i}{\Delta y_i} - \frac{\delta x_i}{\delta y_i}|\right) \qquad (5.2)$$

where N is the number of data points, $\Delta x/\Delta y$ is a implicit derivative estimated from the data, and $\delta x/\delta y$ is the implicit derivative derived from the candidate implicit equation.

5.   Handling Unordered Datasets

The implicit method can also be applied to unordered and non-time series data as there are several ways to estimate implicit derivatives from experimental data. An implicit derivative is simply a local relation of how two variables covary. In 2D, the implicit derivative is the slope of the tangent line. In 3D, the implicit derivatives lie on the tangent plane. In higher dimensions, they lie on the n-dimensional tangent hyperplane.

To generalize this procedure for arbitrary unordered data, one can fit a hyperplane, or higher-order surface such as a conic section (Shpitalni and Lipson, 1995), to local clouds of data points. From each hyperplane, one can then

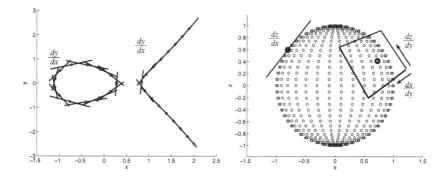

Figure 5-2. Implicit derivatives can be estimated from unordered, or shuffled data, nonpara-metrically by fitting a hyperplane or higher-order surface to neighboring points. After fitting the neighboring points, simply take any of the implicit derivatives of the locally fit surface.

sample implicit derivatives by taking the implicit derivative of the hyperplane equation (Figure 5-2).

We verified that this procedure works in our experimental datasets by randomly shuffling them and discarding their time ordering. The method regresses the same implicit equations as in our results below using this procedure.

6.   Experiments on Implicit Equations

We experimented on six implicit equation problems of varying complexity and difficulty (Figure 5-3). The simplest are the equation of a circle and an elliptic curve. These are well-known two dimensional systems with only two implicit derivatives ($\delta x/\delta y$ and $\delta y/\delta x$) that require implicit equations. A similar but slightly more difficult problem is the 3-dimensional sphere. In each of these systems we can collect data uniformly on their implicit surfaces.

The next three systems are dynamical systems of varying complexity: a simple linear harmonic oscillator, a nonlinear pendulum, and a chaotic spring-pendulum. We simulated single trajectories of each system, recording the positions, velocities, and accelerations for the implicit datasets. In these systems, we are seeking the implicit equation of motion. In the spring-pendulum we are seeking a similar implicit equation, the Hamiltonian, which only uses position and velocity data. The data used for each system is shown in Figure 5-3.

From this data, we estimate the partial derivatives from the data ($\Delta x/\Delta y$) by taking the ratio of the time derivatives. For the circle, elliptic curve, and sphere, we picked an arbitrary time trajectory around their surfaces (two in the case of the elliptic curve). This works because the time component cancels out in the ratio. We could also have fit a local plane to each point to estimate the partial derivatives non-parametrically of unordered data as discussed earlier.

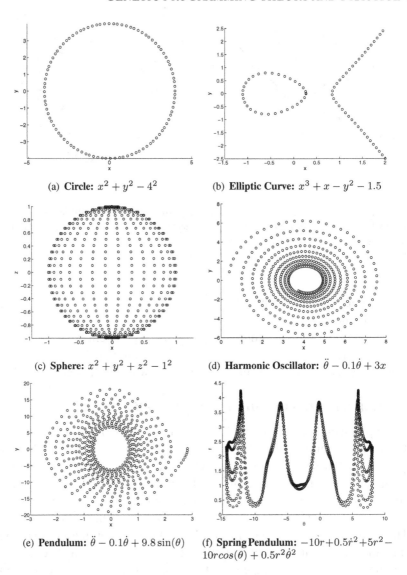

Figure 5-3. Data sampled from six target implicit equation systems. Data is collected uniformly for the geometric systems. In the dynamical systems, the data is a single simulated trajectory from a random initial condition.

We used a basic symbolic regression algorithm (Schmidt and Lipson, 2006) to search the space of implicit equations. We use the deterministic crowding selection method (Mahfoud, 1995), with 1% mutation probability and 75% crossover probability. The encoding is an acyclic graph (Schmidt and Lipson, 2007) with a maximum of 128 operations/nodes. The operation set contains addition, subtraction, multiply, sine, and cosine operations. Fitness was calculated using Equation 5.2.

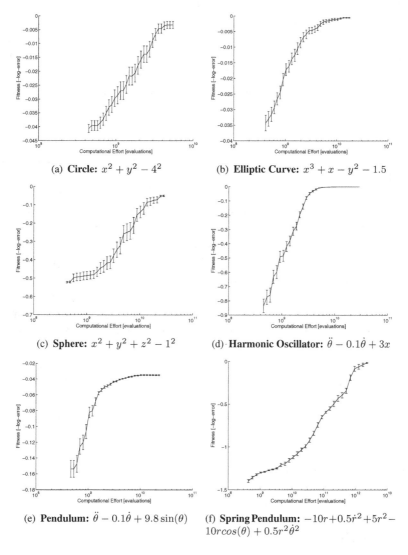

(a) **Circle:** $x^2 + y^2 - 4^2$

(b) **Elliptic Curve:** $x^3 + x - y^2 - 1.5$

(c) **Sphere:** $x^2 + y^2 + z^2 - 1^2$

(d) **Harmonic Oscillator:** $\ddot{\theta} - 0.1\dot{\theta} + 3x$

(e) **Pendulum:** $\ddot{\theta} - 0.1\dot{\theta} + 9.8\sin(\theta)$

(f) **Spring Pendulum:** $-10r + 0.5\dot{r}^2 + 5r^2 - 10r\cos(\theta) + 0.5r^2\dot{\theta}^2$

Figure 5-4. Fitness of the symbolic regression algorithm using the implicit derivatives fitness for each of the six systems. Results are the top ranked solution versus time, averaged over 20 independent trials. Error bars indicate the first standard error.

7.   Results on Implicit Equations

We conducted 20 independent trials on each system, recording fitnesses and solutions overtime. Evolution was stopped after a solution converged onto a near perfect solution. Figure 5-4 shows the mean fitness of the top-ranked solution during the evolutionary runs on a validation dataset.

Each evolutionary run identified the correct implicit equation for these systems, although different systems required more computation than others. The circle took less than a minute to converge on average; the elliptic curve, sphere, and pendulum took five to ten minutes on average; and the spring pendulum took approximately one to two hours.

In comparison, none of the direct methods could find solutions to any of these systems, even with considerably more computational effort. In the case of the circle, the implicit derivatives methods obtained the correct solution 20 out of 20 trials in under one minute per trial. In contrast, the direct methods did not obtain the correct solution even once in 20, one hour trials. The best solution found by the direct method over these runs was $a/(x^2 + b) - y - c = 0$. In the remaining target systems, the direct methods performed even worse.

Over our experiments, we also tracked the Pareto Front of the implicit equation fitness and complexity for each system (Figure 5-5). This front shows the tradeoff between equation complexity and its ability to model the implicit data (Smits and Kotanchek, 2004). Here, we measure the complexity of an equation as the number of nodes in its binary parse tree.

The Pareto fronts tend to contain cliff features where fitness jumps rapidly at some minimum complexity. In the cases where even more complex equations are found on the front, even several times more complex, the improvement in fitness is only marginal.

For each system, the simplest implicit equation to reach the highest qualitative fitness on the Pareto front was the exact target equation. Looking more closely at the higher complexity solutions, we found they were elaborations on the exact solution – for example, extraneous terms with very small coefficients, perhaps compensating for small errors in estimating the partial derivatives from the data.

We also noticed that simpler and lower fitness solutions on the fronts contained approximations to the exact solutions – for example, small angle approximations in the pendulum and spring pendulum systems.

8.   Conclusion

The ability to search for implicit equations enables searching for multi-dimensional surfaces, equations of motion, and other invariant models in experimental data. However, identifying meaningful and nontrivial implicit equations poses difficult challenges.

We explored several naive fitness methods for rewarding implicit equations to model data. These methods, which considered the individual data points and

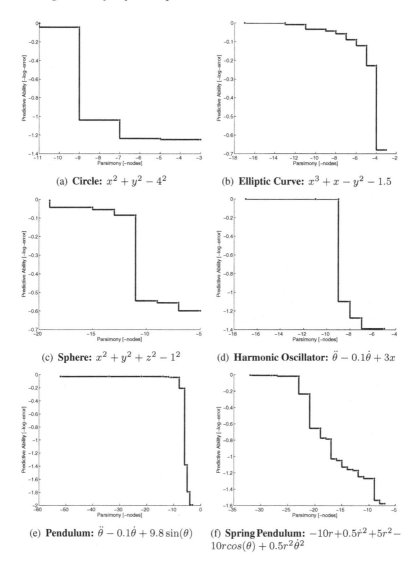

(a) **Circle:** $x^2 + y^2 - 4^2$

(b) **Elliptic Curve:** $x^3 + x - y^2 - 1.5$

(c) **Sphere:** $x^2 + y^2 + z^2 - 1^2$

(d) **Harmonic Oscillator:** $\ddot{\theta} - 0.1\dot{\theta} + 3x$

(e) **Pendulum:** $\ddot{\theta} - 0.1\dot{\theta} + 9.8\sin(\theta)$

(f) **Spring Pendulum:** $-10r + 0.5\dot{r}^2 + 5r^2 - 10r\cos(\theta) + 0.5r^2\dot{\theta}^2$

Figure 5-5. The fitness and equation complexity Pareto fronts found for each of the six systems. The exact solutions are the simplest equations to reach near perfect fitness. More complex solutions show elaborations on the exact solution, improving fitness only marginally.

the zeros of the implicit equations directly, were unable to solve the simplest implicit equations reliably or consistently.

We showed that looking instead at ratios of partial derivatives of local data points provided a reliable search gradient for a variety of implicit systems. This method identified geometric equations such as elliptic curves and 3-dimensional spheres, as well as equations of motions in nonlinear dynamical systems.

Acknowledgment

This research is supported in part by the U.S. National Science Foundation Graduate Research Fellowship and by U.S. Defense Threat Reduction Agency (DTRA) grant HDTRA1-09-1-0013.

References

Bautu, Elena, Bautu, Andrei, and Luchian, Henri (2005). Symbolic regression on noisy data with genetic and gene expression programming. In *Seventh International Symposium on Symbolic and Numeric Algorithms for Scientific Computing (SYNASC'05)*, pages 321–324.

Bongard, Josh and Lipson, Hod (2007). Automated reverse engineering of nonlinear dynamical systems. *Proceedings of the National Academy of Sciences*, 104(24):9943–9948.

De Falco, Ivanoe, Cioppa, Antonio Della, and Tarantino, Ernesto (2002). Unsupervised spectral pattern recognition for multispectral images by means of a genetic programming approach. In Fogel, David B., El-Sharkawi, Mohamed A., Yao, Xin, Greenwood, Garry, Iba, Hitoshi, Marrow, Paul, and Shackleton, Mark, editors, *Proceedings of the 2002 Congress on Evolutionary Computation CEC2002*, pages 231–236. IEEE Press.

Duffy, John and Engle-Warnick, Jim (1999). Using symbolic regression to infer strategies from experimental data. In Belsley, David A. and Baum, Christopher F., editors, *Fifth International Conference: Computing in Economics and Finance*, page 150, Boston College, MA, USA. Book of Abstracts.

Hetland, Magnus Lie and Saetrom, Pal (2005). Evolutionary rule mining in time series databases. *Machine Learning*, 58(2-3):107–125.

Korns, Michael F. (2006). Large-scale, time-constrained symbolic regression. In Riolo, Rick L., Soule, Terence, and Worzel, Bill, editors, *Genetic Programming Theory and Practice IV*, volume 5 of *Genetic and Evolutionary Computation*, chapter 16, pages –. Springer, Ann Arbor.

Koza, John R. (1992). *Genetic Programming: On the Programming of Computers by Means of Natural Selection*. MIT Press, Cambridge, MA, USA.

Mackin, Kenneth J. and Tazaki, Eiichiro (2000). Unsupervised training of Multiobjective Agent Communication using Genetic Programming. In *Proceedings of the Fourth International Conference on Knowledge-Based Intelligent Engineering Systems and Allied Technology*, volume 2, pages 738–741, Brighton, UK. IEEE.

Mahfoud, Samir W. (1995). *Niching methods for genetic algorithms*. PhD thesis, Champaign, IL, USA.

McConaghy, Trent, Palmers, Pieter, Gielen, Georges, and Steyaert, Michiel (2008). Automated extraction of expert domain knowledge from genetic programming synthesis results. In Riolo, Rick L., Soule, Terence, and Worzel,

Bill, editors, *Genetic Programming Theory and Practice VI*, Genetic and Evolutionary Computation, chapter 8, pages 111–125. Springer, Ann Arbor.

Schmidt, Michael and Lipson, Hod (2007). Comparison of tree and graph encodings as function of problem complexity. In Thierens, Dirk, Beyer, Hans-Georg, Bongard, Josh, Branke, Jurgen, Clark, John Andrew, Cliff, Dave, Congdon, Clare Bates, Deb, Kalyanmoy, Doerr, Benjamin, Kovacs, Tim, Kumar, Sanjeev, Miller, Julian F., Moore, Jason, Neumann, Frank, Pelikan, Martin, Poli, Riccardo, Sastry, Kumara, Stanley, Kenneth Owen, Stutzle, Thomas, Watson, Richard A, and Wegener, Ingo, editors, *GECCO '07: Proceedings of the 9th annual conference on Genetic and evolutionary computation*, volume 2, pages 1674–1679, London. ACM Press.

Schmidt, Michael and Lipson, Hod (2009). Distilling Free-Form Natural Laws from Experimental Data. *Science*, 324(5923):81–85.

Schmidt, Michael D. and Lipson, Hod (2006). Co-evolving fitness predictors for accelerating and reducing evaluations. In Riolo, Rick L., Soule, Terence, and Worzel, Bill, editors, *Genetic Programming Theory and Practice IV*, volume 5 of *Genetic and Evolutionary Computation*, chapter 17, pages –. Springer, Ann Arbor.

Shpitalni, M. and Lipson, H. (1995). Classification of sketch strokes and corner detection using conic sections and adaptive clustering. *ASME Journal of Mechanical Design*, 119:131–135.

Smits, Guido and Kotanchek, Mark (2004). Pareto-front exploitation in symbolic regression. In O'Reilly, Una-May, Yu, Tina, Riolo, Rick L., and Worzel, Bill, editors, *Genetic Programming Theory and Practice II*, chapter 17, pages 283–299. Springer, Ann Arbor.

Chapter 6

A STEADY-STATE VERSION OF THE AGE-LAYERED POPULATION STRUCTURE EA

Gregory S. Hornby[1]

[1]*U.C. Santa Cruz, Mail Stop 269-3, Moffett Field, CA 94035, USA.*

Abstract

   The Age-Layered Population Structure (ALPS) paradigm is a novel meta-heuristic for overcoming premature convergence by running multiple instances of a search algorithm simultaneously. When the ALPS paradigm was first introduced it was combined with a generational Evolutionary Algorithm (EA) and the ALPS-EA was shown to work significantly better than a basic EA. Here we describe a version of ALPS with a steady-state EA, which is well suited for use in situations in which the synchronization constraints of a generational model are not desired. To demonstrate the effectiveness of our version of ALPS we compare it against a basic steady-state EA (BEA) in two test problems and find that it outperforms the BEA in both cases.

Keywords:

   Age, Evolutionary Design, Genetic Programming, Metaheuristic, Premature Convergence

1.   Introduction

   One of the main problems with Evolutionary Algorithms (EAs) is that the population will eventually converge on a mediocre solution from which further iterations of the EA are unable to improve upon. Recently, the Age-Layered Population Structure (ALPS) paradigm was proposed as a novel approach for addressing this problem of premature convergence (Hornby, 2006) and, since then, others have also found it to work significantly better than a basic EA (Korns and Nunez, 2008; McConaghy et al., 2007; Willis et al., 2008). In this chapter

R. Riolo et al. (eds.), *Genetic Programming Theory and Practice VII*,
Genetic and Evolutionary Computation, DOI 10.1007/978-1-4419-1626-6_6,
© Springer Science + Business Media, LLC 2010

we describe a steady-state version of the ALPS algorithm and demonstrate its effectiveness by comparing it against a basic EA.

While the ALPS paradigm is a metaheuristic which is applicable to any optimization strategy, the original description of an implementation of ALPS was combined with a generational EA. Since the management of individuals in the different age-layers of an ALPS implementation depends on the measuring of an individual's age, and age was counted using generations as units, modifying the generational ALPS system to a steady-state one requires a revised measure of age. For our combination of ALPS with a steady-state EA (ALPS-SS) we modify the measure of age to be based on the number of evaluations divided by the population size. In addition, since individuals are moved up layers asynchronously, we adjust the algorithm to prevent an individual from replacing one which was just moved up.

The rest of this chapter is organized as follows. In Section 2 we review the problem of *premature convergence*. Next, in Section 3, we review the ALPS paradigm with its measure of age. In Section 4 we present the Steady-State ALPS EA. Then, in Section 5 we describe our experimental setup for evaluating ALPS and then present our comparison on two different test problems in Sections 6 and 7. Finally, in Section 8, we close with a discussion in which we consider a variation to assigning age and give our conclusions in Section 9.

2.   Premature Convergence

One of the main problems with EAs is that after some time they prematurely converge on a mediocre solution and further iterations of evolution do not find any significantly better solutions. Over the years various approaches have been tried for overcoming this problem of premature convergence. Basic approaches are to increase the mutation size or rate or to increase the population size. More sophisticated techniques try to maintain genotypic diversity through an evolutionary run (Cavicchio, 1970; DeJong, 1975; Mahfoud, 1992; Goldberg and Richardson, 1987). While these methods work to varying degrees, so far no approach has solved the problem.

Once an EA has converged and stops improving, the only option is to restart it with a new, randomly generated initial population using a new random number seed. Restarting can be done at fixed intervals with a multi-run EA, which divides a total of n generations into m runs of n/m generations. While regularly restarting the EA can improve search performance (Cantú-Paz and Goldberg, 2003; Luke, 2001), one of the challenges is figuring out when to restart. If too few generations are used, then the population will not have enough time to climb the fitness peak of the global optima, and if too many are used then much time will be wasted while the population has converged on top of a mediocre fitness peak before the next run is started. Alternatively, the population can be

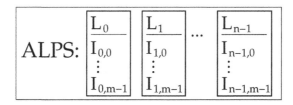

Figure 6-1. The layout of an ALPS system with n layers (L_0 to L_{n-1}) and m individuals in each layer ($I_{i,0}$ to $I_{i,m-1}$).

automatically restarted when no improvements have been detected after some number of generations, but then the problem is deciding how long to wait. All such multistart EAs have the problem that good genetic material found in one solution are not shared with others.

An alternative to restarting the entire EA is to run multiple EAs simultaneously and only restart one of them, and this is what is done with ALPS.

3.   The ALPS Metaheuristic

The Age-Layered Population Structure was developed by Hornby (Hornby, 2006) as a type of meta-EA to overcome the problem of premature convergence. More generally, the ALPS paradigm applies to any stochastic search or optimization technique. With ALPS, several instances of a search algorithm are run in parallel, each in its own age-layer, and the age of solutions is kept track of (see Figure 6-1). The key properties of ALPS are:

- Multiple instances of a search algorithm are run in parallel, with each instance in its own age layer and having its own population of one or more candidate solutions (*individuals*).

- Each age-layer has a maximum age and it may not contain individuals older than that maximum age.

- The age of individuals is based on when the original genetic material was created from random.

- The search algorithm in a given age-layer can look at individuals in its own population and at the populations in younger age layers but it can only replace individuals in its own population.

- At regular intervals, the search algorithm in the first age-layer is restarted.

Measuring Age

Typical optimization algorithms start with a population of one or more random points, or candidate solutions, in the search space. These candidate so-

Table 6-1. Different systems for setting the age-limits for each age-layer and the corresponding maximum age in each layer for an `age-gap` of 1.

Aging-scheme	Max age in layer						
	0	1	2	3	4	5	6
Linear	1	2	3	4	5	6	7
Fibonacci	1	2	3	5	8	13	21
Polynomial (n^2)	1	2	4	9	16	25	49
Exponential (2^n)	1	2	4	8	16	32	64

lutions are also known as *individuals* and the data which encodes a solution is called a *genotype* and what the genotype encodes is called the *phenotype*. Optimization of individuals occurs by making small changes to them (*mutation*) or by combining parts of two or more individuals (*recombination*). With ALPS, age is a measure of how long it has been since an individual's ancestor was randomly created.

Randomly generated individuals start with an age of 1 and individuals created through mutation or recombination inherit the age of their oldest parent. After a new population of individuals has been created, the age of the parents and their offspring is increased by one. For example, if individual Ind_A, age 23, and individual Ind_B, age 28, are selected as parents for recombination then their offspring, Ind_C, will be assigned an age of 28. At the end of the reproduction phase Ind_A will have its age increased to 24 and Ind_B and Ind_C will have their ages increased to 29. More generally, as will be explained later, age is calculated based on the number of evaluations.

The ALPS method of measuring age is different from previous age measures in the EA community (Huber and Mlynski, 1998; Kim et al., 1995; Kubota et al., 1994). With other systems for measuring age, individuals created by modifying existing ones (such as through mutation or recombination) are given an age of 1 and what is measured is the age of that exact genotype. With ALPS, an individual's age is the age of its lineage of genetic material and only the age of individuals created at random start with an age 1.

Maximum Age of Age-Layers

With the ALPS paradigm, there are multiple searches going on in parallel, each in its own age layer and each age layer has its own maximum age. The maximum ages for age layers is monotonically increasing and different methods can be used for setting these values (see Table 6-1). Since there is generally little need to segregate individuals which are within a few "generations" of each other, these values are then multiplied by an `age-gap` parameter. In addition, this allows individuals in the first age-layer some time to be optimized before them, or their offspring, are pushed to the next age layer. Also, the age-gap parameter sets the frequency of how often the first layer, L_0, is restarted. Finally, there is no age-limit to the last layer so as to be able to keep the best individuals from the most promising (longest running) search. Thus with 6 age layers, a polynomial aging-scheme and an age gap of 20 the maximum ages for the layers are: 20, 40, 80, 180, 320 and ∞. With this configuration the search algorithm in the bottom layer is restarted with a new population of randomly created individuals every 20 generations.

ALPS Examples

ALPS can be used with any type of optimizer that has some element of randomness in it, whether the randomness is in selecting the initial starting conditions, in how new candidate solutions are chosen to be tested, or for both. Used with a hill climbing algorithm, each layer L_i would have one individual ($m = 1$) and its own independent hill climbing algorithm running inside it. The ALPS hill climber (ALPS-HC) would cycle through each layer with each hill climbing algorithm performing one hill-climbing step. One way of allowing better individuals to move up layers (from a given L_{i-1} to L_i) is when a hill climber is updated, it checks whether the individual in the previous layer, $I_{i-1,0}$ is better than its own individual $I_{i,0}$. If $I_{i-1,0}$ is better than $I_{i,0}$ then it replaces individual $I_{i,0}$ with a copy of $I_{i-1,0}$. Alternatively, when the individual in layer L_i becomes too old for its current layer then it is replaced with a copy of the individual in layer L_{i-1}. Optionally, a replaced individual can be moved up to the next layer, L_{i+1}, and replace $I_{i+1,0}$ if it is better.

Instead of a hill climbing algorithm, a simulated annealing (SA) algorithm (Kirkpatrick et al., 1983) could be used instead. In this case, along with moving copies of individuals up layers, a copy of the entire search state—the *temperature*—should also be moved up. Also, population based optimizers such as Evolutionary Algorithms can be used in each layer, in which case each layer will have a population of individuals (from $I_{i,0}$ to $I_{i,m-1}$) (Hornby, 2006).

When using an Evolutionary Algorithm in each layer, we have found that using around 10 age layers, each with 20 to 50 individuals, works well. Setting the age gap and aging scheme depends on the desired maximum number of evaluations. It seems useful to set these such that the maximum age for the second oldest layer is some fraction of the maximum age that an individual can reach. For example, if an ALPS-EA with 10 age layers, each with 50 individuals will be run for one million evaluations, then the maximum age an individual can reach is 4000. With a polynomial aging scheme, a good range of values for the age gap is from 3 to 20.

4.   Steady-State ALPS EA

Our proposed combination of a Steady-State EA inside each ALPS layer (ALPS-SS) is much like our original system, which used a generational EA (Hornby, 2006), with one difference being in how age is calculated. In the original system, using a generational EA, age was counted in generations and the age of all individuals was increased after the EAs in all layers had processed one generation. Since there are no explicit generations with ALPS-SS, we keep track of the number of evaluations. Age is then calculated by taking the number of evaluations in which an individual's genetic material has been around and dividing it by the size of the population. Randomly generated individuals store the number of evaluations that have been performed so far, and individuals created through mutation and recombination store the smallest (which is equivalent to "oldest") value of their parents.

The equation for calculating the age of an individual is:

$$age = 1 + (evals_{current} - evals_{created})/popsize \qquad (6.1)$$

Where: $evals_{current}$ is the number of evaluations that have been performed so far; $evals_{created}$ is the number of evaluations that had been performed when the individual's genetic material was first created; and $popsize$ is the total number of individuals in all layers. A constant of 1 is added so that the age of randomly generated individuals is 1 at creation time.

Using this measure of age, ALPS-SS works as follows. The algorithm starts by configuring the age layers and then creating, and evaluating, an initial, random population. Once the initial population is created and evaluated, ALPS-SS enters its main loop which consists of iteratively selecting a layer, L_i to update and then an index in that layer, $I_{i,j}$, for which to create a new individual, creating the new individual, and then inserting it in the population. In more detail, this main loop is shown in Figure 6-2. The algorithm allows for different methods for selecting the parents (eg tournament selection or some form of roulette wheel selection). In addition, elitism can be added either to just the top layer or to all layers.

An additional change that is made to ALPS-SS is the method by which individuals are moved up. In generational ALPS, all individuals that are being replaced in one layer can be moved up as a group at the end of the generation. This means that individuals being moved up cannot overwrite other individuals from their same layer that are also being moved up. To prevent an individual which is being moved up a layer from overwriting an individual that was also just recently moved up, ALPS-SS has an additional check that when moving an individual up it only replaces individuals that were moved more than P (where P is the total size of the population) evaluations ago.

```
 1: procedure ALPSSS( )
 2:    doInit ← false.
 3:    nextInit ← 0.
 4:    while not done do
 5:        Select a layer, L_i.                          ▷ Randomly or sequentially
 6:        if i == 0 & doInit then
 7:            j ← nextInit
 8:            nextInit + = 1
 9:            if nextInit >= m then
10:                doInit ← false
11:            end if
12:            I_new ← randomly created individual.
13:        else
14:            Select a value for j.                      ▷ Randomly or sequentially
15:            Select parents from L_i and L_{i−1}.       ▷ 1 for mut., 2 for recomb.
16:            if No valid parents then                   ▷ Must be in layer L_0.
17:                doInit ← true
18:                nextIndex ← 1
19:                j ← 0
20:                I_new ← randomly created individual.
21:            else
22:                I_new ← offspring of parent(s).
23:            end if
24:        end if
25:        Evaluate(I_new)
26:        TryMoveUp(i, j)
27:        I_{i,j} ← I_new
28:    end while
29: end procedure
30: procedure TRYMOVEUP(i, j)
31:    if i < n then
32:        Look for an individual I_{i+1,k} in L_{i+1} which I_{i,j} can replace.
33:        if A replaceable I_{i+1,k} exists then
34:            TryMoveUp(i + 1, k)
35:            I_{i+1,k} ← I_{i,j}
36:        end if
37:    end if
38: end procedure
```

Figure 6-2. The ALPS-SS algorithm.

5.   Experimental Setup

The objective of these experiments is to compare the performance of the proposed Steady-State ALPS (ALPS-SS) EA against a basic, Steady-State EA (BEA). The ALPS-SS configuration which is used in the following experiments consists of 10 layers of 40 individuals, an exponential aging scheme with an age gap of 3, and an elitism of 5. Parents are selected using a tournament selection with a tournament size of 5 and offspring are created using either mutation or recombination, with equal probability. The BEA is implemented as a single layer version of ALPS-SS, with 400 individuals in its single age-layer. With no maximum age on its single age-layer, this single-layer ALPS system operates exactly like a traditional, steady-state EA. Each of the next two sections presents a comparison of these two EAs on a different test problem.

6.   Evolving Antennas

One of the successes in the Evolutionary Computation community is the evolution of an X-band antenna for NASA's ST-5 Mission (Lohn et al., 2005), which was a co-winner of the Gold Award at the first Human Competitive Competition at GECCO-04. The version of the test problem which we use here is much like that used to evolve the NASA ST-5 antenna. In the rest of this section we describe first the generative representation for encoding an antenna and then give the results of comparing ALPS-SS against the BEA.

Encoding an Antenna

The generative representation used for evolving antennas consists of an antenna-constructing program which is based on a programming language we devised for building objects out of line segments (Hornby et al., 2003). This is the GP-style representation that was used for evolving the antenna for NASA's ST5 mission (Lohn et al., 2005). This language is composed of operators that specify wire segments and perform coordinate system rotations. An antenna design is created by starting with an initial feedwire and creating wires specified by executing the evolved antenna-constructing program. The operator forward(length, radius) adds a wire with the given length and radius. The operator rotate-x(angle) changes the coordinate system orientation by rotating it the specified amount about the x-axis. Similar operators are defined for the y and z axes. For example, in executing the program rotate-z(0.5236) forward(1.0,0.000406), the rotate-z() operator causes the current orientation to rotate 0.5236 radians ($30°$) about the Z axis. The forward() operator adds a wire of length 1.0 cm and radius 0.000406 cm (which corresponds to a 20 gauge wire) in the current forward direction. In the instance of the problem used here, all antennas start with a feed-element segment from (0.0, 0.0, 0.0) to (0.0, 0.0, 0.001) (units are in meters).

Antenna Results

To evaluate antenna designs we use the same fitness function which Lohn et al. (Lohn et al., 2005) used for their GA implementation, although here we are optimizing for a single frequency (2106.0 MHz) whereas in their work they were optimizing for two frequencies. This fitness function sums the squared difference of gain values for those values below a given level (here we use 0.5 dBic) and the objective is to find an antenna which minimizes this function:

$$Fitness = \sum_{\substack{0° < \phi < 360° \\ 0° < \theta < 90°}} (\text{gain}_{\phi,\theta} - T)^2 \quad \text{if gain}_{\phi,\theta} < T \qquad (6.2)$$

where $\text{gain}_{\phi,\theta}$ is the gain of the antenna in dBic (right-hand polarization) at a particular angle, T is the target gain (0.5 dBic), ϕ is the azimuth, and θ is the elevation. The gain component of the fitness function takes the gain (in dBic) in 5° increments about the angles of interest: from $0° \le \theta \le 90°$ and $0° \le \phi \le 360°$. These angles of interest are for a hemispherical pattern.

In addition, there are two qualifications to this fitness function. Frequently the software for analyzing an antenna, NEC, fails to evaluate an antenna (this happens with about one quarter of randomly generated antennas but with much lower frequency on offspring of successfully evaluated antennas) in which case a worst score of 1.0e+8 is returned. Also, antennas are constrained to fit in a box of $\pm 0.04m$ in the X and Y direction and 0-$0.041m$ in the Z (up) direction; this dimensional constraint approximates what might be given for commercial antennas at this frequency. Those designs which have segments that go outside this box are also given the worst fitness value of 1.0e+8.

Using the fitness function just described, both EAs were run 30 times with one million evaluations in each trial. A graph comparing the performance of ALPS-SS and the BEA is shown in Figure 6-3. While ALPS-SS starts off slightly slower then the BEA, it quickly achieves much better fitness scores. Averaged over the 30 trials ALPS-SS scores 2.738e+03±4.21e+02 and the BEA scores 6.709e+03±1.37e+03 and this difference in performance is highly significant (P < 0.001, using a two-tailed Mann-Whitney test).

7. Evolving Tables

The second test problem uses both a different design domain and a different generative representation. This second domain consists of constructing 3D solid objects out of cubes and the objective we use is to evolve tables. Here, the generative representation we use is a more powerful encoding system with

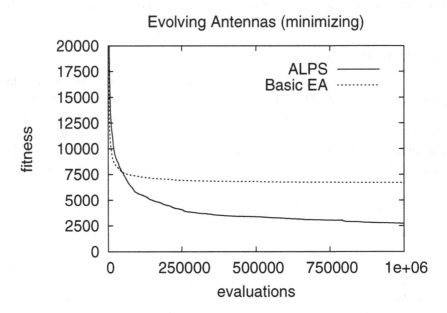

Figure 6-3. Comparison between ALPS-SS and the Basic EA on the antenna design problem. Plots are of the best individual found, averaged over 30 trials.

conditionals, loops and parameterized procedures. We first describe this more advanced generative representation used to encode table designs and then give the results of our comparison.

Encoding a Table

The generative representation language used in this substrate is a kind of linear, computer-programming language inspired by L-systems. The language consists of a framework for object-construction rules and a set of these rules defines a program for an object. Objects are created by compiling a program into an assembly procedure of construction operators and then executing this assembly procedure in the module which constructs objects. The rules for constructing an object consist of a rule head followed by a number of condition-body pairs. For example in the following rule,

$$A(n0, n1) : n1 > 5 \rightarrow B(n1+1)cD(n1+0.5, n0-2)$$

the rule head is A($n0$, $n1$), the condition is $n1 > 5$ and the body is B($n1+1$) c D($n1+0.5$, $n0-2$). A complete encoding of an object consists of a starting operator and a sequence of rules. For example an object could be encoded as,

$P0(4)$
$P0(n0):$ $\quad n0 > 1.0 \rightarrow [\,P1(n0 * 1.5)\,]\; up(1)\; forward(3)$
$\qquad\qquad down(1)\; P0(n0 - 1)$

$P1(n0):$ $\quad n0 > 1.0 \rightarrow \{\,[\,forward(n0)\,]\,left(1)\,\}(4)$

Through an iterative sequence of replacing rule heads with the appropriate body
this program compiles as follows,

1. *P0(4)*
2. *[P1(6)] up(1) forward(3) down(1) P0(3)*
3. *[{ [forward(6)] left(1) }(4)] up(1) forward(3) down(1) [P1(4.5)
   ] up(1) forward(3) down(1) P0(2)*
4. *[{ [forward(6)] left(1) }(4)] up(1) forward(3) down(1) [{ [
   forward(4.5)] left(1) }(4)] up(1) forward(3) down(1) [P1(3)] up(1)
   forward(3) down(1) P0(1)*
5. *[{ [forward(6)] left(1) }(4)] up(1) forward(3) down(1) [{ [
   forward(4.5)] left(1) }(4)] up(1) forward(3) down(1) [{ [forward(3)
   ] left(1) }(4)] up(1) forward(3) down(1)*
6. *[[forward(6)] left(1) [forward(6)] left(1) [forward(6)] left(1)
   [forward(6)] left(1)] up(1) forward(3) down(1) [[forward(4.5)]
   left(1) [forward(4.5)] left(1) [forward(4.5)] left(1) [forward(4.5)]
   left(1)] up(1) forward(3) down(1) [[forward(3)] left(1) [forward(3)
   ] left(1) [forward(3)] left(1) [forward(3)] left(1)] up(1) forward(3)
   down(1) forward(3)*

The particular language used in this example is an encoding for three-
dimensional objects that are constructed out of cubes in a three-dimensional
grid. The operators in this language are: $back(n)$, move in the negative X
direction n units; $clockwise(n)$, rotate heading $n \times 90°$ about the X axis;
$counter\text{-}clockwise(n)$, rotate heading $n \times -90°$; about the X axis; $down(n)$,
rotate heading $n \times -90°$ about the Z axis; $forward(n)$, move in the positive X
direction n units; $left(n)$, rotate heading $n \times 90°$ about the Y axis; $right(n)$,
rotate heading $n \times -90°$ about the Y axis; $up(n)$, rotate heading $n \times 90°$ about
the Z axis; [, push the current state to the stack; and], pop the top state off the
stack and makes it the current state.

With this construction language an object starts with a single cube in a three-
dimensional grid and new cubes are added with the operators forward() and
back(). The current state, consisting of location and orientation, is maintained
and the operators clockwise(), counter-clockwise(), down(), left(),
right(), and up() change the orientation. A branching in object construction
is achieved through the use of the operators [and], which push (save) and pop
(restore) the current state onto a stack.

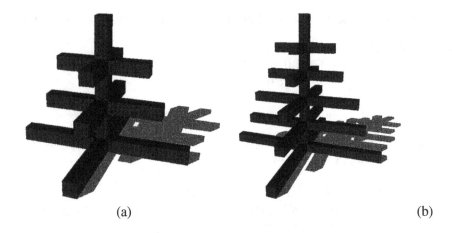

(a)   (b)

Figure 6-4. Two tree structures produced from the same set of rules with different starting operators.

Executing the final assembly procedure produced by the example program results in the structure shown in figure 6-4.a. Interestingly, the rules of this program encode for a family of objects and by using a different value as the parameter to the starting operator different objects can be created. The object in Figure 6-4.b is created by using the starting operator $P0(6)$ instead of $P0(4)$.

Results on Evolving Tables

The fitness function to score tables is a function of their height, surface structure, stability and number of excess cubes used. Height, f_{height}, is the number of cubes above the ground. Surface structure, $f_{surface}$, is the number of cubes at the maximum height. Stability, $f_{stability}$, is a function of the volume of the table and is calculated by summing the area at each layer of the table. Maximizing height, surface structure and stability typically results in table designs that are solid volumes, thus a measure of excess cubes, f_{excess}, is used to reward designs that use fewer bricks. To produce a single fitness score for a table these four criteria are combined together:

$$\text{fitness} = f_{height} \times f_{surface} \times f_{stability}/f_{excess} \qquad (6.3)$$

In our comparison we setup the design space to consist of a grid of $40 \times 40 \times 40$ cubes and performed thirty trials with each algorithm. For each trial the evolutionary algorithm was configured to run for one million evaluations with a population of 400 individuals. As with the evolutionary algorithm for evolving antennas, table designs are bred by selecting as parents the better ones to reproduce and then performing mutation and recombination on the table-constructing programs to produce new table designs. The graph in figure 6-5

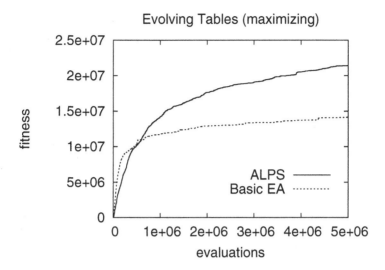

Figure 6-5. Comparison between ALPS-SS and the Basic EA on the antenna design problem. Plots are of the best individual found, averaged over 30 trials.

contains the results of these experiments. ALPS-SS had superior performance (2.14e+07±3.84e+06) than the BEA (1.42e+07±7.63e+06) and this difference is highly significant (P < 0.001, using a two-tailed Mann-Whitney test).

8. Discussion: Rethinking Aging

In re-working the basic EA into an age-layered system, ALPS introduces more variables to be set by the user: the number of age layers and the maximum ages for each layer. As noted in Section 3.0, one method for assigning maximum age values for each layer is to use some aging scheme whereby the maximum values for each layer increase by some constant (the *age-gap*) times a series of monotonically increasing numbers (the *aging scheme*). In tweaking ALPS to improve its performance, choosing the value for the age-gap and the aging scheme can have a noticeable impact on evolutionary performance. One of the main issues is ensuring that the maximum age of the second-to-last layer, L_{i-2}, is high enough that individuals have enough time to compete with individuals in the last (and oldest) layer, L_{i-1}.

In the process of implementing this version of ALPS, a mistake was made when assigning the age of an individual created through recombination. Instead of setting its age of creation to be that of its oldest parent, they were assigned that of their youngest parent. This had the fortuitous benefit that ages of individuals stayed quite low—they seem to top out at roughly one or two times the age gap

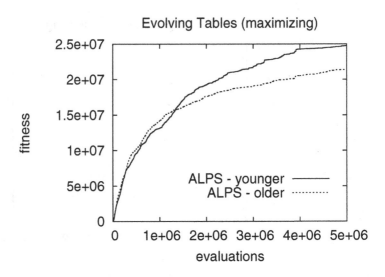

Figure 6-6. Comparison between two versions of ALPS: in the original version (ALPS - older), the age of a child created through recombination is based on its oldest parent; in the new variation (ALPS - younger) the age of such a child is based on the age of its youngest parent. Plots are of the best individual found, averaged over 30 trials.

times the number of age layers. Using such an age-assignment system may make setting the aging-scheme and age gap easier.

To determine if using the age value of the younger parent can also produce as good evolutionary results as when age is based on the value of the older parent, we performed an additional set of runs on the table design problem. Results of our runs are shown in Figure 6-6 and show that both systems achieve comparable fitness levels. Taking the age of the older parent averaged $2.14e+07\pm3.84e+06$ and taking the age of the younger parent averaged $2.48e+07\pm1.22e+06$, with the difference being highly significant ($P <= 0.001$, using a two-tailed Mann-Whitney test). This suggests that a possible direction for future research is to more thoroughly compare these two methods of age assignment.

9.   Conclusion

When the Age-Layered Population Structure (ALPS) was introduced, a generational version was shown to work well on an antenna design problem with a GP-style representation (Hornby, 2006). More recent work has found it to work well with other GP systems and different problems. One of the main interests in this paper was devising a version of ALPS to work with a steady-state EA. Necessary for this steady-state implementation was the development of a way for calculating age that does not rely on explicit generations.

We compared our ALPS with a steady-state EA (ALPS-SS) implementation against a steady-state, basic EA (BEA), on two different test problems, each with its own generative representation. On both test problems we found that ALPS-SS greatly outperformed the BEA. This version of ALPS is likely to be of interest to those who need, or prefer, a steady-state algorithm rather than a generational one.

Acknowledgment

This material is supported in part by the National Science Foundation's Creative-IT grant 0757532.

References

Cantú-Paz, E. and Goldberg, D. E. (2003). Are multiple runs of genetic algorithms better than one? In et al., E. Cantu-Paz, editor, *Proc. of the Genetic and Evolutionary Computation Conference*, LNCS 2724, pages 801–812, Berlin. Springer-Verlag.

Cavicchio, D. J. (1970). *Adaptive Search using simulated evolution*. PhD thesis, University of Michigan, Ann Arbor.

DeJong, K. A. (1975). *Analysis of the Behavior of a Class of Genetic Adaptive Systems*. Dept. Computer and Communication Sciences, University of Michigan, Ann Arbor.

Goldberg, David E. and Richardson, Jon (1987). Genetic algorithms with sharing for multimodal function optimization. In Grefenstette, John J., editor, *Proc. of the Second Intl. Conf. on Genetic Algorithms*, pages 41–49. Lawrence Erlbaum Associates.

Hornby, Gregory S. (2006). ALPS: the age-layered population structure for reducing the problem of premature convergence. In Keijzer, Maarten, Cattolico, Mike, Arnold, Dirk, Babovic, Vladan, Blum, Christian, Bosman, Peter, Butz, Martin V., Coello Coello, Carlos, Dasgupta, Dipankar, Ficici, Sevan G., Foster, James, Hernandez-Aguirre, Arturo, Hornby, Greg, Lipson, Hod, McMinn, Phil, Moore, Jason, Raidl, Guenther, Rothlauf, Franz, Ryan, Conor, and Thierens, Dirk, editors, *GECCO 2006: Proceedings of the 8th annual conference on Genetic and evolutionary computation*, volume 1, pages 815–822, Seattle, Washington, USA. ACM Press.

Hornby, Gregory S., Lipson, Hod, and Pollack, Jordan B. (2003). Generative representations for the automated design of modular physical robots. *IEEE transactions on Robotics and Automation*, 19(4):709–713.

Huber, A. and Mlynski, D. A. (1998). An age-controlled evolutionary algorithm for optimization problems in physical layout. In *International Symposium on Circuits and Systems*, pages 262–265. IEEE Press.

Kim, J.-H., Jeon, J.-Y., Chae, H.-K., and Koh, K. (1995). A novel evolution-ary algorithm with fast convergence. In *IEEE International Conference on Evolutionary Computation*, pages 228–29. IEEE Press.

Kirkpatrick, S., Gelatt, C.D., and Vecchi, M.P. (1983). Optimization by simu-lated annealing. *Science*, 220:671–680.

Korns, M. F. and Nunez, L. (2008). Profiling symbolic regression-classification. In Riolo, R. L., Soule, T., and Worzel, B., editors, *Genetic Programming Theory and Practice VI*, Genetic and Evolutionary Computation, chapter 14, pages 215–229. Springer, Ann Arbor.

Kubota, N., Fukuda, T., Arai, F., and Shimojima, K. (1994). Genetic algorithm with age structure and its application to self-organizing manufacturing sys-tem. In *IEEE Symposium on Emerging Technologies and Factory Automa-tion*, pages 472–477. IEEE Press.

Lohn, Jason D., Hornby, Gregory S., and Linden, Derek S. (2005). Rapid re-evolution of an X-band antenna for NASA's space technology 5 mission. In Yu, Tina, Riolo, Rick L., and Worzel, Bill, editors, *Genetic Programming Theory and Practice III*, volume 9 of *Genetic Programming*, chapter 5, pages 65–78. Springer, Ann Arbor.

Luke, Sean (2001). When short runs beat long runs. In Spector, Lee, Goodman, Erik D., Wu, Annie, Langdon, W. B., Voigt, Hans-Michael, Gen, Mitsuo, Sen, Sandip, Dorigo, Marco, Pezeshk, Shahram, Garzon, Max H., and Burke, Edmund, editors, *Proceedings of the Genetic and Evolutionary Computation Conference (GECCO-2001)*, pages 74–80, San Francisco, California, USA. Morgan Kaufmann.

Mahfoud, S. W. (1992). Crowding and preselection revisited. In Männer, R. and Manderick, B., editors, *Parallel Problem Solving from Nature, 2*, pages 27–36. North-Holland.

McConaghy, Trent, Palmers, Pieter, Gielen, Georges, and Steyaert, Michiel (2007). Genetic programming with reuse of known designs. In Riolo, Rick L., Soule, Terence, and Worzel, Bill, editors, *Genetic Programming Theory and Practice V*, Genetic and Evolutionary Computation, chapter 10, pages 161–186. Springer, Ann Arbor.

Willis, A., Patel, S., and Clack, C. D. (2008). GP age-layer and crossover effects in bid-offer spread prediction. In *Proceedings of the 10th annual conference on Genetic and Evolutionary Computation Conference*, Atlanta, GA.

Chapter 7

LATENT VARIABLE SYMBOLIC REGRESSION FOR HIGH-DIMENSIONAL INPUTS

Trent McConaghy[1]

[1]*Solido Design Automation Inc., Canada*

Abstract

This paper explores symbolic regression when there are hundreds of input variables, and the variables have similar influence which means that variable pruning (*a priori*, or on-the-fly) will be ineffective. For this problem, traditional genetic programming and many other regression approaches do poorly. We develop a technique based on latent variables, nonlinear sensitivity analysis, and genetic programming designed to manage the challenge. The technique handles 340-input variable problems in minutes, with promise to scale well to even higher dimensions. The technique is successfully verified on 24 real-world circuit modeling problems.

Keywords: symbolic regression, latent variables, latent variable regression, LVR, analog, integrated circuits

1. Introduction

Symbolic regression (SR) is the automated extraction of static whitebox models that map input variables to output variables. Genetic programming (GP) (Koza, 1992) is a popular approach to do SR, with successful applications to industrial problems such as industrial processing (Kordon et al., 2005), medicine (Moore et al., 2008; Almal and al., 2006), finance (Korns, 2007; Becker et al., 2007), and robotics (Schmidt and Lipson, 2006).

In most GP-based SR applications, there are one to ten input variables, and hundreds to thousands of training samples. GP-based approaches are quite good at handling these. There are two approaches to handling more input variables. The first is to prune the variables beforehand, e.g. from neural networks (Kordon

R. Riolo et al. (eds.), *Genetic Programming Theory and Practice VII*,
Genetic and Evolutionary Computation, DOI 10.1007/978-1-4419-1626-6_7,
© Springer Science + Business Media, LLC 2010

et al., 2002). The second is to let GP prune the variables on-the-fly during the
SR run (Smits et al., 2005; Korns, 2007).

Pruning is reasonable when the significant variables are just a fraction of the
overall set of variables. But what about when *most* variables have a degree of
influence that cannot be ignored? Consider Figure 7-1 left, which is the output
of a nonlinear sensitivity analysis from input/output X/y training data. Here,
the input variables are ordered from highest to lowest impact. The cumulative
sum of impacts vs. variable number is plotted. While the first 10 variables
explain about 50% of the total variation in y, **almost all of the variables are
needed in order to capture 95% of the total variation**.

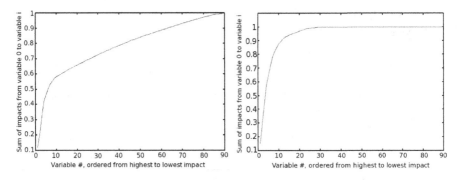

Figure 7-1. Cumulative relative impacts of input variables on a target output variable. The
nonlinear impacts on the left plot were extracted using the impact-extraction technique in (Mc-
Conaghy et al., 2008) where the regression models are Random Forests (Breiman, 2001). The
impacts on the right plot are the weights on the model found by gradient directed regularization
(Friedman and Popescu, 2004).

Because most variables are needed for a reasonable model, pruning variables
will be ineffective. Even if we try a different technique that places extra bias on
the most important variables (Figure 7-1 right), we still see that 1/3 of variables
– the same order of magnitude as total number of variables – are needed in order
to capture 95% of the total variation.

This is the problem we face when modeling analog circuit performances as
a function of manufacturing process variations. This matters, because better
models allow higher-quality circuits to be designed in less time. The impact
plots of Figure 7-1 were for the "AV" output of circuit in Figure 7-2 left. It
has approximately 10 process variables per transistor (Drennan and McAndrew,
1999), which leads to 90 input variables overall.

In this paper, we test on 24 benchmark problems having up to **341 input
variables** with impact profiles similar to Figure 7-1. Section 3 will show that
a modern GP-based SR technique and several other state-of-the-art regression
techniques will fail, badly, on even the easiest 16 problems. A different way to
think about the symbolic regression problem is needed. So, in section 4 we in-

troduce the perspective brought by *latent variable regression* (LVR)(Friedman and Tukey, 1974). Each "latent variable" t_i in an LVR model is a linear combination of the input variables $t_i = w_i^T x$; and the model's output is a nonlinear function of the latent variables $\hat{f}(x) = \sum_i g_i(w_i^T x)$. Latent variables can be thought of as auto-discovered "hidden intermediate variables" which transform the inputs into a reduced-dimensionality space. An LVR technique recently introduced in circuits (Li and Cao, 2008) is promising, but assumes a quadratic model when setting w_i's and does not return a symbolic model.

The contributions of this paper are the use of an LVR framework for solving this challenging SR problem, a means to determine the LVR linear-combination vectors w_i without assuming quadratic mapping, and, most particularly, a means to find the *symbolic* nonlinear functions g_i. We determine w_i's by building models of $x \mapsto f$, extracting variable impacts from those models, and using those impacts as the basis for setting w_i. Once w_i is determined, a (trivial for GP) one-dimensional SR run is performed having $t_i = w_i^T x$ as the input variable and f as the output. The process is repeated on the residuals of f until a stopping criteria is hit.

We dub our approach LVSR: Latent Variable Symbolic Regression.

This paper is organized as follows. Section 2 describes the problem setup. Section 3 gives experimental results of a modern GP technique and state-of-the-art regression techniques on the 16 benchmark problems. Section 4 introduces LVR in the context of a recent approach (Li and Cao, 2008), highlighting the promise of LVR and the current shortcomings. Section 5 introduces LVSR, which is designed to overcome the issues of past SR, regression, and LVR approaches. Section 6 has experimental validation of LVSR on 24 real-world circuit modeling problems. Section 7 concludes.

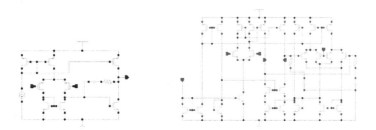

Figure 7-2. Schematics of 10-device (left) and 30-device operational amplifier (right).

2. Modeling Problems

The modeling problems come from two analog circuits as shown in Figure 7-2. These circuits are well-known to the domain experts (analog circuit designers). Each circuit's device sizes were set to have "reasonable" values by an analog circuit designer, leading to "reasonable" performance values. Each circuit has 8 performance measures of interest: AV (gain), BW (bandwidth), GBW (gain-bandwidth), GM (gain margin), OS (overshoot), PM (phase margin), SR (slew rate), ST (settling time) (Sansen, 2006).

The variations in the circuit performance due to manufacturing imprecision can be modeled as a joint probability density function (jpdf). We use the well-known model (Drennan and McAndrew, 1999) where the random variables are "process variables" which model quantities like "substrate doping concentration". Variations in these quantities affect the electrical behavior of the circuit, and therefore its performances. In this model, there are about 10 normal independent identically-distributed (NIID) random variables per transistor. In total, the 10-transistor amp had 90 random variables, and the 30-transistor amp had 215 random variables. (Section 6 will introduce an even larger problem, a 50-transistor amp with 431 input variables.)

To simulate the effect of manufacturing variations, a "Monte Carlo" (MC) analysis was performed on each circuit. In MC analysis, we draw $N = 600$ points from the jpdf. At each random point, we simulate the circuit at several sets of environmental conditions (combinations of high/low temperature, high/low power supply V_{dd}, high/low load). Each random point will get a "worst-case" value of each performance across the environmental points, which is either the minimum or maximum value (e.g. worst-case for gain "AV" is minimum value because we want to maximize gain).[1]

For our modeling problem, each random point is the model's input vector x. Each worst-case performance metric is a model's scalar output, e.g. y_{AV}. Therefore we have 8 modeling problems with $n = 90$ input variables (for the 10T circuit), 8 modeling problems with $n = 215$ input variables (for the 30T circuit), and $N = 600$ input/output pairs per problem.

We need a scheme to assess the ability of the final models to predict on previously-unseen data. A popular approach is k-fold cross-validation, which is accurate but requires kx more computational approach than a single pass of learning. Another approach is to set aside a random subset of $\approx 25\%$ of the data for testing. This has the virtue of speed but inconsistent results, because the chosen test samples may not be representative of the whole dataset. We employ a technique which has both speed and consistency: sort the data according to the y-values, then take every 4th point for testing.[2]

---

[1] The specific technology was TSMC $0.18\mu m$ CMOS. The simulator was a proprietary SPICE-like simulator of a leading analog semiconductor company, with accuracy and runtime comparable to HSPICE^{TM}.

[2] This was inspired by vertical slicing (Korns, 2007) which used sorted y-values for a different purpose.

3. Experiments Using Traditional Regressors

This section gives results from applying a modern GP-based SR technique and several other state-of-the-art regression techniques to the problems. We test the following regressors, which range from simple linear techniques to progressively more nonlinear approaches:

- **Least-squares (LS) linear regression**.

- **Regularized linear regression** via gradient directed regularization (**GDR**), in which a regularization term limits the variance among the linear model's weights. GDR is a generalization of both the lasso and ridge regression (Friedman and Popescu, 2004).

- **Quadratic modeling** using **PROBE**, which models the variable interactions as a rank-reduced weight matrix which improves scaling from $O(n^2)$ to $O(k * n)$ (k=rank, typically 2-10; n = number of input variables) (Li et al., 2007).

- **GP** using **CAFFEINE**, a modern SR approach which restricts the search space to interpretable-by-construction models and has demonstrated ability to scale to 100+ input variables (it *does* prune variables) (McConaghy and Gielen, 2009; McConaghy and Gielen, 2006).

- **Boosted trees** using Stochastic Gradient Boosting (**SGB**), which builds a shallow CART tree at each boosting iteration. Iterations zoom in on hard-to-model regions (Friedman, 2002).

- **Bootstrapped trees** using Random Forests (**RF**), in which each CART tree in an ensemble is greedily built from a different bootstrapped sample of the training data (Breiman, 2001; Breiman et al., 1984).

Settings for each regressor were as follows. In the notation of (Friedman and Popescu, 2004), GDR had threshold parameter $\tau = 0.2$ and stepsize $\delta\mu = 0.002$. PROBE had $max\_rank = 2$. CAFFEINE had settings like (McConaghy and Gielen, 2009), except population size of 250, population initialization size 250, and 1000 generations. SGB parameters were: learning rate $\alpha = 0.10$, minimum tree depth = 2, maximum tree depth = 7, target training error = 5%. RF had 200 CARTs; CART-building would consider $\sqrt{n}$ input variables at each split; and splitting would continue until no possible splits remained.

Table 7-1 gives the results of the regressors on the 16 modeling problems (2 circuits x 8 problems per circuit) on the test data. Root-mean squared error $rmse(\boldsymbol{y}, \hat{\boldsymbol{y}}) = \sqrt{1/N * \sum_j^N ((\hat{y}_j - y_j)/\sigma_y)^2}$ reports the difference between y and $\hat{y}$ on testing data. Note that $rmse$ is scaled by y's standard deviation σ_y. Because SGB and RF are stochastic, for each problem we do 30 independent runs and report the median value. (We report median and not mean because the worst $rmse$ values are significantly higher, in a Poisson-like distribution.)

Table 7-1. Test RMSE values with traditional regressors. 10T = 10-transistor circuit. 30T = 30-transistor circuit. AV, BW, etc. are different circuit output metrics.

Problem	LS-lin	Reg-lin (GDR)	Quad (PROBE)	GP (CAFF-EINE)	Boost tree (SGB)	Bootstr. tree (RF)
10T AV	0.4377	0.4430	0.1384	≫10.0	0.5947	0.7419
10T BW	0.6175	0.6131	0.2417	3.0170	0.7300	0.8716
10T GBW	0.4257	0.4290	0.2826	0.6016	0.5696	0.7052
10T GM	0.4404	0.4381	0.3416	0.2189	0.5524	0.6782
10T OS	0.2397	0.2506	0.2913	≫10.0	0.4830	0.7002
10T PM	0.6028	0.5907	0.6710	≫10.0	0.7842	0.9190
10T SR	0.0132	0.0151	0.0205	0.0555	0.4260	0.6818
10T ST	0.0566	0.0607	0.0765	≫10.0	0.4379	0.6839
30T AV	0.1141	0.1158	0.1281	≫10.0	0.6282	0.8118
30T BW	0.0766	0.0760	0.0949	≫10.0	0.5780	0.7540
30T GBW	0.0675	0.0675	0.0766	≫10.0	0.5687	0.7516
30T GM	0.1099	0.1102	0.1204	≫10.0	0.6043	0.8055
30T OS	0.2165	0.2009	0.2209	≫10.0	0.6101	0.7801
30T PM	0.0782	0.0844	0.1026	≫10.0	0.6085	0.7665
30T SR	0.1963	0.1744	0.1903	≫10.0	0.5651	0.7258
30T ST	0.1658	0.1640	0.1681	≫10.0	0.6165	0.7903

Let us examine the results, one regressor at a time. As a reference, $rmse$ values of <0.10 are quite good, and values of >0.20 are very poor. The LS-linear regressor did very poorly on about half the problems, including the first six. However, it got $rmse$ <0.10 in some problems, indicating that some of them have nearly-linear mappings. The regularized-linear regressor performed comparably to LS. The quadratic modeling approach improved upon the linear approaches for some problems, but still had very poor performance for 6/16 problems. This improved behavior that while the modeling is not quite linear and not quite quadratic, it may not be significantly more nonlinear.

The GP technique did very poorly in all but two problems. Remember that this technique did well on other 100+ variable problems. But the difference is that on those problems, pruning variables was helpful. In examining GP's behavior on the 16 problems at hand, we found that GP prunes out variables fairly aggressively, which explains its poor performance.

Both tree-based approaches did very poorly in predicting on previously-unseen inputs. There is a straightforward explanation. The quadratic models do fairly well on 10/16 problems, indicating that an assumption a continuous mapping holds fairly well. Yet the tree-based approaches, with their piecewise-discontinuous nature, do not make this continuity assumption, making the modeling problem unnecessarily difficult.

Not shown in the table, we also tested two variants of radial basis functions (RBFs) (Poggio and Girosi, 1990) (with renormalization (Hastie et al., 2001)). The first variant used Euclidian distance measure and Gaussian kernels. It gave $rmse$ values comparable to the tree-based approaches (very poor). Such performance is unsurprising, because with 100 or 200 input variables, all points are effectively far apart from all other points, rendering the Euclidian distance ineffective (Hastie et al., 2001; Smits et al., 2005). The second RBF variant used the Fractional distance measure which has been hypothesized to handle dimensionality better (Vladislavleva, 2008), but it had poor $rmse$ results too.

In summary, none of the eight "traditional" approaches tested could adequately capture the target circuit mappings. Even the best one did poorly on 6/16 problems. We need to examine the problem from a different perspective.

4. Latent Variable Regression

This section introduces latent variable regression (LVR). The general regression problem is to find a model $\hat{y} = \hat{f}(X)$ which minimizes $rmse(y, \hat{y})$ on testing data X. In *symbolic* regression, we also want $\hat{f}$ to be interpretable, i.e. can be inspected by a human to gain insight into the mapping.

In LVR, the mapping $\hat{f}$ is decomposed into a sum of k one-dimensional functions g_i:

$$\hat{f}(x) = g_1(w_1^T x) + g_2(w_1^T x) + \ldots + g_k(w_k^T x) \qquad (7.1)$$

where each g_i takes in a scalar value $t_i = w_i^T x$ that has been transformed from x-space by projection vector w_i. k is the model's *rank*; $i = 1 \ldots k$.

The power of LVR techniques is that a high-dimensional input vector x may be transformed into a one-dimensional (scalar) value t, and that nonlinear processing g is deferred until after the transformation. The LVR challenges are to find the projection vectors $\{w_i\}\forall i$ and the nonlinear mappings $\{g_i\}\forall i$.

LVR is not new. For linear functions, it was introduced decades ago as projection pursuit (Friedman and Tukey, 1974), and related forms are called partial least squares (PLS).

The PROBE quadratic-modeling approach (Li et al., 2007) tested in section 3 can actually be interpreted as an LVR approach, where the g_i's are quadratic. Of course, the quadratic g_i's are also PROBE's weakness.

The work (Baffi et al., 1999) uses neural networks, which can handle arbitrary nonlinear mappings. However, it is slow because it iterated between finding w_i's, and finding g_i's. The approach (Malthouse et al., 1997) uses three coupled neural networks, which is complex and therefore severely prone to overfitting. The SiLVR approach of (Singhee and Rutenbar, 2007) needs just one neural network, but it only has a local optimizer for weight tuning and remains prone to overfitting. In (Jordan and Jacobs, 1994), each t_i is a neural network, and each g_i is a normalized output from an overall "gating" network. A problem with all neural-network approaches is that the g_i mapping is opaque due to the hard-to-interpret sigmoidal squashing function(s).

The recent P2M approach (Li and Cao, 2008) is of particular interest to us, because of how it decomposes the problem. In P2M, the first projection vector w_1 is chosen by (1) building a PROBE model, and (2) extracting w_1 from either the linear or the quadratic component of the model. Then $t_1 = w_1^T x$ is computed for each input/output pair $j = 1 \ldots N$. Finally, an M=10-segment piecewise-linear (PWL) model of $t_1 \mapsto y$ is fit using LS, to complete the rank-1 LVR model. To build a rank-k model, the target y updates the residual $y_{target} = y_{prev} - \sum_i g_i(w_i^T x)$, and the process re-loops to the first step. P2M is particularly interesting because it demonstrated that if an algorithm could choose *good* projection vectors w_i, then one could decouple learning the w_i's from the g_i's, simplifying and speeding the algorithm.

P2M has issues. First, it could choose the wrong projection vector because of the quadratic assumption, or because it must choose between quadratic vs. linear without reconciling them. Second, while the PWL model is first-order continuous, it is not second-order continuous despite experimental evidence indicating this is the case. Finally, like the neural network approaches, the PWL model is hard to interpret, which is against our *symbolic* regression goals.

With a thorough search of the GP literature, we found just one set of work using LVR (McKay et al., 1999). However, that work was tuned for low-dimensional problems (just 4 dimensions in the paper), and the output expressions were hard to interpret (e.g. $g_1 = 2.61 * exp(tanh(tanh(exp(4 * t_1)))) - 4.58$). We seek a more focused approach with more interpretable results.

5.   Latent Variable *Symbolic* Regression

This section introduces latent variable symbolic regression (LVSR). Generalizing upon P2M's approach, LVSR decomposes the problem into finding projection vectors w_i, finding nonlinear mappings g_i, and iterating one rank at a time. The choices within that framework are:

- To enable the *symbolic* part of latent variable symbolic regression, the g_i's are determined via GP-based symbolic regression. We use CAFFEINE (McConaghy and Gielen, 2006; McConaghy and Gielen, 2009), but any almost GP-based SR system would do here since the problem is a simple 1-d mapping.

- To choose the projection vectors, we test multiple options, each for a different reason. For a nonlinear model having discontinuities, we use Random Forests (bootstrapped trees) (Breiman, 2001) where we set each projection variable w_i, l as the impact of the lth variable in the Random Forest. Its sign is computed by observing the change in y going from $x_{nominal} = \{0, 0, ..., 0\}$ to a 1-σ perturbation in the lth variable with $x = \{0, 0, ..., 1, ..., 0\}$. We call this LVSR-RF. For a model having continuous mapping that is robust to mild nonlinearities, we use regularized linear learning with aggressive weight pruning (GDR, where $\tau = 0.95$). We call this LVSR-GDR. A bonus of using aggressive weight pruning is to reduce the final number of variables, at the possible expense of model accuracy. For completeness in comparison to P2M, we also test a quadratic model-based approach to projection-vector extraction. We call this LVSR-PROBE.

Figure 7-3 left gives the algorithm flow for LVSR.

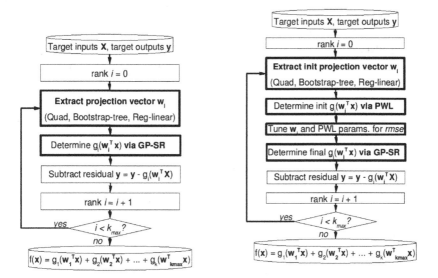

Figure 7-3. Left: Algorithm flow for Latent Variable Symbolic Regression (LVSR). The key steps are extracting the projection vector w_i, and determining 1-d mapping g_i. Right: LVSR with tuning.

We have also designed a further variant of LVSR, which adds tuning as shown in Figure 7-3 right. It starts by getting w_i and a *PWL*-extracted g_i. It then tunes those values, minimizing $rmse$ by changing the w_i (with n parameters) and the PWL parameters α and β (each with $M + 1$ parameters, $M = 10$). We tune with a simple, fast, and derivative-free local optimizer (Nelder and Mead, 1965). Up to 50,000 evaluations are allowed. Each evaluation is cheap, needing just one vector-matrix product of $t = w_i * X^3$, followed by simulation of the 1-d PWL model $g_i(t)$ at the N values in t.

We found that, for this application, models of rank > 2 did not improve test rmse (similar to the results of (Singhee and Rutenbar, 2007)), so results shown are from max rank = 2. Runtime for all LVSR variants is on the order of a few minutes on a single-core 2 GHz CPU, with the SR portion taking the majority of time.

6.   Experiments Using Latent Variable Regression

Let us first examine LVR in action, with the P2M algorithm. Figure 7-4 illustrates P2M on the 10T AV problem, where it performed the best of any regressor. The left plot shows the outcome after the first round. At any given t-value (x-axis value), the spread of points is quite tight, which indicates that the direction w_1 can account for a major part of the variation. Also note that the curve on the left plot cannot be readily modeled by a linear mapping; this corresponds to the poor performance exhibited by the linear models on 10T AV seen in section 3 ($rmse$ values of 0.4377 and 0.4430). The curve can be fit fairly well by a quadratic, though not perfectly, which is why the quadratic approach PROBE did reasonably well ($rmse$ of 0.1384). On this plot, a PWL curve is able to capture the trend well, to complete the first iteration (final $rmse$ of P2M was 0.0915).

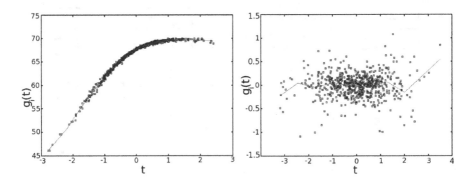

Figure 7-4. Left: Result after first round of P2M (rank=1) on 10 AV problem. The y-axis is g_1; the x-axis is the projection $t_1 = w_1^T x$ which in this case was found via quadratic modeling (PROBE). The scatter points are the 450 training samples projected onto the g_1-t_1 plane. The line among the scatter points is a 10-segment PWL model. Right: Result second round of P2M (rank=2) on 10T AV problem, g_2 vs. t_2.

---

[3] Actually, since the optimizer changes just a subset of variables in w_i, only those changes need to propagate through X to update t.

The second P2M iteration learns on the residuals of the first round. Since the first round captured most of the variation, the y-range for the second round is significantly smaller (g_2 ranges from just $\approx$-1 to $\approx$+1, whereas g_1 was from $\approx$45 to $\approx$70). The PWL model captures this as best it can, though this second round helps little. However, it illluminates a risk of PWL modeling: the model is not second-order continuous and goes to a more extreme value when extrapolating to large values of t (right hand side of the plot). This will hurt prediction ability.

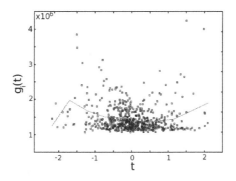

Figure 7-5. For P2M on 10T BW problem, g_1 vs. t_1.

On the next problem, 10T BW, P2M did *not* capture the direction well, as Figure 7-5 illustrates. The rank-1 projection of BW vs. $t_1 = w_1^T x$ has a very weak pattern, with much spread in BW at any given x-axis value t. This contrast sharply with the tightly-spread rank-1 projection we just observed for AV in Figure 7-4 left. For 10T BW, the PWL model attempts to capture the weak trend, but of course results in a poor model. The rank-2 projection helps little. The final $rmse$ was 0.9077, which is the worst of any regressor.

In contrast to P2M's approach of capturing projection vectors using quadratic modeling, the LVSR approaches use impacts from either Random Forests or regularized linear learning (LVSR-RF and LVRS-GDR, respectively). Figure 7-1 is worth re-examining: it shows relative variable impacts as extracted by RF or GDR. We see that GDR needs sharply fewer variables to capture the majority of variation. This is due to the nature of the respective model-building algorithms. RF has no bias to reduce the number of variables – given two variables causing the same effect, RF will "democratically" keep both. In contrast, GDR has bias to reduce variables – given two variables with the same effect, just one will be kept.

Recall that P2M did poorly on the 10T BW problem. Figure 7-6 shows the rank=1 projections from LVSR-RF (left plot), and from LVSR-GDR (right plot). Both approaches captured the trend, and GDR captured it very tightly. This is reflected in the final $rmse$ values: whereas P2M had an $rmse$ of 0.9077,

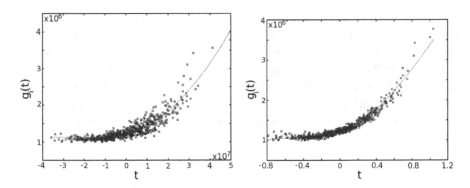

Figure 7-6. Left: For LVSR-RF on 10T BW problem, g_1 vs. t_1. Right: For LVSR-GDR on 10T BW problem, g_1 vs. t_1.

LVSR-RF had $rmse$ of 0.4331E, and LVSR-GDR had $rmse$ of 0.1728 (the lowest $rmse$ for 10T BW).

Table 7-2. Test RMSE values with LVR regressors

Problem	P2M: PROBE/PWL	LVSR-PROBE	LVSR-RF	LVSR-GDR	LVSR-GDR-tune
10T AV	0.0915	0.3297	0.4914	0.4012	0.1167
10T BW	0.9077	0.7018	0.6802	0.2767	0.4671
10T GBW	0.4202	0.3997	0.5271	0.4050	0.4091
10T GM	0.2723	0.3614	0.5348	0.4017	0.3738
10T OS	0.2527	0.2549	0.3807	0.2316	0.2370
10T PM	0.7188	0.5817	0.6933	0.6077	0.5937
10T SR	0.0136	0.0376	0.2913	0.0448	0.0464
10T ST	0.0574	0.0600	0.3293	0.0716	0.0556
30T AV	0.1499	0.1758	0.3744	0.1107	0.1023
30T BW	0.1058	0.1232	0.2887	0.0868	0.0777
30T GBW	0.1147	0.1038	0.3119	0.0459	0.0525
30T GM	0.1623	0.1752	0.3732	0.6198	0.1056
30T OS	0.3533	0.3393	0.3640	0.2017	0.1933
30T PM	0.1120	0.1236	0.3665	0.0856	0.0712
30T SR	0.2885	0.3749	0.3096	0.1648	0.1676
30T ST	0.2021	0.1950	0.3317	0.1673	0.1583

Table 7-2 gives test $rmse$ values for the various LVSR approaches. Because the LVSR approaches are stochastic, for each problem we do 30 independent runs and report the median value. P2M is hit and miss – sometimes it gets excellent performance but sometimes it is abysmal (e.g. $rmse$ of 0.9077).

LVSR-PROBE, which uses quadratic models like P2M, performs similarly to P2M, except avoiding the abysmal failures. Because the only difference is in g_i approach, the abysmal failures are almost certainly due to the PWL mappings' poor extrapolations. LVSR-RF approach is mediocre everywhere. This is not surprising: RF tends to "soften" (lowpass filter) the variable impacts due to its "democratic" variable selection (lack of bias in choosing variables).

LVSR-GDR-tune and LVSR-GDR do the best, with comparable $rmse$ values. They both have low $rmse$ in most cases, and never have abysmal performance. LVSR-GDR-tune and LVSR-GDR does better on 10T AV and 30T GM, and LVSR-GDR does better on 10T BW. So, tuning can help, but not always. There are three remaining problems that resist good models in the median (10T GBW, 10T GM, 10T PM). However, since the runs' best (minimum) $rmse$ values are 0.3797, 0.2992, and 0.3428 respectively, good models are achievable.

The final rank-1 symbolic model for one run of 10T BW, via LVSR-GDR, is given in Table 7-3. The projection vector has too many terms to interpret, but that is compensated by visualizing the g_i vs. t_i projections, the symbolic models of g_i, and if desired, a cumulative impact plot like Figure 7-1.

Table 7-3. Final model for 10T BW, as found by LVSR-GDR

$$g_1(t_1) = 1.184e+06 + 0.871e+6 * \max(0, 5.214 * t_1)^{1/2} * t_1 + 0.213e+6 * t_1$$
$$t_1 = 1.338e+06 + 6.683e+03 * DP1\_M2\_nsmm\_TOX + (40 \text{ other terms})$$

To test scalability to larger problems yet, we tested LVSR-GDR-tune on the 50-transistor circuit shown in Figure 7-7. Each modeling problem has 341 input variables. Like 10T and 30T problems, the outputs are AV, BW, etc. The rest of the setup was the same. Runtime was about the same (minutes), because the 1-d SR takes the majority of time. 30 runs were performed for each problem.

Table 7-4 gives median $rmse$ values for each of the 8 modeling problems. We see that in most cases, the $rmse$ is acceptable, and it is never abysmal. The rmse of the best run's 50T GBW was 0.2721. This signifies that LVSR has scaled very nicely to this problem with more variables; which the non-LVR approaches would have had extreme difficulty with. We expect LVSR to scale to problems of much higher dimensionality, e.g. circuits with $\approx$1,000 transistors and $\approx$10,000 input variables. We leave that to future research.

Table 7-4. Test $rmse$ values for LVSR-GDR-tune, for 50T-amp problems having 316 input variables.

AV	BW	GBW	GM	OS	PM	SR	ST
0.2852	0.4047	0.2379	0.2265	0.2549	0.1742	0.1772	0.2162

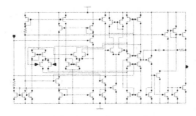

Figure 7-7. Schematic of 50-device operational amplifier.

7.   Conclusion

This paper described a new challenge for GP-based symbolic regression: handling high-dimensional inputs when pruning does not work because too many variables have significant impact. This challenge matters for the real-world problem of variation-aware analog circuit design. This paper showed how how traditional GP-based SR performed poorly on such problems, alongside the poor performance of other state-of-the-art regression techniques. Then this paper introduced the latent variable regression (LVR) view of the regression problem, reviewed existing LVR techniques and their shortcomings, and introduced latent variable *symbolic* regression (LVSR). LVSR provides a symbolic model and useful visualizations of the projection vectors. On real-world circuit modeling problems, LVSR demonstrated significantly lower prediction error than traditional non-LVR approaches and a modern LVR approach (P2M).

8.   Acknowledgment

Funding for the reported research results is acknowledged from Solido Design Automation Inc.

References

Almal, Arpit A. and al. (2006). Using genetic programming to classify node positive patients in bladder cancer. In *Proc. Genetic and Evolutionary Computation Conference*, pages 239–246.

Baffi, G., Martin, E.B., and Morris, A.J. (1999). Non-linear projection to latent structures revisited (the neural network pls algorithm). *Computers in Chemical Engineering*, 23(9).

Becker, Y.L., Fox, H., and Fei, P. (2007). An empirical study of multi-objective algorithms for stock ranking. In Riolo, R.L., Soule, T., and Worzel, B., editors, *Genetic Programming Theory and Practice V*, pages 241–262. Springer.

Breiman, L. (2001). Random forests. *Machine Learning*, 45(1):5–32.

Breiman, L., Friedman, J.H., Olshen, R.A., and Stone, C.J. (1984). *Classification and Regression Trees*. Chapman & Hall.

Drennan, P. and McAndrew, C. (1999). A comprehensive mosfet mismatch model. In *Proc. International Electron Devices Meeting*.

Friedman, J.H. (2002). Stochastic gradient boosting. *Journal of Computational Statistics & Data Analysis*, 38(4):367–378.

Friedman, J.H. and Popescu, B.E. (2004). Gradient directed regularization for linear regression and classification. Technical report, Stanford University, Department of Statistics.

Friedman, J.H. and Tukey, J.W. (1974). A projection pursuit algorithm for exploratory data analysis. *IEEE Trans. Computers*, C-23:881.

Hastie, T., Tibshirani, R., and Friedman, J.H. (2001). *The Elements of Statistical Learning*. Springer.

Jordan, Michael I. and Jacobs, Robert A. (1994). Hierarchical mixtures of experts and the em algorithm. *Neural Computation*, 6:181–214.

Kordon, A., Castillo, F., Smits, G., and Kotanchek, M. (2005). Application issues of genetic programming in industry. In Yu, T., Riolo, R.L., and Worzel, B., editors, *Genetic Programming Theory and Practice III*, chapter 16, pages 241–258. Springer.

Kordon, A., Smits, G., Jordaan, E., and Rightor, E. (2002). Robust soft sensors based on integration of genetic programming, analytical neural networks, and support vector machines. In Fogel, D.B. and al., editors, *Congress on Evolutionary Computation*, pages 896–901. IEEE Press.

Korns, M.F. (2007). Large-scale, time-constrained symbolic regression-classification. In Riolo, R.L., Soule, T., and Worzel, B., editors, *Genetic Programming Theory and Practice V*, chapter 4, pages 53–68. Springer.

Koza, John R. (1992). *Genetic Programming: On the Programming of Computers by Means of Natural Selection*. MIT Press, Cambridge, MA, USA.

Li, X. and Cao, Y. (2008). Projection-based piecewise-linear response surface modeling for strongly nonlinear vlsi performance variations. In *IEEE/ACM International Symposium on Quality Electronic Design*.

Li, X., Gopalakrishnan, P., Xu, Y., and Pileggi, L. (2007). Robust analog/rf circuit design with projection-based performance modeling. *IEEE Trans. Comput.-Aided Design of Integr. Circuits and Systems*, 26(1):2–15.

Malthouse, C., Tamhane, A.C., and Mah, R.S.H. (1997). Nonlinear partial least squares. *Computers in Chemical Engineering*, 21(8).

McConaghy, T. and Gielen, G.G.E. (2006). Canonical form functions as a simple means for genetic programming to evolve human-interpretable functions. In *Proc. Genetic and Evolutionary Computation Conference*, pages 855–862.

McConaghy, T. and Gielen, G.G.E. (2009). Template-free symbolic performance modeling of analog circuits via canonical form functions and genetic programming. *IEEE Trans. Comput.-Aided Design of Integr. Circuits and Systems (to appear)*.

McConaghy, T., Palmers, P., Gielen, G.G.E., and Steyaert, M. (2008). Automated extraction of expert domain knowledge from genetic programming synthesis results. In Riolo, R.L., Soule, T., and Worzel, B., editors, *Genetic Programming Theory and Practice VI*, pages 111–125. Springer.

McKay, B., Willis, M., Searson, D., and Montague, G. (1999). Non-linear continuum regression using genetic programming. In Banzhaf, W. and al., editors, *Proc. Genetic and Evol. Comput. Conference*, pages 1106–1111.

Moore, J.H., Greene, C.S., Andrews, P.C., and White, B.C. (2008). Does complexity matter? artificial evolution, computational evolution and the genetic analysis of epistasis in common human diseases. In Riolo, R.L., Soule, T., and Worzel, B., editors, *Genetic Programming Theory and Practice VI*, Genetic and Evolutionary Computation, chapter 9, pages 125–145. Springer.

Nelder, J.A. and Mead, R. (1965). A simplex method for function minimization. *Computer Journal*, 7:308–313.

Poggio, T. and Girosi, F. (1990). Networks for approximation and learning. *Proc. of the IEEE*, 78(9):1481–1497.

Sansen, W. (2006). *Analog Design Essentials*. Springer.

Schmidt, M.D. and Lipson, H. (2006). Co-evolving fitness predictors for accelerating and reducing evaluations. In Riolo, R.L., Soule, T., and Worzel, B., editors, *Genetic Programming Theory and Practice IV*, chapter 17. Springer.

Singhee, A. and Rutenbar, R.A. (2007). Beyond low-order statistical response surfaces: Latent variable regression for efficient, highly nonlinear fitting. In *Proc. Design Automation Conference*.

Smits, G., Kordon, A., Vladislavleva, K., Jordaan, E., and Kotanchek, M. (2005). Variable selection in industrial datasets using pareto genetic programming. In Yu, T., Riolo, R.L., and Worzel, B., editors, *Genetic Programming Theory and Practice III*, volume 9 of *Genetic Programming*, pages 79–92. Springer.

Vladislavleva, E. (2008). *Model-based Problem Solving through Symbolic Regression via Pareto Genetic Programming*. PhD thesis, Tilburg University.

Chapter 8

ALGORITHMIC TRADING WITH DEVELOPMENTAL AND LINEAR GENETIC PROGRAMMING

Garnett Wilson[1] and Wolfgang Banzhaf[1]

[1]*Memorial University of Newfoundland, St. John's, NL, Canada.*

Abstract   A developmental co-evolutionary genetic programming approach (PAM DGP) and a standard linear genetic programming (LGP) stock trading system are applied to a number of stocks across market sectors. Both GP techniques were found to be robust to market fluctuations and reactive to opportunities associated with stock price rise and fall, with PAM DGP generating notably greater profit in some stock trend scenarios. Both algorithms were very accurate at buying to achieve profit and selling to protect assets, while exhibiting both moderate trading activity and the ability to maximize or minimize investment as appropriate. The content of the trading rules produced by both algorithms are also examined in relation to stock price trend scenarios.

Keywords: Developmental Genetic Programming, Linear Genetic Programming, Computational Finance

1.   Introduction

Algorithmic trading examines a stock's past price movements in order to anticipate what effect they will have on its future price. Such analysis uses technical indicators like price fluctuations and trading volume to identify these changes in an asset's price. Evolutionary Computation techniques, such as genetic programming (GP), have been applied to the analysis of financial markets with a reassuring degree of success (Brabazon and O'Neill, 2006). This chapter explores the application of a developmental GP system, Probabilistic Adaptive Mapping Developmental Genetic Programming (PAM DGP), and linear genetic programming (LGP), to interday stock trading. PAM DGP uses co-operative co-evolution of genotype solutions and genotype-phenotype map-

R. Riolo et al. (eds.), *Genetic Programming Theory and Practice VII*,
Genetic and Evolutionary Computation, DOI 10.1007/978-1-4419-1626-6_8,
© Springer Science + Business Media, LLC 2010

pings and permits emphasis of certain functions over others, while LGP uses a single genotype population and the encoding of functions is static.

The following section discusses previous GP-related approaches to stock market analysis. Section 3 describes the stock trading implementations of LGP and PAM DGP, including function set and interpretation of trading rules as genotype individuals. The ability of both algorithms to generate profit when applied to a number of stocks across market sectors is examined in Section 4. Section 5 examines the general trading activity and its profitability for the two algorithms. Section 6 presents an analysis of the actual function set content of the trading rules. Conclusions and future work follow in Section 7.

2.   Related Approaches to Stock Prediction

Genetic programming is pervasive in the field of financial analysis , and a number of implementations are described in the literature. The system described here was first introduced in (Wilson and Banzhaf, 2009). In this work, we examine a much more substantial variety of stocks and price trends, and also the trading rules generated by the different implementations. The first implementation we consider is traditional linear GP (Brameier and Banzhaf, 2007). LGP has been applied to stock market analysis previously by (Grosan and Abraham, 2006), where a LGP hybrid (with multi-expression systems) outperformed neural networks and neuro-fuzzy systems for interday prediction of stock prices for NASDAQ and Nifty indices. The second implementation we examine is PAM DGP, a co-evolutionary developmental approach. While the authors are not aware of any previous approaches to stock market analysis using developmental approaches, a co-evolutionary process has been applied to the evolution of trading rules by (Drezewski and Sepielak, 2008). In their co-evolutionary system, one species represented entry strategies and one species represented exit strategies. Both a multi-agent version of the co-evolutionary algorithm and an evolutionary algorithm were created, where the multi-agent co-evolutionary approach generated the most profit.

In terms of the application of the GP algorithms to interday trading, some modified elements of the grammatical evolution (GE) approach of (Brabazon and O'Neill, 2006) were adopted. In their approach, after initial evolution during a training period, the best rules in the population traded live for a window of *n* days. The training window then shifted and the current population was retrained using the data in the window on which it was previously trading live. The algorithm then traded live on the following *n* days, and so on. The authors compared two versions of the GE system, one where the final population from the last window was used as the starting population for the current window, and one that re-initialized the population with each window shift. The authors found that maintaining the population, rather than re-initializing it, provided more profitable performance (and better rules). Similarly, our populations were not re-initialized with each window shift. Our technique uses a shifting window of length 5 days, but shifts only in increments of 1 day.

3.   LGP and PAM DPG Algorithm for Stock Analysis

LGP is a very popular form of genetic programming, where instead of the most traditionl form of trees being used as individuals, genotypes consist of binary strings and registers to store subresults. These binary strings are interpreted as instructions of a program, where a unique binary sequence encodes for only one member of the function set. Throughout program execution in standard LGP, the mapping of binary sequence to instruction does not change.

In PAM DGP (Wilson and Heywood, 2007), there is a population of genotypes that cooperatively coevolves with a separate population of mappings. A probability table is updated throughout algorithm execution with entries corresponding to each pairing of individual genotype and mapping from both populations. The table entries represent frequencies that dictate the probability that roulette selection in a steady state tournament will choose the genotype-mapping pairing of individuals determined by the indices of the table. The genotype and mapping individual that are members of the current best genotype-mapping pairing are immune to mutation and crossover to maintain the current best solution discovered. Each tournament round involves the selection of four unique genotype-mapping pairings. Following fitness evaluation and ranking, the probability table columns associated with the winning combinations have the winning combination in that column updated using Equation (8.1) and the remaining combinations in that column updated using Equation (8.2)

$$P(g,m)_{new} = P(g,m)_{old} + \alpha(1 - P(g,m)_{old}) \qquad (8.1)$$

$$P(g,m)_{new} = P(g,m)_{old} - \alpha(P(g,m)_{old}) \qquad (8.2)$$

where g is the genotype individual/index, m is the mapping individual/index, α is the learning rate (corresponding to how much emphasis is placed on current values versus previous search), and $P(g,m)$ is the probability in table element $[g, m]$. To prevent premature convergence, the algorithm uses a noise threshold. If an element in the table exceeds the noise threshold following a tournament round, a standard Gaussian probability in the interval $[0, 1]$ is placed in that element and all values in its column are re-normalized so the column elements sum to unity. The PAM DGP algorithm and selection mechanism are summarized in Figure8-1.

Genotypes in PAM DGP are binary strings, with interpretation of sections of the binary string being instruction-dependent. Mappings in this work are redundant such that individuals are composed of $b \geq s$ 10-bit binary strings, where b is the minimum number of binary sequences required to represent a function

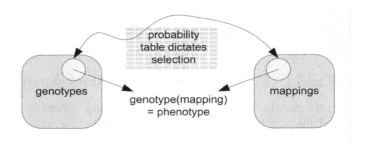

Figure 8-1. Probabilistic Adaptive Mapping Developmental Genetic Programming (PAM DGP).

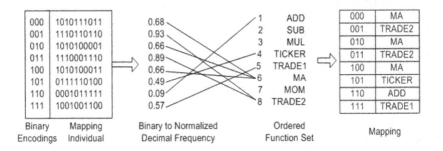

Figure 8-2. PAM DGP mapping process.

set of s symbols. Each 10 bit mapping section is interpreted as its decimal equivalent, normalized to the range [0, 1], and mapped to an ordered function set index by multiplying by s and truncating to an integer value (allowing redundant encoding of symbols). The process whereby a particular mapping is used to isolate and emphasize certain members of the function set when interpreting genotype is depicted in Figure 8-2. Using this mapping mechanism with co-evolutionary selection, PAM DGP will emphasize the most useful members of the function set, ignore members of the function set which are not pertinent, and simultaneously evolve an appropriate genotype solution.

PAM DGP is compared to the standard LGP implementation (Brameier and Banzhaf, 2007) in this study. LGP individuals are also bit strings, and there is naturally only a genotype population. The interpretation of instructions for PAM DGP is the same for LGP, where LGP here can be seen as a special case of PAM DGP that uses a static mapping and constant function set. (PAM DGP extends LGP such that members of a function set are adaptively emphasized.) Additional details of PAM DGP, along with its original motivations and comparisons to related developmental systems, are available in (Wilson and Heywood, 2007).

The PAM DGP and LGP implementations are applied to several stocks across market segments, including technology: Google Inc. (GOOG), Apple Inc. (AAPL), and Microsoft Corporation (MSFT), energy: Chevron Co. (CVX) and Ballard Power Systems (BLDP), consumer: PepsiCo Inc. (PEP), automobile: Ford Motor Co. (F), and finance: Bank of Montreal (BMO). The initial exchange portion of the ticker symbols were removed in all cases for brevity. High, low, open, and close data was provided as input for 200 day periods throughout 2007 and 2008, with different dates chosen to test the implementations' performance. The first 16 days of the 200 days were reserved as a basis on which to draw initial data for the technical indicators. After those dates, GP fitness was evaluated on data corresponding to a moving window of n days. Individuals represent sets of trading rules, based on functions in the function set. For each window of n days corresponding to trading days m to n, each of m to $n - 1$ days were used for calculation of a trading decision given the individual's rule set, with $m + 1$ to n being used to evaluate the recommendation based on the immediately preceding day. Days used for the calculation of a trading decision were normalized using two-phase preprocessing as in (Brabazon and O'Neill, 2006): All daily values were transformed by division by a lagged moving average, and then normalized using linear scaling into the range [0, 1] using

$$v_{scaled} = \frac{v_t - l_n}{h_n - l_n} \tag{8.3}$$

where v_{scaled} is the normalized daily trading value, v_t is the transformed daily trading value at time step t, h_n is highest transformed value in the last n time steps, l_n is the lowest transformed value in the last n time steps, and n is length of the time lag chosen for the initial transformation.

In addition to an instruction set, each individual consists of a set of four registers, a flag for storing the current value of logical operations, and a separate output (trade) register for storing a final value corresponding to a trade recommendation. Following the execution of the trading rules of a GP individual, if the value of the trade register is 0, no action is recommended. Otherwise, the final value in the trade register corresponds to a value in the range [0, 1]. This value was multiplied by a maximum dollar amount to be bought or sold per trade ($10,000 was used here based on an initial account balance of $100,000 with which to trade) to give some portion of $10,000 to be traded. For each trade conducted, there is a $10 commission penalty. The trading system is permitted to run a small deficit >= $10 to either handle a sell recommendation when maximally invested (where the deficit would be immediately recouped) or, similarly, to allow a buy in order to be maximally invested. Fitness of an individual is the value of the cash and shares held.

The best individual consisting of the best trading rule set is used by a "live" trading algorithm. That is, the live trader provides known information to the GP for days m to n. The GP algorithm returns a recommendation on which the live trading system bases its decision to trade on the following day, $n + 1$. In particular, the net number of shares bought and sold by the best evolved individual (trading rules) given the recommendation of the trade register over all the fitness cases is the buy or sell recommendation to the "live" trading system. The transactions of the live trading system are thus based on unknown data, and determine the success of the algorithms.

While PAM DGP uses co-evolution to refine function set composition, the appropriate initial function set members must be provided as a basis upon which the algorithm can select its optimum function set. In the case of standard GP, this initial function set remains constant throughout execution. The function set includes standard mathematical operators, and instructions to trade based on logical operators applied to the four internal registers. In addition, there are established financial analysis metrics used: moving average, momentum, channel breakout, and current day high, low, open, or close price. The financial technical indicator moving average (MA) is the mean of the previous n share prices. The momentum indicator (MOM) provides the rate of change indicator, and is the ratio of a particular time-lagged price to the current price. Channel breakout (BRK) establishes a trading range for a stock, and reflects its volatility. The most popular solution places Bollinger bands around a n-day moving average of the price at ± 2 standard deviations of the price movement.

4.   Profit Analysis

The worth of the live trading system's assets over 184 days of trading is examined (200 fitness cases in total were actually used, with the first 16 reserved to provide initial values for technical indicators). Fifty trials over the 184 trading days were conducted for the four stocks using an Apple iMac Intel Core 2 Duo 2.8 GHz CPU and 4GB RAM using OS X Leopard v10.5.4. With an initial account of $100,000, the mean worth (with standard error) of all assets (cash and shares) of the live trading system for PAM DGP, LGP, and naive buy-and-hold strategies is given in Figure 8-3. Naive buy-and-hold is simply the strategy of maximally investing on the first trading day and staying invested for the entire time period.

It is evident from Figure 8-3 that PAM DGP and LGP are both robust to share price fluctuations (where the buy and hold trend line is a direct indication of share price fluctuations). The evolved solutions seem to take advantage of the upward trends, although the solutions reflect a conservative strategy overall, adept at anticipating and buffering against sharp share price declines and volatility in general. In terms of specific upward trends, GOOG and AAPL exhibit moderately volatile behavior followed by fairly sharp declines (from approximately day 60 to 80), proceeded by climbing stock prices. In both of these instances, LGP and PAM DGP outperform buy-and-hold, with PAM DGP outperforming LGP. Given PEP and CVX, a general upward climbing trend can be examined. Here, the performance of LGP and PAM DGP is much closer. While the more steady upward climb of PEP does not allow LGP or PAM DGP to outperform buy-and-hold, the price drops of CVX between days 60 and 120 allow PAM DGP and LGP to outperform buy-and-hold by the end of the time period. Note that in the instance of PEP, both algorithms are naturally not invested to the (maximal) extent of buy-and-hold prior to the steep price climb, and thus have less final profit (but are still competitive and almost as profitable).

In terms of the ability of the algorithms to handle downward market trends, BLDP and MSFT show downward trending stock prices. MSFT exhibits a fairly gradual downward trending slope. PAM DGP and LGP perform relatively on par with buy-and-hold, with all implementations generating comparable losses at the end of the time period. BLDP, in contrast, features some volatility with spiking near the end. This volatility allows LGP and PAM DGP to end the time period with greater profit than buy-and-hold (although all algorithms suffer losses when investing in these downward trending stocks). While we see in all stocks in Figure 8-3 that LGP and PAM DGP are typically able to recognize steep downward trends, and sell assets to protect investments, general downward trends with consistent moderate volatility (see MSFT especially) can prevent the algorithm from pulling out assets to a large degree because there are brief episodes of profit. F and BMP exhibit an upward trend, followed by punctuated steeper downward trends. During the downward trends, LGP and PAM DGP will typically sell to protect investments (although PAM DGP does get caught in a very sudden drop at the end of the time period for BMO). Final and cumulative measures of profit are shown in Figures 8-4 and 8-5, respectively.

In the boxplots of Figures 8-4 and 8-5, each box indicates the lower quartile, median, and upper quartile values. If the notches of two boxes do not overlap, the medians of the two groups differ at the 0.95 confidence interval. Points represent outliers to whiskers of 1.5 times the interquartile range. In Figure 8-4, a comparison of final profit indicates that stocks that were well-chosen (were profitable overall during the time period) generated profit for both algorithms. Note that time period end is arbitrary and profits are a direct reflection of underlying market trend. If a stock is losing value, direct buying and selling of the stock cannot generate profit.

Figure 8-5 is more informative, as it shows the mean daily cumulative profit (%) greater than buy-and-hold for the LGP and PAM DGP live trading systems over all trading days. Both PAM DGP and LGP were generally more profitable than buy-and-hold at any given time for all stocks. Exceptions included, naturally, the case of PEP where naïve buy-and-hold is a very good strategy, and

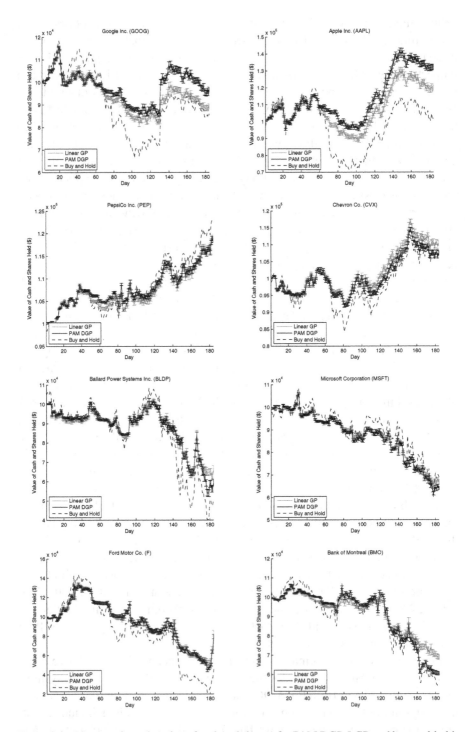

Figure 8-3. Mean total worth (value of cash and shares) for PAM DGP, LGP, and buy-and-hold strategies over 50 trials with standard error given initial $100,000 cash value.

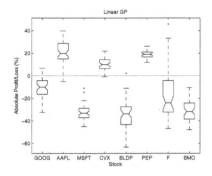
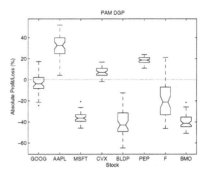

Figure 8-4. Boxplot of mean final profit (%) greater than buy-and-hold for PAM DGP and LGP over 50 trials. Value of 0 indicates the breakeven point.

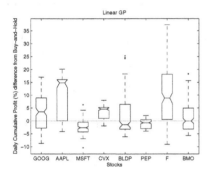
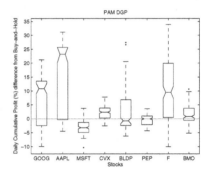

Figure 8-5. Boxplot of mean daily cumulative profit (%) difference from buy-and-hold for PAM DGP and LGP over 50 trials. Value of 0 indicates the breakeven point.

BLDP and MSFT where high volatility combined with a drawn out downward trend caused losses. In all cases where buy-and-hold was cumulatively more profitable, the performance was only lower for LGP or PAM DGP by a very slight amount (0–1% for BLDP and PEP, less than 5% for MSFT). PAM DGP was more profitable than LGP at any given time by a large margin for GOOG and AAPL and a very small margin for PEP. LGP slightly outperformed PAM DGP for CVX. Given the behavior in Figures 8-3 and 8-5, PAM DGP provides increased robustness to market downturns and quickly takes advantage of growth opportunities later in evolution. Also, we can see in Figure 8-5 that LGP slightly outperforms PAM DGP for CVX by not selling quite as much stock during a market dip immediately preceding a steady climb starting at approximately day 100 (Figure 8-3). Thus PAM DGP is slightly more reactive in its selling to prevent loss, where this benefits performance for GOOG and AAPL, but not CVX. There was no substantial statistically significant difference in cumulative profit for the other stocks.

5.   Trading Activity

Trading activity is shown in Figure 8-6, expressed as the number of shares retained daily as a percentage of the live system's total worth. Comparing Figures 8-3 and 8-6, it is evident that both PAM DGP and LGP are capable of efficiently reacting to the market: they will both sell if a stock price starts to drop and buy if the stock price appears to be rising. Figures 8-3 and 8-6 collectively show that both algorithms will stay maximally invested during sustained profitable periods.

The performance of these trades can be further examined by analysis of how many trades were conducted and their benefit. Proportion of profitable trades is a common metric for evaluation of trading activity, although it can be deceptive: it does not even reflect the overall ability of an algorithm in terms of actual profit generated (Brabazon and O'Neill, 2006). Many trades are beneficial in preventing loss during market downturns, and generate no profit at all. Thus, rather than the standard measure of percentage of profitable trades, the percentage of profitable buy trades and percentage of sell trades preventing loss for each algorithm are given in Figures 8-7 and 8-8, respectively. Figure 8-9 shows the percentage of trading opportunities where a trade was actually conducted. The number of trading opportunities not taken when the system was maximally or minimally invested, out of all possible trades, is shown in Figure 8-10.   Figure 8-7 reveals that both LGP and PAM DGP are very accurate when buying for profit: LGP exhibited medians of 96–100% profitable buys across all stocks, and PAM DGP exhibited 87% to 100% profitable buys across all stocks (with the vast majority above 96%). Figure 8-8 shows that LGP was extremely good at selling to prevent loss; all medians were 100%. PAM DGP did not perform quite as well, but still exhibited very impressive results by selling to prevent loss with 94–100% accuracy. Overall, both algorithms were very good at both buying for profit and selling to prevent loss. Even outliers in either buying for profit or selling to prevent loss were acceptably high percentages.

Figure 8-9 shows the trading activity behind all the performance measures we have considered so far. PAM DGP generally conducted more trades (based on spread of data) than LGP for all stocks. For all stocks with a general upward trend (GOOG, AAPL, CVX, and PEP), a lower number of trades were conducted for both LGP and PAM DGP. In particular, LGP conducted approximately 28–35% (based on median) of possible trades for (generally) rising stocks, while approximately 37–42% of possible trades were conducted for the (generally) falling stocks (MSFT, BLDP, F, BMO). PAM DGP conducted approximately 30–40% of available trades for rising stocks and 44–50% for falling

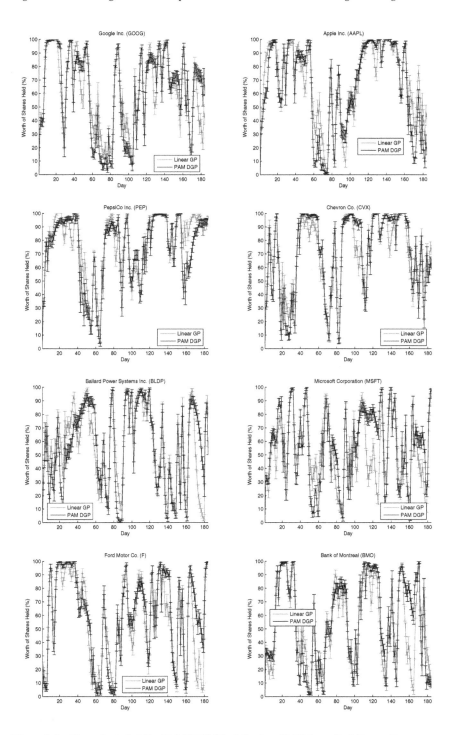

Figure 8-6. Mean shares held by PAM DGP (black line) and LGP (grey line) live trading systems as a percentage of total worth over 50 trials with standard error.

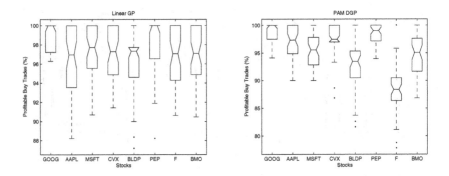

Figure 8-7. Percentage of profitable buy trades for 184 trading days over 50 trials.

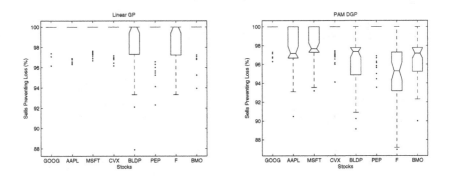

Figure 8-8. Percentage of sell trades preventing losses for 184 trading days over 50 trials.

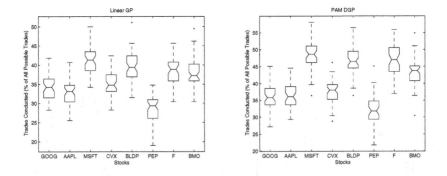

Figure 8-9. Percentage of trades executed overall for each stock for 184 trading days over 50 trials.

stocks. Overall, the groups of falling stocks caused both algorithms to trade more actively than they would for the rising stocks, where this was statistically

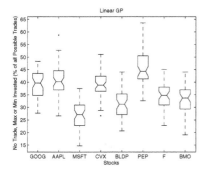 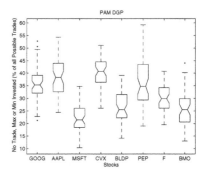

Figure 8-10. Trades not conducted while maximally or minimally invested as a percentage of all trades for 184 trading days over 50 trials.

significant for both LGP and PAM DGP. Figure 8-10 indicates the percentage of all trades where the system wished to maintain a maximally or minimally invested position. For both LGP and PAM DGP, the system would maximize (or minimize) investment for all rising stocks between approximately 35 and 45% (based on median) of the time for rising stocks. Compared with Figure 8-6, it is evident that most of these positions were maximal investment to generate profit. However, again for both algorithms, the system would maximize or minimize investment for only approximately 20 to 35% (median) of the time for falling stocks. Overall, Figures 8-7 to 8-10 indicate that the proportion of beneficial trades (generating profit or protecting the investor from further losses) was impressive, where this occurred in the context of moderate levels of trading.

6.   Trading Rules

The actual content of the trading rules will vary between trading days and across general stock price trends. Since populations are kept across training windows, as recommended in (Brabazon and O'Neill, 2006) (see Section 3), the content of an individual at the arbitrary end of a time period is a reflection of trading rules for that stock built up over the entire time period. Thus, we examine the proportion of each member of the function set in the final best individual at the end of the time period over all 50 trials. The composition of individuals for two stock price trend types are examined: a rising stock (AAPL) that achieved profit and a falling stock (BMO) that suffered losses. The percentage of each function set member in the final individuals over all 50 trials is provided for AAPL and BMO in Figure 8-11 and 8-12, respectively. Standard mathematical operators, a logical operator (*logical*), moving average (*ma*), momentum (*mom*), a measure of the turbulence (*trb*), measures based on stock ticker data (*ticker*), and different trading mechanisms (*trade1* to *trade4*) are shown.

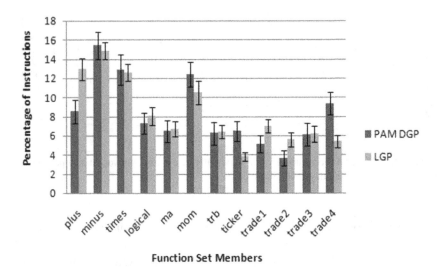

Figure 8-11.   Percentage composition corresponding to function set members in final day trading rules after 184 trading days over 50 trials for AAPL.

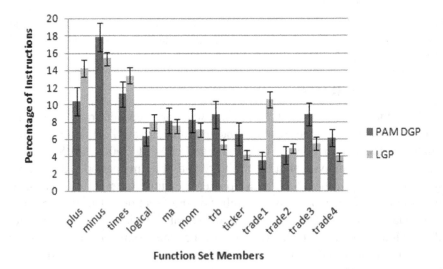

Figure 8-12.   Percentage composition corresponding to function set members in final day trading rules after 184 trading days over 50 trials for BMO.

We can note from Figure 8-11 that there are only statistically significant differences in the trading rules of LGP and PAM DGP for 5 of the 12 function set members, but never by a margin of more than 5%. In terms of interesting quantitative measures, momentum analysis dominates the instruction sets for the dropping followed by rising stock (AAPL) where profits were greatest. For the mean number of instructions in the sets over all trials for the falling BMO stock in Figure 8-12, there is a more even distribution of instruction types. However, PAM DGP does provide greater emphasis on certain instructions that execute trades (*trade3* and *trade4*). As with AAPL, only 5 of the 12 function set members differ statistically for BMO between LGP and PAM DGP, but never by more than 5% (with the exception of *trade1*). Overall, there appears to be no substantial difference in proportional function set composition seen in Figures 8-11 and 8-12, averaging content within all final instructions sets.

7.   Conclusions and Future Work

This work examined the trading performance of a co-evolutionary developmental GP model (PAM DGP) using a genotype-phenotype mapping and more traditional LGP on eight stocks across market sectors. Both implementations were found to be robust to stock price fluctuations, and outperformed naïve buy-and-hold strategies in almost all scenarios (with the exceptions of steady rise, where buy-and-hold cannot be beaten, and volatile moderate downturn). Even for a stock with a steady rise in price, LGP and PAM DGP are still very competitive and a less risky strategy for shorter time periods than buy-and-hold. Both algorithms evolved so that they protected investments during price drops with impressive accuracy, and they very accurately made buying decisions to generate profit. The beneficial trades by both algorithms were conducted with moderate trading activity and periods of maximal investment to capitalize on rising stock prices. Analysis of trading rules for two chosen stock trends showed that, overall, both algorithms picked similar levels for the majority of functions over all trials. Future work will examine index trading, intraday trading, incorporation of additional quantitative metrics, and extension of the algorithms for trading portfolios of multiple stocks.

Acknowledgment

We would like to thank the reviewers for their helpful comments, especially Michael Korns and Gregory Hornby.

References

Brabazon, Anthony and O'Neill, Michael (2006). *Biologically Inspired Algorithms for Financial Modelling*. Natural Computing Series. Springer.

Brameier, Markus and Banzhaf, Wolfgang (2007). *Linear Genetic Programming*. Number XVI in Genetic and Evolutionary Computation. Springer.

Drezewski, Rafal and Sepielak, Jan (2008). Evolutionary system for generating investment strategies. In Giacobini, Mario, Brabazon, Anthony, Cagnoni, Stefano, Caro, Gianni Di, Drechsler, Rolf, Ekárt, Anikó, Esparcia-Alcázar, Anna, Farooq, Muddassar, Fink, Andreas, McCormack, Jon, O'Neill, Michael, Romero, Juan, Rothlauf, Franz, Squillero, Giovanni, Uyar, Sima, and Yang, Shengxiang, editors, *EvoWorkshops*, volume 4974 of *Lecture Notes in Computer Science*, pages 83–92. Springer.

Grosan, Crina and Abraham, Ajith (2006). Stock market modeling using genetic programming ensembles. In Nedjah, Nadia, de Macedo Mourelle, Luiza, and Abraham, Ajith, editors, *Genetic Systems Programming*, volume 13 of *Studies in Computational Intelligence*, pages 131–146. Springer.

Wilson, Garnett and Banzhaf, Wolfgang (2009). Prediction of interday stock prices using developmental and linear genetic programming. In Giacobini, Mario, De Falco, Ivanoe, and Ebner, Marc, editors, *Applications of Evolutionary Computing, EvoWorkshops2009: EvoCOMNET, EvoENVIRONMENT, EvoFIN, EvoGAMES, EvoHOT, EvoIASP, EvoINTERACTION, EvoMUSART, EvoNUM, EvoPhD, EvoSTOC, EvoTRANSLOG*, LNCS, Tubingen, Germany. Springer Verlag.

Wilson, Garnett and Heywood, Malcolm (2007). Introducing probabilistic adaptive mapping developmental genetic programming with redundant mappings. *Genetic Programming and Evolvable Machines*, 8(2):187–220. Special issue on developmental systems.

Chapter 9

HIGH-SIGNIFICANCE AVERAGES OF EVENT-RELATED POTENTIAL VIA GENETIC PROGRAMMING

Luca Citi[1], Riccardo Poli[1], and Caterina Cinel[1]

[1]*School of Computer Science and Electronic Engineering, University of Essex, Wivenhoe Park, CO4 3SQ, UK*

Abstract   In this paper we use register-based genetic programming with memory-with-memory to discover probabilistic membership functions that are used to divide up data-sets of event-related potentials recorded via EEG in psycho-physiological experiments based on the corresponding response times. The objective is to evolve membership functions which lead to maximising the statistical significance with which true brain waves can be reconstructed when averaging the trials in each bin. Results show that GP can significantly improve the fidelity with which ERP components can be recovered.

Keywords: Event-related potentials, Averaging, Register-based GP, Memory-with-Memory

1.   Introduction

The electrical activity of the brain is typically recorded from the scalp using Electroencephalography (EEG). This is used in electrophysiology, in psychology, as well as in Brain-Computer Interface (BCI) research. Particularly important for these purposes are Event-Related Potentials (ERPs). ERPs are relatively well defined shape-wise variations to the ongoing EEG elicited by a stimulus and/or temporally linked to it (Luck, 2005). ERPs include early exogenous responses, due to the primary processing of the stimulus, as well as later endogenous responses, which are a reflection of higher cognitive processing induced by the stimulus (Donchin and Coles, 1988).

While the study of *single-trial* ERPs has been considered of great importance since the early days of ERP analysis, in practice the presence of noise and artifacts has forced researchers to make use of *averaging* as part of their standard investigation methodology (Donchin and Lindsley, 1968). Even today, despite

R. Riolo et al. (eds.), *Genetic Programming Theory and Practice VII*,
Genetic and Evolutionary Computation, DOI 10.1007/978-1-4419-1626-6_9,
© Springer Science + Business Media, LLC 2010

enormous advances in acquisition devices and signal-processing equipment and techniques, ERP averaging is still ubiquitous (Handy, 2004; Luck, 2005).

ERP averaging is also a key element in many BCIs. BCIs measure specific signals of brain activity intentionally and unintentionally induced by the participant and translate them into device control signals (see, for example, (Farwell and Donchin, 1988; Wolpaw et al., 1991; Pfurtscheller et al., 1993; Birbaumer et al., 1999; Wolpaw et al., 2000; Furdea et al., 2009)). Averaging is frequently used to increase accuracy in BCIs where the objective is to determine which of the stimuli sequentially presented to a user is attended. This is achieved via the classification of the ERP components elicited by the stimuli. This form of BCI — which effectively started off with the seminal work of (Farwell and Donchin, 1988) who showed that it was possible to spell words through the detection of P300 waves — is now one of the most promising areas of the discipline (e.g., see (Bostanov, 2004; Rakotomamonjy and Guigue, 2008; Citi et al., 2008)).

Averaging has empirically been shown to improve the accuracy in ERP-based BCIs. However, the larger the number of trials that need to be averaged, the longer it takes for the system to produce a decision. So, only a limited number of trials can be averaged before a decision has to be taken. A limitation on the number of trials one can average is also present in psychophysiological studies based on ERPs: the larger the number of trials that are accumulated in an average, the longer an experiment will last, potentially leading to participants fatiguing, to increases in noise due to variations in electrode impedances, etc. So, both in psychophysiological studies and in BCIs it would be advantageous to make the absolute best use of all the information available in each trial. However, as we will discuss in Section 2, standard averaging techniques do not achieve this.

In recent work (Poli et al., ress) we proposed, tested and theoretically analysed an extremely simple technique which can be used in forced-choice experiments. In such experiments response times are measured via a button press or a mouse click. Our technique consists of binning trials based on response times and then averaging. This can significantly alleviate the problems of other averaging methods, particularly when response times are relatively long. In particular, results indicated that the method produces clearer representations of ERP components than standard averaging, revealing finer details of components and helping in the evaluation of the true amplitude and latency of ERP waves.

The technique relies on dividing an ERP dataset into bins. The size and position of these bins is extremely important in determining the fidelity with which bin averages represent true brain waves. In (Poli et al., ress) we simply used standard (mutually exclusive) bins. That is, each bin covered a particular range of response times, the ranges associated to different bins did not overlap and no gaps were allowed between the bins. As we will explain in Section 3, this implies that, in bin averages, true ERP components are distorted via the convolution with a kernel whose frequency response is itself a convolution between the frequency response of the original latency distribution $\ell(t)$ and the Fourier transform of a *rectangular window* (a $sinc$ function).

While provably this has the effect of improving the resolution with which ERPs can be recovered via averages, it is clear that the convolution with $sinc$ will produce distortions due to the Gibbs phenomenon. Also, the width and position of the bins we used in (Poli et al., ress) was determined heuristically. We chose bins as follows: one gathered the lower 30% of the response time distribution, one the middle 30% and one the longer 30%.[1] However, it is clear that neither the choice of crisp mutually exclusive membership functions for bins (leading to convolution with $sinc$) nor the position and width of the bins is optimal.

So, although our binning method is a marked improvement over traditional techniques, it still does not make the best use of the information available in an ERP dataset. It is arguable, for example, that doing binning using gradual membership functions would provide even better ERP reconstruction fidelity. Similarly, setting the size of the bins on the basis of the noise in the data and the particular shape of the response time distribution would be beneficial to make best use of the available trials. Finding bin membership functions which satisfy these criteria, however, is difficult. It is also difficult to specify what notion of optimality one should use. In this paper we solve both problems.

The paper is organised as follows. After the reviews of previous work provided in Sections 2 and 3, we define what an optimal set of binning functions is (Section 4). As we will see this involves the use of statistical tests on the data belonging to different bins. Then (Section 5), we apply Genetic Programming (Poli et al., 2008) to the task of identifying optimal membership functions for bins in such a way as to get the best possible reconstruction of real ERP components from bin averages. The results of this process, as described in Section 6, provide significant improvements over the original technique. We give some conclusions and indications of future work in Section 7.

2. Averaging Techniques for ERPs

There are essentially three classes of methods that are commonly used to resolve ERP components via averaging. *Stimulus-locked averaging* requires extracting epochs of fixed duration from the EEG signal starting at the stimulus presentation and averaging the corresponding ERPs (Lindsley, 1968). An important problem with this form of averaging is that any ERP components whose latency is not phase-locked with the presentation of the stimuli may be

---

[1] Since extremely long response times are typically the sign of the participant being distracted or having had some other problem with providing a response, the 10% of the trials with the longest response times were discarded.

significantly distorted as a result of averaging (Spencer, 2004; Luck, 2005). This is because the average, $a(t)$, of randomly shifted versions of a waveform, $w(t)$, is the convolution between the original waveform and the latency distribution, $\ell(t)$, for that waveform, i.e., $a(t) = w(t) \star \ell(t) = \int w(t - \tau)\ell(\tau)\,d\tau$, e.g., see (Zhang, 1998). This typically means that a stimulus-locked average can only show a smoothed (low-pass filtered) version of each variable-latency component.

The problem is particularly severe when the task a subject needs to perform after the presentation of the stimuli is relatively difficult since the variability in the latencies of endogenous ERP components and in response times increase with the complexity of the task (Luck, 2005; Polich and Comerchero, 2003). In these cases, multiple endogenous variable-latency components may appear as a single large blurred component in the average; a synthetic example is shown in Figure 9-1 (left).[2] This makes it very difficult to infer true brain area activity for any response occurring after the early exogenous potentials typically elicited by (and synchronised with) a stimulus.

In experiments in which the task requires participants to provide a specific behavioural response (e.g., in the form of a button press or a spoken response), *response-locked averaging* can be used as an alternative to stimulus-locked averaging to help resolve variable-latency ERP components that are synchronised with the response; see, for example, (Luck and Hillyard, 1990; Keus et al., 2005; Spencer, 2004; Töllner et al., 2008). In this case, however, the early responses associated and phase-locked with the stimulus will end up being blurred and hard to distinguish, since they are represented in the average by the convolution of their true waveform with the response-time distribution; see (Zhang, 1998). A synthetic example illustrating this problem is shown in Figure 9-1 (right).

Thus, inferring whether a component in an average represents a true effect or it is due to averaging biases can then be very difficult. Note that averaging more data does not help increase the fidelity of the reconstructed signals because there is a *systematic error* in the averaging process.

A third alternative to resolve variable-latency waves is to attempt to identify such components in each trial and estimate their latency. Then, shifting trials on the basis of estimated latencies and averaging may bring out the desired component from its noise background. However, most methods of this kind require prior knowledge of what type of component to expect and at what times. What if this knowledge is not available? Without this information automated detection algorithms have very little hope of finding the latency of the waves of interest. Also, latency detection algorithms assume that the component of

---

[2]Real EEG signals are extremely noisy. So, synthetic data illustrate the problem more clearly.

STIMULUS LOCKED   RESPONSE LOCKED

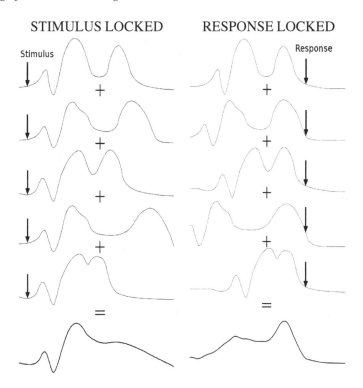

Figure 9-1. Example of distortions produced by averaging: the five sample ERPs at the top present two positive and one negative deflections each, which are phase-locked with a stimulus, as well as one positive component, which is of variable latency. Averaging them (plots at the bottom) preserves the exogenous components when trials are stimulus-locked (left). This, however, turns the variable-latency component into an inconspicuous plateau which could easily be misinterpreted as a continuation of the preceding positive wave. A response-locked average (right), on the other hand, preserves the variable-latency endogenous component but smears out the details of early potentials turning them into a single, wide positive deflection.

interest is present in every trial and we just need to find its latency in the trial. What if an ERP component is not always elicited by the stimuli? The presence of a component might be, for example, condition-dependent, or dependent on whether or not a participant attended a stimulus, whether a participant was rested or tired, whether there was habituation to the stimuli, etc. (Bonala et al., 2008; Wagner et al., 2000). If a component was absent frequently, running a latency-measuring algorithm on trials where the component did not occur would inundate the averaging process with bias and noise. And, unfortunately, thresholds or even more sophisticated algorithms for the detection of the *presence* of the component, which in principle could be used to properly handle trials that do not contain it, produce large numbers of mis-classification errors. So, the composition of detection errors with latency-estimation errors may render component-locked averaging very unreliable in many situations.

Note also that all methods that realign trials based on component latencies can potentially suffer from a *clear-centre/blurred-surround problem*. That is, after shifting trials based on the latency of a particular ERP component, all instances of that component will be synchronised, thereby effectively becoming fixed-latency elements. However, stimulus-locked components will now become variable-latency components. Also, all (other) components that are phase-locked with some other event (e.g., the response), but not with the component of interest, will remain variable-latency. Not surprisingly, then, they will appear blurred and distorted in a component-locked average.

It is clear that the standard averaging techniques reviewed above are not entirely satisfactory and that a more precise and direct way of identifying variable-latency components as well as measuring their latency and amplitude is needed. In the following section we describe the binning technique we developed in (Poli et al., ress), which significantly improves on previous methods.

3. Averaging Response-time Binned ERPs

In (Poli et al., ress) we proposed an extremely simple technique — binning trials based on their recorded response time and then applying averaging to the bins. This has the potential of solving the problems with the three main ways of performing averages (stimulus-locked, component-locked and response-locked) discussed above, effectively reconciling the three methods. In particular, response-time binning allows one to significantly improve the resolution with which variable-latency waves can be recovered via averaging, even if they are distant from the stimulus-presentation and response times. The reason for this is simple to understand from a qualitative point of view.

The idea is that if one selects out of a dataset all those epochs where a participant was presented with qualitatively identical stimuli and gave the same response within approximately the same amount of time, it is reasonable to assume that similar internal processes will have taken place. So, within those trials, ERP components that would normally have a widely variable latency might be expected to, instead, present a much narrower latency distribution, i.e., they should occur at approximately the same time in the selected subset of trials. Thus, if we bin epochs on the basis of stimuli, responses and response times, we would then find that, for the epochs within a bin, the stimulus, the response, as well as fixed- and variable-latency components are much more synchronised than if one did not divide the dataset. Averaging such epochs should, therefore, allow the rejection of noise while at the same time reducing the undesirable distortions and blurring (the systematic errors) associated with averaging. Response-time binning and averaging should thus result in the production of clearer, less biased descriptions of the activity which really takes place in the brain in response to the stimuli *without the need for prior knowledge* of the phenomena taking place and ERP components present in the EEG recordings.

In (Poli et al., ress) we assessed the binning technique both empirically and theoretically. For empirical validation we modified and used an experiment originally designed by (Esterman et al., 2004) in which the task was relatively difficult, since target detection is based on specific combinations of multiple features (i.e., requiring feature binding), and where response times varied from around 400ms to over 2 seconds. We evaluated the empirical results in a number of ways, including: (a) a comparison between stimulus-locked and response-locked averages which showed how these are essentially identical under response-time binning; (b) an analysis of differences between bin means, medians and quartiles of the amplitude distributions and an analysis of statistical significance of amplitude differences using Kolmogorov-Smirnov tests which showed that bins indeed captured statistically different ERP components; and (c) an analysis of the signal-to-noise ratio (SNR) with and without binning which showed that the (expected) drop in SNR due to the smaller dataset cardinality associated with bins is largely compensated by a corresponding increase due to the reduction in systematic errors.

From the theoretical point of view, we provided a comprehensive analysis of the resolution of averages with and without binning, which showed that there are resolution benefits in applying response-time binning even when there is still a substantial variability in the latency of variable-latency components after response-time binning. We summarise this analysis below since this is the starting point for our fitness function, as we will show in Section 4.

Let us assume that there are three additive components in the ERPs recorded in a forced-choice experiment — a stimulus-locked component, $s(t)$, a response-locked component, $r(t)$, and a variable-latency component, $v(t)$. Let R be a stochastic variable representing the response time in a trial and let $\rho(t)$ be its density function. Similarly, let L be a stochastic variable representing the latency of the component $v(t)$ and let $\ell(t)$ be the corresponding density function. Let us further assume that response time and latency do not affect the shape of these components. Under these assumptions we obtain the following equation for the stimulus-locked average $a_s(t)$:

$$a_s(t) = s(t) + v(t) \star \ell(t) + r(t) \star \rho(t) \tag{9.1}$$

where $\star$ is the convolution operation.

Let us consider the most general conditions possible. Let L and R be described by an unspecified joint density function $p(l, r)$. So, the latency and response-time distributions are marginals of this joint distribution:

$$\ell(l) = \int p(l,r)\, dr \quad \text{and} \quad \rho(r) = \int p(l,r)\, dl.$$

Note that by the definition of conditional density function, we have that

$$p(l,r) = p(r|l)\ell(l) \quad \text{and} \quad p(l,r) = p(l|r)\rho(r)$$

where $p(r|l)$ is the pdf of R when $L = l$ and $p(l|r)$ is the pdf of L when $R = r$.

In (Poli et al., ress) we showed that if one considers a classical "rectangular" bin collecting the subset of the trials having response times in the interval $[\chi_1, \chi_2)$, i.e., such that $\chi_1 \leq R < \chi_2$, the joint distribution of L and R transforms into

$$p^{[\chi_1,\chi_2]}(l,r) = \frac{\delta(\chi_1 \leq r < \chi_2)p(l,r)}{\int_{\chi_1}^{\chi_2} \rho(r)\, dr},$$

where the $\delta(x)$ returns 1 if x is true and 0 otherwise. So, it has the function of zeroing the distribution outside the strip $[\chi_1, \chi_2)$. The denominator normalises the result so that $p^{[\chi_1,\chi_2]}(l,r)$ integrates to 1.

We also showed that taking the marginal of this distribution w.r.t. l gives us the response time distribution for response-time bin $[\chi_1, \chi_2)$:

$$\rho^{[\chi_1,\chi_2]}(r) = \frac{\delta(\chi_1 \leq r < \chi_2)\,\rho(r)}{\int_{\chi_1}^{\chi_2} \rho(r)\, dr}.$$

The marginal of the distribution $p^{[\chi_1,\chi_2]}(l,r)$ w.r.t. r, which gives us the latency distribution for the trials in response-time bin $[\chi_1, \chi_2)$, is:

$$\ell^{[\chi_1,\chi_2]}(l) = \frac{\Pr\{\chi_1 \leq R < \chi_2 \,|\, l\}\,\ell(l)}{\int_{\chi_1}^{\chi_2} \rho(r)\, dr}.$$

These two marginals are important because we can express the stimulus-locked bin average as follows:

$$a_s^{[\chi_1,\chi_2]}(t) = s(t) + v(t) \star \ell^{[\chi_1,\chi_2]}(t) + r(t) \star \rho^{[\chi_1,\chi_2]}(t).$$

The marginals determine in what ways and to what extent $v(t)$ and $r(t)$ appear distorted and blurred in the average. So, in order to understand why $a_s^{[\chi_1,\chi_2]}(t)$ provides a better representation of $r(t)$ and $\ell(t)$ than $a_s(t)$, we need to analyse the differences between the distribution $\rho^{[\chi_1,\chi_2]}(t)$ and $\rho(t)$ and between the distribution $\ell^{[\chi_1,\chi_2]}(t)$ and $\ell(t)$. We will concentrate on the former pair since the arguments for the latter are almost symmetric.

The key difference between $\rho^{[\chi_1,\chi_2]}(t)$ and $\rho(t)$ is that, apart from a scaling factor, $\rho^{[\chi_1,\chi_2]}(t)$ is the product of $\rho(t)$ and a rectangular windowing function, $\delta(\chi_1 \leq t < \chi_2)$. In the frequency domain, therefore, the spectrum of

$\rho^{[\chi_1,\chi_2]}(t)$, which we denote with $\mathcal{R}^{[\chi_1,\chi_2]}(f)$, is the convolution between the spectrum of $\rho(t)$, denoted as $\mathcal{R}(f)$, and the spectrum of a translated rectangle, $\Delta(f)$. This is a scaled and rotated (in the complex plane) version of the *sinc* function (i.e., it behaves like $\sin(f)/f$). The function $|\Delta(f)|$ has a large central lobe whose width is inversely proportional to the bin width $\chi_2 - \chi_1$. Thus, when convolved with $\mathcal{R}(f)$, $\Delta(f)$ behaves as a low pass filter. As a result, $\mathcal{R}^{[\chi_1,\chi_2]}(f) = \mathcal{R}(f) \star \Delta(f)$ is a smoothed and enlarged version of $\mathcal{R}(f)$. In other words, while $\rho^{[\chi_1,\chi_2]}(t)$ is still a low-pass filter, it has a higher cut-off frequency than $\rho(t)$. So, $a_s^{[\chi_1,\chi_2]}(t)$ *provides a less blurred representation of* $r(t)$ *than* $a_s(t)$.

We will modify this analysis in the next section for the purpose of defining a suitable fitness measure the optimisation of which would lead to maximising the statistical significance with which ERP components can be reconstructed via binning and averaging.

4. Binning Optimality and Fitness Function

As described in the previous section, in (Poli et al., ress) we used the function $\delta(\chi_1 \leq R < \chi_2)$ to bin trials. To get the best out of the binning technique, here we will replace this function with a *probabilistic membership function* which gives the probability that a trial characterised by a response time R would be accepted in a particular bin b. Let us denote this probabilistic membership function as

$$\mathcal{P}_b(r) = \Pr\{\text{accept trial in bin } b \,|\, \text{trial response time } R = r\}.$$

Naturally, when $\mathcal{P}_b(r) = \delta(\chi_1 \leq R < \chi_2)$, then b is a traditional (crisp, rectangular) bin.

Let us denote with a binary stochastic variable A the event $\{$accept trial for averaging in bin $b\}$. Let $p(a, l, r)$ be the joint distribution of the events $R = r$, $L = l$ and $A = a$. This can be decomposed as follows

$$p(a, l, r) = p(a|l, r)p(l, r).$$

Since A does not depend on L but only on R (we base the decision to accept trials in a bin only on their associated response time), we have that $p(A = \text{true}|l, r) = \mathcal{P}_b(r)$ and $p(A = \text{false}|l, r) = 1 - \mathcal{P}_b(r)$.

Focusing our attention on the subset of the trials falling within bin b, we obtain the following joint distribution of L and R

$$p^b(l, r) = p(l, r \,|\, A = \text{true}) = \frac{p(A = \text{true}, l, r)}{p(A = \text{true})} = \frac{p(A = \text{true} \,|\, l, r)p(l, r)}{p(A = \text{true})}$$

Hence

$$p^b(l, r) = \frac{\mathcal{P}_b(r)p(l, r)}{\int\int \mathcal{P}_b(r)p(l, r) \, dr \, dl} = \frac{\mathcal{P}_b(r)p(l, r)}{\int \mathcal{P}_b(r)\rho(r) \, dr}.$$

So,

$$\rho^b(r) = \int p^b(l, r) \, dl = \frac{\mathcal{P}_b(r) \int p(l, r) \, dl}{\int \mathcal{P}_b(r) \rho(r) \, dr} = \frac{\mathcal{P}_b(r) \rho(r)}{\int \mathcal{P}_b(r) \rho(r) \, dr}.$$

Also,

$$\ell^b(l) = \int p^b(l, r) \, dr = \frac{\int \mathcal{P}_b(r) p(l, r) \, dr}{\int \mathcal{P}_b(r) \rho(r) \, dr} = \frac{\ell(l) \int \mathcal{P}_b(r) p(r|l) \, dr}{\int \mathcal{P}_b(r) \rho(r) \, dr}.$$

Again these two marginals are important because we can express the stimulus-locked bin average as follows:

$$a_s^b(t) = s(t) + v(t) \star \ell^b(t) + r(t) \star \rho^b(t).$$

From the equations above, one can clearly understand how different definitions of the probabilistic membership function $\mathcal{P}_b(r)$ can lead to radically different results in terms of the resolution of true ERP components in bin averages.

Naturally, one will generally use multiple probabilistic response-time bins for the purpose of analysing ERP trials. For each, a membership function $\mathcal{P}_b(r)$ must be defined. Our objective is to use GP to discover these membership functions in such a way as to maximise the information extracted from the raw data. To do so, we need to define an appropriate fitness function.

While we form bins based on response times, each data element in a bin actually represents a fragment of EEG signal recorded at some electrode site. The question we need to ask is: what do we mean by extracting maximal information from these data? Naturally, alternative definitions are possible. Here we want to focus on the *getting ERP averages which are maximally significantly different*.

An ERP bin average, $a_s^b(t)$, is effectively a vector, each element of which is the signal amplitude recorded at a particular time after stimulus presentation averaged over all the trials in a bin. Because we use probabilistic membership functions for the bins, the composition of a bin is in fact a stochastic variable. Let us denote the stochastic variable representing bin b with $\mathcal{B}_b$. The probability distribution of $\mathcal{B}_b$ is determined by the membership function $\mathcal{P}_b(r)$ and by the response time distribution $\rho(r)$. An instantiation of $\mathcal{B}_b$, β_b, is effectively an array with as many rows as there are trials in bin b and as many columns as there are time steps in each epoch. An element in β_b represents the voltage amplitude recorded in a particular trial and in a particular time step in that trial at the chosen electrode. Let $\beta_b(t)$ represent the set of the amplitudes recorded at time t in the trials in bin b.

Let us consider two bins, b_1 and b_2. If β_{b_1} is an instantiation of $\mathcal{B}_{b_1}$ and β_{b_2} is an instantiation of $\mathcal{B}_{b_2}$, one could check whether the signal amplitude distributions recorded in bins b_1 and b_2 at a particular time step t are statistically different by applying the Kolmogorov-Smirnov test for distributions to the data-sets $\beta_{b_1}(t)$ and $\beta_{b_2}(t)$. The test would return a p value, which we will call

$p_{b_1,b_2}(t)$. The smaller $p_{b_1,b_2}(t)$, the better the statistical separation between the signal amplitude distributions in bins b_1 and b_2 at time step t. Naturally to get an indication of how statistically different the ERPs in different bins are one would then need to somehow integrate the $p_{b_1,b_2}(t)$ values obtained at different t's and for different pairs of bins.

Since we are interested in obtaining bins (via the optimisation of their membership functions $\mathcal{P}_b(r)$) which contain maximally mutually statistically different trials, we require that the sum of the p values returned by the Kolmogorov-Smirnov test when comparing the signal amplitudes in each pair of bins over the time steps in an epoch be as small as possible. So, we want to maximise the following *fitness function*:

$$f = \sum_{b_1 \neq b_2} \sum_t (1 - E[p_{b_1,b_2}(t)]), \qquad (9.2)$$

where the expectation operator $E[\cdot]$ is required because $p_{b_1,b_2}(t)$ is a stochastic variable in that we can only apply the Kolmogorov-Smirnov test to amplitude measurements obtained from *instantiations* of the stochastic variables $\mathcal{B}_{b_1}$ and $\mathcal{B}_{b_2}$. For this reason, the use of Equation (9.2) as a fitness function would require repeatedly assigning trials to bins based on their membership functions, assessing the mutual statistical independence of the trials, and averaging the results. However, this repeated sampling is a very expensive operation (see Section 5). Therefore, we adopted a noisy fitness function, where the expectation operator is omitted. In other words, we only sample the stochastic variables $\mathcal{B}_{b_1}$ and $\mathcal{B}_{b_2}$ once per fitness evaluation. Fitness, however, gets re-evaluated periodically, as described in the next section. So, general and robust solutions to the problem are favoured by evolution.

5. GP System and Settings

We did our experiments using a linear register-based GP system. The system uses a steady-state update schedule.

The primitive set used in our experiments is shown in Table 9-1. The instructions refer to four registers: the input register `ri` which is loaded with the response time, r, of a trial before a program is evaluated, the two general-purpose registers `r0` and `r1` that can be used for numerical calculations, and the register `rs` which can be used as a swap area. `r0`, `r1` and `rs` are initialised to 0. The output of the program is read from `r0` at the end of its execution. In the addition and multiplication instructions we used the memory-with-memory technique proposed in (McPhee and Poli, 2008) with a memory coefficient of 0.5. So, for example the instruction `r0 <- r0 + ri` is actually implemented as `r0 = 0.5 * r0 + 0.5 * ( r0 + ri )` while `r1 <- r0 * r1` is implemented as `r1 = 0.5 * r1 + 0.5 * ( r0 * r1 )`.

Table 9-1. Primitive set used in our experiments.

NOP	r0 <- -1	r1 <- r0 + r1
r0 <- 0	r1 <- 1	r0 <- r0 * r1
r1 <- 0	r0 <- -r0	r1 <- r0 * r1
r0 <- 0.5	r1 <- -r1	r0 <- r0 * r0
r1 <- -0.5	r0 <- r0 + ri	r1 <- r1 * r1
r0 <- -0.1	r1 <- r1 + ri	rs <-> r0
r1 <- 0.1	r0 <- r0 + r1	rs <-> r1

As in (Poli et al., ress), in our tests we consider three bins. So, we need to evolve three membership functions, which we will call $P_1(r)$, $P_2(r)$ and $P_3(r)$. To help GP in this difficult task we constrained the family of functions from which the membership functions could be drawn. So, instead of evolving the three functions $P_1(r)$, $P_2(r)$ and $P_3(r)$, we decomposed each function into three components and we asked GP to evolve the components used in the formulation of each $P_i(r)$. So, each GP individual was actually made up of nine programs. All nine must be run to decide with which probability an element of an ERP dataset should belong to each response-time bin.

More specifically, our membership functions had the following form:

$$P_i(x) = \left(\mathrm{pcos} \left(\frac{r - c(r)}{w(r)} \right) \right)^{|e(r)|}$$

where $c(r) = c_i + p_{ic}(r)$, $w(r) = w_i + p_{iw}(r)$, $e(r) = e_i + p_{ie}(r)$ and $\mathrm{pcos}(x) = \cos\left(\frac{\pi}{2} x\right)$ if $|x| < 1$, and 0 otherwise. Here $p_{1c}(r)$, $p_{2c}(r)$, $p_{3c}(r)$, $p_{1w}(r)$, $p_{2w}(r)$, $p_{3w}(r)$, $p_{1e}(r)$, $p_{2e}(r)$, and $p_{3e}(r)$ are the nine programs forming a particular individual. The terms $c_1, c_2, c_3, w_1, w_2, w_3, e_1, e_2$ and e_3 are constants which we defined so as to give meaningful bins even if $p_{ic}(r) = p_{iw}(r) = p_{ie}(r) = 0$ for all i and r. Since we initialised the programs in the population with a high proportion of NOP operations, this ensured that even individuals in the first generation could obtain reasonable fitness levels. More specifically, c_1, c_2 and c_3 were set to be the medians of the three bins chosen using the heuristic method described in (Poli et al., ress) (where each bin gathered 30% of the response-time distribution), while w_1, w_2 and w_3 were set to twice the standard deviation of the data in such bins. Standard deviations were estimated using the robust estimator provided by 1.4826 times the median absolute deviation from the median (or MAD for short) (Wilcox, 2005). Finally, the constants e_1, e_2 and e_3 were all set to 0.5. This value is half-way between 0, which would give an perfectly rectangular bin, and 1, which gives bins a perfectly sinusoidal shape.

The system initialised the population as follows. All nine programs in an individual had identical length (50 instructions). The length was fixed, but through the use of NOP instructions, the active code was effectively of variable size. The nine programs were concatenated, so effectively an individual was an array of 450 instructions. Programs were initially all made up only of NOP instructions, but they were immediately mutated with point mutation with a mutation rate of 8% so that on average approximately 4 instructions in each of the 9 programs were non-NOP. When an instruction was mutated, the instruction was replaced with a random instruction from the whole primitive set. These choices of parameters were based on some preliminary tests.

The system used tournament selection with tournament size 10. At each iteration, the system randomly decided whether to perform reevaluation of the fitness of an individual (keep in mind that our fitness function is noisy) or to create a new individual. It reevaluated fitness with probability 0.1 and performed crossover with a probability of 0.9. When fitness reevaluation was chosen, the new fitness value was blended with the old one using the formula: $f = 0.8f_{old} + 0.2f_{new}$. This effectively low-pass filters the fitness values using a simple IIR filter, thereby eventually leading to fitness values to stabilise around the expected value for each program. When crossover was performed, two parent individuals were selected, and 9-point crossover was performed. The 9 points were not constrained to fall within the 9 programs that form an individual. Crossover returned one offspring after each application. The offspring was mutated using point mutation with a mutation rate of 4% (so, on average each program was hit by two mutations) and then was evaluated. The offspring was then inserted in the population, replacing an individual which was selected using a negative tournament (with tournament size 10). Given the heavy computational nature of the task we used populations of size 1,000 and 5,000 and we performed 50 generations in each run. To see what kind of results could be obtained with smaller runs, we also performed runs with a population size of 50 run for 20 generations (for a total of 1,000 fitness evaluations).

The data used for our experiments were obtained as follows. We modified an experiment originally designed by (Esterman et al., 2004). In the experiment a composite stimulus is presented at a randomly chosen location (out of four possible locations) on a display for a very short time (between 50 and 150ms depending on conditions). The task of the subject is to identify whether the stimulus represented a target or a non-target stimulus. To correctly perform the task participants needed to identify and conjoin multiple features of the stimulus and then they needed to click a button to signal their response. While the participant performed the task they were connected to electroencephalographic equipment so that the waves generated during the task in different areas of the brain could be recorded. We used a BioSemi ActiveTwo system with 64 pre-amplified electrodes plus additional electrodes on the earlobes, the external canthi and infra-orbital positions. Signals were acquired at 2048 samples per second, were then bandpass-filtered between 0.15 and 40 Hz and, finally, were down-sampled to 512 samples per second. We tested six students from the University of Essex, all with normal or corrected-to-normal vision. Each experiment lasted about one hour, and took about one further hour for preparation and for practice.

Trials were classified according to whether the target was present or absent and according to whether the response was 'Correct' or 'Incorrect'. This resulted in four conditions: true positives (target present, correct response), true negatives (target absent, correct response), false positives (target absent, incorrect response) and false negatives (target present, incorrect response). For the tests reported in this paper we focused on the largest class, the True Negatives, which included a total of 2967 trials. We used epochs of approximately 1200ms (614 samples). That is, each trial contained a vector of 614 signal amplitude samples for each electrode. Each trial had an associated response/reaction time which represents the time lapsed between the presentation of the stimulus and the response provided by the user in the form of a mouse click. Following (Poli et al., ress), the 10% of the trials with the longest response times were discarded. This left 2670 trials. In order to evaluate the fitness of an individual in the population, we needed to run the nine programs included in the individual on each of the trials in the dataset, i.e., the GP interpreter was invoked over 24,000 times before the fitness function could start executing.

With the fitness function defined in Section 4, the objective of evolution is to identify three membership functions which allow one to divide up this dataset into bins based on response times in such a way as to maximise the mutual statistical significance of differences in the bins' amplitude averages. Note that evolution can choose to evolve functions that discard certain ranges of response times if this is advantageous.

With 3 bins (i.e., 3 bin-vs-bin comparisons), 64 electrodes and 614 samples per epoch evaluating our fitness function would require running 117,888 Kolmogorov-Smirnov tests per fitness evaluation. Since such tests are rather computationally expensive, we decided to scale down the problem by concentrating on one particular electrode ('Pz') and by further sub-sampling the amplitude data by a factor of 16. So, after performing the binning of the dataset, we needed to run the Kolmogorov-Smirnov test $3 \times 38 = 114$ times per fitness evaluation.

6.   Results

We show the response-time distribution recorded in our experiments for the True Negatives in Figure 9-2 (note that amplitudes have been normalised so that the curves are density functions; abscissas are in seconds). The boundaries of the 30%-quantile fixed-size bins produced with the method described in (Poli et al., ress) are shown as vertical lines in Figure 9-2. The medians and standard

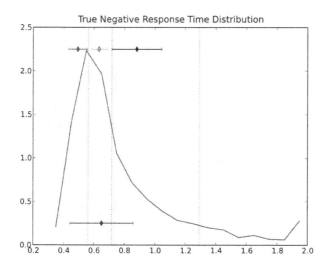

Figure 9-2. Response time distributions for true negative trials recorded in our experiments. Response times of 2000ms or longer have been grouped in the rightmost bin. The vertical lines within each plot represent the boundaries of the bins produced by the standard binning method described in (Poli et al., ress). In each plot medians and standard deviations are also shown both for the bins (top) and for the overall distribution (bottom).

deviations, estimated using MAD, for the whole distribution and for the bins are also shown in Figure 9-2. As indicated above, the objective of GP is to probabilistically divide up this distribution into bins using appropriate membership functions in such a way to maximise the statistical significance of bin averages.

The fitness value for the standard membership functions (rectangular bins) is approximately 0.8297, which corresponds to a mean Kolmogorov-Smirnov p-value of 0.1703. This implies that only for a fraction of the time steps in an epoch differences between bin averages are statistically significant at the standard confidence levels of 0.10 and 0.05. We want GP to improve on this.

We performed 50 runs with populations of size 50 and 1,000, and 10 runs with populations of size 5,000 on 182-core Linux cluster with Xeon CPUs. We report the mean, standard deviation, min and max of best fitnesses as well as the quartiles of the fitness distribution recorded in out experiments in Table 9-2. As one can see in all conditions, the method is very reliable, all standard deviations being very small. Even with the smallest population GP improved over the standard binning technique *in all runs*. This is particularly remarkable given that such runs required only approximately 2 minutes of CPU time each. Naturally, only runs with 1,000 and 5,000 individuals consistently achieved best fitnesses close to or exceeding 0.9, which corresponds to average p values of 0.1 or less. This is a very significant improvement over the p value associated with rectangular bins. Now, for a large proportion of the time in an epoch differences between bin averages are statistically significant. CPU time was approximately 4 hours for runs of 1,000 individuals and approximately one day for runs of 5,000 individuals. Note that these long training times are not a problem in the domain of ERP analysis, since setting up an experiment, trialling it, then collecting the data with independent subjects, preparing the data for averaging and finally interpreting them after averaging require many weeks of work.

In order to achieve this high level of performance and reliability in the ERP binning problem, GP has discovered how to partition the data based on response times in such a way as to optimally balance two needs: (a) the need to include as many trials as possible in each bin so as to reduce noise in both variable-latency and fixed-latency ERP components, and (b) the need to make the bins as narrow as possible so as to reduce the systematic errors associated with averaging variable-latency components.

Table 9-2. Mean, standard deviation, min and max of best and quartiles of the fitness distribution recorded in out experiments.

Population size 50, 20 generations					
Statistic	Best	Qrtl 1	Qrtl 2	Qrlt 3	Qrtl 4
Mean	0.87750	0.86354	0.86020	0.85613	0.17514
StdDev	0.008868	0.006952	0.007123	0.008249	0.272409
Max	0.900335	0.877868	0.876486	0.872651	0.753881
Min	0.855929	0.845703	0.842577	0.837546	0.000000
Population size 1,000, 50 generations					
Statistic	Best	Qrtl 1	Qrtl 2	Qrlt 3	Qrtl 4
Mean	0.89862	0.88161	0.88056	0.87910	0.00000
StdDev	0.00396	0.00293	0.00288	0.00307	0.00000
Max	0.91348	0.89096	0.88979	0.88922	0.00000
Min	0.89197	0.87720	0.87526	0.87346	0.00000
Population size 5,000, 50 generations					
Statistic	Best	Qrtl 1	Qrtl 2	Qrlt 3	Qrtl 4
Mean	0.90431	0.88301	0.88214	0.88091	0.00000
StdDev	0.0060682	0.0039270	0.0038899	0.0040199	0.00000
Max	0.91763	0.89148	0.89053	0.88947	0.00000
Min	0.89914	0.88039	0.87956	0.87794	0.00000

As an example, we plot the best evolved bin membership functions in the 50 runs with a population of 1,000 individuals in Figure 9-3. These correspond to the following equations:

$$\mathcal{P}_1(r) \;=\; \left(\mathrm{pcos}\left(\frac{r - 0.394}{0.127} \right) \right)^{0.375} \tag{9.3}$$

$$\mathcal{P}_2(r) \;=\; \left(\mathrm{pcos}\left(\frac{r - 0.633}{0.129 - 0.5r} \right) \right)^{0.4 + 0.5r} \tag{9.4}$$

$$\mathcal{P}_3(r) \;=\; \left(\mathrm{pcos}\left(\frac{r - 1.381}{0.327} \right) \right)^{0.688} \tag{9.5}$$

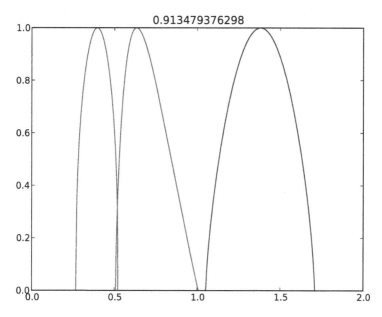

Figure 9-3. Best membership functions evolved in 50 runs with a population of 1,000 individuals.

These were obtained by analysing and then symbolically simplifying the nine programs making up the best individual evolved in such runs. The listing of the nine programs is shown in Table 9-3.

Table 9-3. The nine programs forming the best evolved solution to the ERP binning problem (NOP instructions have been edited out).

Bin 1			Bin 2			Bin 3		
Centre	Width	Exponent	Centre	Width	Exponent	Centre	Width	Exponent
r1 <- 0	rs <-> r1	r1 <- r1 + ri	r1 <- r1 + ri	r1 <- -.5	r1 <- -.5	r0 <- -1	r1 <- 1	r1 <- -r1
r1 <- -.5	r0 <- r0 + r1	r0 <- r0 + r1	rs <-> r0	r0 <- -r0	r1 <- r1 + ri	r0 <- r0 + r1	r1 <- r0 + r1	r0 <- -r0
r1 <- .1	rs <-> r1	r0 <- .5	r0 <- r0 * r1	r1 <- 0	r0 <- r0 + ri	r1 <- .1	r1 <- -.5	r1 <- r1 * r1
r0 <- .5	r0 <- r0 + ri	rs <-> r0	rs <-> r0	r0 <- -r0	r1 <- -r1	r0 <- 0	r1 <- r1 + ri	r1 <- 0
r0 <- r0 + ri	r1 <- .1	r1 <- 0	r1 <- -.1	r0 <- r0 + r1	rs <-> r1	r0 <- r0 + r1	r0 <- r0 * r1	r0 <- .5
r0 <- -1	r0 <- r0 * r0	rs <-> r0	r1 <- -1	r0 <- -r0	r0 <- r0 * r0	r0 <- 0	r1 <- r0 + r1	r1 <- r0 * r1
r0 <- r0 + r1	r1 <- r0 + r1	r1 <- r1 + ri	r0 <- r0 + r1	r1 <- r1 + ri	r1 <- 0	r1 <- -r1	r1 <- r0 + r1	r1 <- r0 + r1
r0 <- r0 + r1	r1 <- -.5	r0 <- -r0	r1 <- 0	r1 <- -.5	r0 <- -.1	r0 <- -r0	r0 <- r0 * r0	r1 <- 1
r0 <- r0 * r1	r0 <- .5	rs <-> r1	r0 <- r0 * r0	r0 <- r0 + r1	r0 <- .5	r1 <- r0 * r1	r1 <- 1	r0 <- r1 * r1
r1 <- r1 * r1	r0 <- 0	r1 <- r0 + ri	r1 <- -r1	r1 <- r0 + r1	rs <-> r1	r1 <- r1 + ri	r1 <- 0	r0 <- r0 * r1
r0 <- r0 + ri	r1 <- r1 + ri	r0 <- r0 + r1	rs <-> r1	r0 <- r0 * r1	r0 <- r0 * r0	rs <-> r0	r0 <- -1	r0 <- r1 + r1
r0 <- -.1	r1 <- r1 * r1	r0 <- r0 * ri	r1 <- 0	r1 <- -.5	r0 <- r0 + r0	r0 <- r0 + ri	r0 <- .5	r1 <- r1
r1 <- 0	r1 <- 0	r0 <- r0 + r1	r0 <- -r0	r1 <- .5	rs <-> r0	r0 <- 0	r0 <- r0 + ri	rs <-> r1
r1 <- r1 * r1	r1 <- r0 * r1	r1 <- r1 * r1	r1 <- 0	r0 <- -1	r0 <- -1	r0 <- -.1	r0 <- r0 * r0	r0 <- -1
r0 <- r0 * ri	r0 <- r0 + r1	r1 <- r0 + r1	rs <-> r1	rs <-> r0	r0 <- r0 + r1	r0 <- -r0	r1 <- r1 + ri	r0 <- -.5
r0 <- -r1	r0 <- -.1	rs <-> r0	r0 <- r0 + r1	r1 <- -.5	r0 <- -.1	r0 <- .5	r0 <- r0 * r0	r0 <- r0 + r1
rs <-> r1	rs <-> r1	r0 <- r0 * r0	r1 <- 1	r0 <- -.1	r1 <- r0 + r1	r1 <- r0 + r1	r1 <- -1	r0 <- r0 * r0
r0 <- r0 * r0	r0 <- 0	r0 <- .5	rs <-> r1	r0 <- r0 * r1	r0 <- -r1	r1 <- r0 + r1	r0 <- -.1	r0 <- -1
r0 <- r0 * r1	r1 <- .1	r0 <- -r0	r1 <- r1 + ri	r0 <- r0 * r1	r0 <- 0	r0 <- r0 + r1	r0 <- r1 * r1	r0 <- .5
r1 <- -.5	r1 <- r1 + r1	r1 <- r1 + ri	r0 <- r0 * r1	r1 <- 0	r0 <- -.1	r0 <- -1	r0 <- r0 + r1	r1 <- r1 * r1
r1 <- .1	r1 <- .1	r1 <- r1 + r0	r1 <- -1	r1 <- r0 * r1	r0 <- -.1	r1 <- 1	r1 <- 0	r1 <- -r1
r0 <- -r1	r0 <- r0 * r0	r1 <- -r1	r0 <- 0	r1 <- r1 + ri	r0 <- .5	r0 <- .1	r1 <- -1	r0 <- r0 + r1
r0 <- r0 + r0	r1 <- r1 + ri	r1 <- 1		r0 <- -r0	r0 <- r0 + ri	rs <-> r0	r0 <- r0 + ri	r0 <- r0 + r0
r0 <- 0	r0 <- -r1			r1 <- .1	r0 <- r0 + ri	r0 <- -r0	r0 <- 0	r0 <- -r0
r0 <- r0 + ri	r1 <- 1			r1 <- 0	r0 <- r0 * r0	r1 <- r0 + r1	r0 <- -r0	r1 <- r0 + r1
r0 <- 0	r0 <- r0 * r0			r1 <- 1	r1 <- r1 + ri	r0 <- r0 + r1	r1 <- .1	rs <-> r1
r0 <- .1	r0 <- r0 * r0				r1 <- .5	r0 <- .5		rs <-> r0
r0 <- -r0	r1 <- 0				r1 <- -r1	r1 <- r1 * r1		rs <-> r1
r0 <- -.1	r0 <- -r0					r1 <- r0 + r1		
r1 <- -r1						r1 <- r1 * r1		

The ERP averages produced by this solution are shown in Figure 9-4. For reference we show the averages obtained with traditional rectangular bins in Figure 9-5. As one can see the ERP averages for the middle bins are almost identical to the full average in both cases. This is because both the reference bin and the GP-evolved bin capture the median response time and surrounding samples, which are representative of the central tendency of the whole distribution. However, when comparing the ERP averages for bins 1 and 3 with the corresponding reference averages, we see that the membership functions evolved by GP are more selective in their choice of trials. This produces bigger (and hence more statistically significant) variations between groups. Particularly interesting is the case of bin 3, which, with the standard binning method, is adjacent to bin 2 and is very broad. This led to averaging ERP components having an excessively wide distribution of latencies, leading to an ERP average where late endogenous components, which are typically associated with the preparation of the response, are hardly discernible. Instead, GP has produced a much narrower bin 3 and a large gap between bins 2 and 3. As one can see from Figure 9-4, this yields a much clearer representation of such late potentials.

7. Conclusions

In this paper we used a multi-program form of register-based GP to discover probabilistic membership functions for the purpose of binning and then averaging ERP trials based on response times. The objective was to evolve membership functions which could significantly improve the mutual statistical significance of bin averages thereby capturing more accurately true brain waves than when using simple rectangular bins.

Our results are very encouraging. GP can consistently evolve membership functions that almost double the statistical significance of the ERP bin averages with respect to the standard binning method.

In future work we will test the generality of evolved solution, by applying the bins found by GP to newly acquired (unseen) data. We also intend to make use of our new bin averaging technique in BCIs. Indeed, the work presented in this paper originated from the need to understand in exactly what ways stimulus features and task complexity, as well as cognitive errors, modulate ERP components in BCI (Cinel et al., 2004; Citi et al., 2004; Citi et al., 2008). Our long term objective is to formally link quantitative psychological models of feature binding and perceptual errors (Humphreys et al., 2000; Cinel et al., 2002; Cinel and Humphreys, 2006) with the presence of specific ERP components and the modulation of their latency and amplitude. This knowledge could then be used to design a new generation of BCIs where the behaviour and features of human cognitive systems are best exploited.

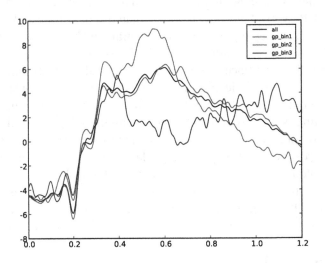

Figure 9-4. Averages obtained with the GP-evolved bin membership functions in Equations 9.3–9.5 and shown in Figure 9-3.

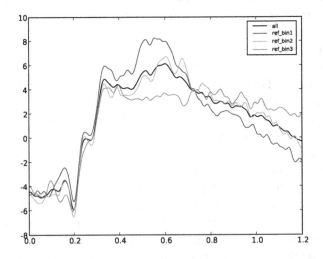

Figure 9-5. Averages obtained with traditional rectangular bins.

Acknowledgements

We would like to thank the Engineering and Physical Sciences Research Council (grant EP/F033818/1) and by the Experimental Psychological Society (UK) (grant "Binding Across the Senses") for financial support and Francisco Sepulveda for helpful comments and suggestions.

References

Birbaumer, N., Ghanayim, N., Hinterberger, T., Iversen, I., Kotchoubey, B., Kübler, A., Perelmouter, J., Taub, E., and Flor, H. (1999). A spelling device for the paralysed. *Nature*, 398(6725):297–298.

Bonala, B., Boutros, N.N., and Jansen, B.H. (2008). Target probability affects the likelihood that a P300 will be generated in response to a target stimulus, but not its amplitude. *Psychophysiology*, 45(1):93–99.

Bostanov, V. (2004). BCI competition 2003–data sets Ib and IIb: feature extraction from event-related brain potentials with the continuous wavelet transform and the t-value scalogram. *IEEE transactions on bio-medical engineering*, 51(6):1057–1061.

Cinel, C. and Humphreys, G.W. (2006). On the relations between implicit and explicit spatial binding: evidence from Balint's syndrome. *Cognitive, affective & behavioral neuroscience*, 6(2):127–140.

Cinel, C., Humphreys, G.W., and Poli, R. (2002). Cross-modal illusory conjunctions between vision and touch. *Journal of experimental psychology. Human perception and performance*, 28(5):1243–1266.

Cinel, C., Poli, R., and Citi, L. (2004). Possible sources of perceptual errors in P300-based speller paradigm. *Biomedizinische Technik*, 49:39–40. Proceedings of 2nd International BCI workshop and Training Course.

Citi, L., Poli, R., Cinel, C., and Sepulveda, F. (2008). P300-based BCI mouse with genetically-optimized analogue control. *IEEE transactions on neural systems and rehabilitation engineering*, 16(1):51–61.

Citi, L., Poli, R., and Sepulveda, F. (2004). An evolutionary approach to feature selection and classification in P300-based BCI. *Biomedizinische Technik*, 49:41–42. Proceedings of 2nd International BCI workshop and Training Course.

Donchin, E. and Coles, M.G.H. (1988). Is the P300 a manifestation of context updating? *Behavioral and Brain Sciences*, 11:355–372.

Donchin, E. and Lindsley, D.B., editors (1968). *Average Evoked Potentials: Methods, Results, and Evaluations*, number NASA SP-191, San Francisco, California. NASA, NASA.

Esterman, M., Prinzmetal, W., and Robertson, L. (2004). Categorization influences illusory conjunctions. *Psychonomic bulletin & review*, 11(4):681–686.

Farwell, L.A. and Donchin, E. (1988). Talking off the top of your head: toward a mental prosthesis utilizing event-related brain potentials. *Electroencephalography and clinical neurophysiology*, 70(6):510–523.

Furdea, A., Halder, S., Krusienski, D.J., Bross, D., Nijboer, F., Birbaumer, N., and Kübler, A. (2009). An auditory oddball (P300) spelling system for brain-computer interfaces. *Psychophysiology*.

Handy, T.C., editor (2004). *Event-related potentials. A Method Handbook.* MIT Press.

Humphreys, G. W., Cinel, C., Wolfe, J., Olson, A., and Klempen, N. (2000). Fractionating the binding process: neuropsychological evidence distinguishing binding of form from binding of surface features. *Vision research*, 40(10-12):1569–1596.

Keus, I.M., Jenks, K.M., and Schwarz, W. (2005). Psychophysiological evidence that the SNARC effect has its functional locus in a response selection stage. *Brain research. Cognitive brain research*, 24(1):48–56.

Lindsley, D.B. (1968). Average evoked potentials – achievements, failures and prospects. In Donchin, Emanuel and Lindsley, Donald B., editors, *Average Evoked Potentials: Methods, Results, and Evaluations*, chapter 1. NASA.

Luck, S.J. (2005). *An introduction to the event-related potential technique.* MIT Press, Cambridge, Massachusetts.

Luck, S.J. and Hillyard, S.A. (1990). Electrophysiological evidence for parallel and serial processing during visual search. *Perception & psychophysics*, 48(6):603–617.

McPhee, N.F. and Poli, R. (2008). Memory with memory: Soft assignment in genetic programming. In Keijzer, Maarten, Antoniol, Giuliano, Congdon, Clare Bates, Deb, Kalyanmoy, Doerr, Benjamin, Hansen, Nikolaus, Holmes, John H., Hornby, Gregory S., Howard, Daniel, Kennedy, James, Kumar, Sanjeev, Lobo, Fernando G., Miller, Julian Francis, Moore, Jason, Neumann, Frank, Pelikan, Martin, Pollack, Jordan, Sastry, Kumara, Stanley, Kenneth, Stoica, Adrian, Talbi, El-Ghazali, and Wegener, Ingo, editors, *GECCO '08: Proceedings of the 10th annual conference on Genetic and evolutionary computation*, pages 1235–1242, Atlanta, GA, USA. ACM.

Pfurtscheller, G., Flotzinger, D., and Kalcher, J. (1993). Brain-computer interface: a new communication device for handicapped persons. *Journal of Microcomputer Applications*, 16(3):293–299.

Poli, R., Cinel, C., Citi, L., and Sepulveda, F. (In Press). Reaction-time binning: a simple method for increasing the resolving power of erp averages. *Psychophysiology*.

Poli, R., Langdon, W.B., and McPhee, N.F. (2008). *A field guide to genetic programming.* Published via http://lulu.com and freely available at http://www.gp-field-guide.org.uk. (With contributions by J. R. Koza).

Polich, J. and Comerchero, M.D. (2003). P3a from visual stimuli: typicality, task, and topography. *Brain topography*, 15(3):141–152.

Rakotomamonjy, A. and Guigue, V. (2008). BCI competition III: dataset II-ensemble of SVMs for BCI P300 speller. *IEEE transactions on bio-medical engineering*, 55(3):1147–1154.

Spencer, K.M. (2004). Averaging, detection and classification of single-trial erps. In Handy, Todd C., editor, *Event-related potentials. A Method Handbook*, chapter 10. MIT Press.

Töllner, T., Gramann, K., Müller, H.J., Kiss, M., and Eimer, M. (2008). Electrophysiological markers of visual dimension changes and response changes. *Journal of experimental psychology. Human perception and performance*, 34(3):531–542.

Wagner, P., Röschke, J., Grözinger, M., and Mann, K. (2000). A replication study on P300 single trial analysis in schizophrenia: confirmation of a reduced number of 'true positive' P300 waves. *Journal of psychiatric research*, 34(3):255–259.

Wilcox, R.R. (2005). *Introduction to Robust Estimation and Hypothesis Testing*. Academic Press, second edition.

Wolpaw, J.R., Birbaumer, N., Heetderks, W.J., McFarland, D.J., Peckham, P.H., Schalk, G., Donchin, E., Quatrano, L.A., Robinson, C.J., and Vaughan, T.M. (2000). Brain-computer interface technology: a review of the first international meeting. *IEEE Transactions on Rehabilitation Engineering*, 8(2):164–173.

Wolpaw, J.R., McFarland, D.J., Neat, G.W., and Forneris, C.A. (1991). An EEG-based brain-computer interface for cursor control. *Electroencephalography and Clinical Neurophysiology*, 78(3):252–259.

Zhang, J. (1998). Decomposing stimulus and response component waveforms in ERP. *Journal of neuroscience methods*, 80(1):49–63.

Chapter 10

USING MULTI-OBJECTIVE GENETIC PROGRAMMING TO SYNTHESIZE STOCHASTIC PROCESSES

Brian Ross[1] and Janine Imada[1]

[1]*Brock University, Department of Computer Science, St. Catharines, Ontario, Canada L2S 3A1.*

Abstract   Genetic programming is used to automatically construct stochastic processes written in the stochastic π-calculus. Grammar-guided genetic programming constrains search to useful process algebra structures. The time-series behaviour of a target process is denoted with a suitable selection of statistical feature tests. Feature tests can permit complex process behaviours to be effectively evaluated. However, they must be selected with care, in order to accurately characterize the desired process behaviour. Multi-objective evaluation is shown to be appropriate for this application, since it permits heterogeneous statistical feature tests to reside as independent objectives. Multiple undominated solutions can be saved and evaluated after a run, for determination of those that are most appropriate. Since there can be a vast number of candidate solutions, however, strategies for filtering and analyzing this set are required.

Keywords: genetic programming, stochastic processes, process algebra, time-series feature tests, multi-objective gp

1.   Introduction

Bionetwork modeling, for example, of gene expression networks and metabolic reactions, is an active research area (Bower and Bolouri, 2001). Such computer based models have been used for modeling gene expression networks and metabolic reactions. There is an ongoing effort to automate the synthesis of such process models (Markowetz and Spang, 2007). For example, given time-series data obtained from gene microarrays in the laboratory, a goal is the automatic generation of functional models that explain the genetic processes behind that data.

R. Riolo et al. (eds.), *Genetic Programming Theory and Practice VII*,
Genetic and Evolutionary Computation, DOI 10.1007/978-1-4419-1626-6_10,
© Springer Science + Business Media, LLC 2010

Process models are characterized by being either deterministic or stochastic in nature. Although deterministic models can exhibit noisy behaviours, they benefit from the fact that they will behave predictably when started in a given environment. On the other hand, stochastic process behaviours are determined dynamically by stochastic factors, and they can behave unpredictably during different simulations. These differences between deterministic and stochastic processes impact machine learning. Deterministic process learning can often use sums of errors between generated and target time series. Stochastic processes, however, must often consider different strategies for characterizing and evaluation behaviour.

Evolutionary computation has been applied to the deterministic process synthesis problem. (Koza et al., 2003) use genetic programming to synthesize metabolic networks. (Kitagawa and Iba, 2003) evolve Petri net models of metabolic networks using genetic algorithms. Genetic algorithms have been used to evolve nonlinear differential equation models of time series data (Cho et al., 2006; Streichert et al., 2004). Research involving the evolution of models for noisy time series is also relevant to the process modeling problem (Borrelli et al., 2006; Imada and Ross, 2008; Rodriguez-Vazquez and Fleming, 2005; Zhang et al., 2004).

In terms of stochastic process synthesis, (Leier et al., 2006) use GP to evolve algebraic models of oscillating behaviour. (Ross and Imada, 2009) use GP to evolve stochastic processes denoted by process algebra. (Imada, 2009) evolves stochastic gene regulatory networks, using GP with a gene gate language that is implemented in a stochastic process algebra. GAs are used to evolve stochastic models for biological networks (Drennan and Beer, 2006; Chu, 2007).

This paper extends work in (Ross and Imada, 2009) by considering the use of multi-objective optimization in the evolution of stochastic process models. The formalism considered is a subset of the stochastic π-calculus (Priami, 1995; Phillips and Cardelli, 2004). Feature-based evaluation of process behaviour is employed. The goal is to evolve a process whose feature values are similar to those of the target process. We posit that multi-objective optimization will be an effective means for evaluating processes with different feature scores, since heterogeneous features do not need to be artificially combined into a single objective. Since stochastic processes can exhibit variable behaviours, multi-objective ranking may be a means for accounting for variations of performance.

A secondary goal is to show the benefit of grammatical evolution in this application. Syntactic constraints are shown to promote effective evolution.

A stochastic process algebra is reviewed in Section 2. Statistical feature evaluation and time series analysis is discussed in Section 3. Grammar-guided evolution is overviewed in Section 4. Experimental methodologies are explained in Section 5, and the processes being investigated are presented in

Section 6. Results are shown in Section 7, and some concluding remarks are given in Section 8.

2.   A Stochastic Process Algebra

Table 10-1. Process Algebra Syntax

$$P ::= 0 \ \| \ P|P \ \| \ Repl(\pi : P) \ \| \ \Sigma$$
$$\Sigma ::= \pi.P \ \| \ delay(t).P \ \| \ \Sigma + \Sigma$$
$$\pi ::= ?c \ \| \ !c$$

Process algebra are mathematical systems for modeling and reasoning about concurrent systems (Milner, 1999). Stochastic process algebra, such as the stochastic π-calculus, incorporate a probabilistic component in their semantics, which permits the modeling of complex chaotic behaviours that are probabilistic in nature. The stochastic π-calculus is effective for modeling various natural phenomena, for example, chemical reactions and gene regulatory processes (Blossey et al., 2006; Priami et al., 2001; Phillips, 2008).

Many bionetwork models are *reaction-based*, in which elements in the model define all the possible reactions. Such models explicitly encapsulate the complexity of the process reactions, as no reaction is possible that is not accounted for in the model (Koza et al., 2003; Kitagawa and Iba, 2003).

Conversely, stochastic π-calculus systems are *component-based*. The actual process definitions are simple to construct. However, they do not directly encode the dynamic interactions and reactions that ensue when the processes are combined together. This results in a rich and robust execution semantics, stemming from fairly rudimentary process definitions. On the other hand, reactions can be difficult to predict, depending on the the contexts in which such processes are placed.

The full stochastic π-calculus is a process algebra that models concurrency, stochastic behaviour, and mobility (dynamic network changes) (Priami, 1995). We consider here a subset of the stochastic π-calculus (Table 10-1), which is similar in syntax to the CCS algebra (Milner, 1989). The main feature of interest is its stochastic semantics, which permits many complex behaviours to be modelled in a quantitative manner.

The operators used in Table 10-1 are as follows. A null process is *0*. The concurrent operator ("$\|$") permits expressions to interact concurrently. The replication operator (*Repl*) recursively defines an indefinite number of copies of an expression. The choice operator (Σ or $+$) permits the stochastic selection and execution of one or more behaviours. A term is an input ($?x$) or output ($!x$) action (often called *channels*). Each channel c has a rate associated with it. A delay term of time t, if selected, advances the clock by a stochastically-determined duration. A notation $K@P$ means $P|P|...|P$ repeated K times.

The process algebra semantics are based on the Gillespie algorithm (Gillespie, 1977), which is used in chemical simulations. Consider the following transition of an expression:

$$(?x.P_1 + \Sigma_1)|(!x.P_2 + \Sigma_2)|P_3 \overset{rate(x)}{\to} P_1|P_2|P_3$$

Here, $?x$ and $!x$ are *active*. If these terms are selected by the Gillespie process, a handshake arises. The expression transforms by discarding these communications and alternate choice terms Σ_i. The Gillespie algorithm selects the execution of x stochastically, by considering its probability in relation to the probabilities of all other active communications. This is known in evolutionary computation as roulette wheel selection (Goldberg, 1989). A global time counter is updated, by an amount inversely proportional to the probability of a selected action. This reflects the higher frequency of more probable actions.

A higher-level characterization of process behaviour is possible, by recording the plot of changing quantities of active channels over time. Behavioural time plots can be unpredictable, however, and highly sensitive to the stochastic effects arising from small details of expressions. For example, editing a channel rate or delay time can result in widely varying behaviours, and changing a channel label can result in a deadlocked, inactive expression. This makes process specification challenging, both for humans and GP.

3.   Time Series and Statistical Features

The study of time series is a well-established research discipline (Chatfield, 2004). Time series can denote stock market activity, predator-prey relationships, and gene expression rates. Since time series are often complex and chaotic, significant effort in the field of statistics has been dedicated towards defining suitable measurement techniques for such data. More recently, research in data mining and machine learning has investigated the value of using univariate feature tests for characterizing complex time series (Nanopoulos et al., 2001; Wang et al., 2006). Besides offering the possibility of effective characterization of data, being able to use few feature test scores is much more efficient than examining the actual time series data itself.

Note that the characterization of generalized time series with feature tests is intractable in general. Turing machine computations are encodable as time series, and hence undecidability and complexity issues will immediately arise.

We characterize process behaviour by analyzing the generated time series with a suite of univariate feature tests, taken from (Nanopoulos et al., 2001; Wang et al., 2006). Experiments in this paper select from the following six tests: (1) *Raw mean*: The mean of all v_t is computed. (2) *Raw standard deviation*: The

Table 10-2. A grammar for stochastic processes

$$
\begin{aligned}
Expr ::=\ & Rates,\ Procs(in)\ \|\ Procs(out) \\
Rates ::=\ & Float,\ Float,\ \dots\ (1\ per\ channel) \\
Procs(dir) ::=\ & Proc_i = Choice\ \|\ Procs(dir)|Procs(dir) \\
Choice ::=\ & Term\ \|\ Choice + Choice \\
Term ::=\ & Pi\ \|\ Pi.Pi\ \|\ Pi.Call\ \|\ Pi.Pi.Call\ \|\ Pi.(Call|Call) \\
Call ::=\ & Proc\ Int \\
Pi ::=\ & ?Ch\ \|\ !Ch\ (if\ dir = in\ or\ out) \\
Ch ::=\ & c\ (c \in \text{channels}) \\
Float ::=\ & min_f \le \mathbf{f} \le max_f \\
Int ::=\ & min_i \le \mathbf{i} \le max_i
\end{aligned}
$$

standard deviation of v_t is computed. (3) *Skew*: If the data values are put into histogram bins, this measures the symmetry, or lack thereof, of the histogram. (4) *Serial correlation*: This measures the degree of fit to a white noise model. (5) *Chaos*: This measures the sensitivity to initial values. It calculates the rate of divergence of nearby points, averaged over many measures. (6) *Periodicity*: This denotes cyclic activity which might vary in frequency. The periodicity is the time interval of the shortest detected cycle.

Given a process to be evolved with GP, the statistical feature values for its output behaviour are computed. Hundreds of plots are generated, the feature values of all the plots are determined, and the means and standard deviations of these values are calculated. Next, a meaningful set of features must be chosen that competently characterizes the time series. We first tabulate all the feature tests scores and compute the *stability* for each: stability = μ/σ. A high stability indicates that the standard deviation is low compared to the mean, and hence this may be an accurate measurement. Next, we manually select from the feature tests that are both stable, and seem *reasonable* for the behaviour at hand. For example, an oscillating time series would likely require an account of its periodicity.

4. Grammar-Guided Genetic Programming

Whigham showed that grammars can introduce positive bias in evolutionary search (Whigham, 1996). By using a context-free grammar to encode possible program structures, the program space can be constrained to enable reasonable, higher level constructs to be considered. This also inhibits the consideration of less useful, and often nonsensical, program forms.

It might seem controversial whether syntactically constraining the stochastic π-calculus is warranted. The grammar in Table 10-1 is simple and elegant, and constraining it may be counterproductive. We address this issue in one experiment (NaCl), by evolving the natural "generic" algebra. It is worth considering that different denotations of formal languages have their own particular linguistic advantages and weaknesses. For example, a regular language denoted by a finite automaton may require a complex, unwieldy regular expression (Hopcroft and Ullman, 1979). The same effect may apply to process algebra.

Our grammar-guided GP system encodes the process algebra with a context-free grammar (CFG). The grammar permits the inclusion of grammatical constraints for evolved expressions, and it can be tailored according to the complexity of the process to evolve. The DCTG-GP system is used, in which logic-based attribute grammars are used to specify GP languages (Ross, 2001). The stochastic π-calculus interpreter is written in Prolog. It is based on an efficient abstract machine definition in (Phillips and Cardelli, 2004).

A typical CFG used in this paper is in Table 10-2. This grammar evolves channel rates, which is a list of floats. Two partitions of processes are defined, each of which incorporates a direction (in or out) for channel terms. The direction is passed to the channel actions in *Ch* (not shown). This reduces the chances for deadlock. Process definitions are indexed with an integer value, and calls to them use modulo arithmetic to resolve to a process definition. The *Choice* rule defines the main body of expressions. The *Term* rule shows the different kinds of expression sequences allowed. Terms are guarded so that each recursive call to a sub-process involves at least one action *Pi* beforehand.

5.   Methodology

Genetic programming evaluates processes by running simulations on them, and comparing their resultant time series with the target process. The most accurate analyses require multiple time plots. This is too computationally expensive to do for many processes, including some of those studied here. Our point of view is that repeated process sampling happens implicitly via a population pool of related expressions evaluated over many generations. Weak expressions that obtain strong time plot fitnesses by sheer luck will not likely remain strong during subsequent generations.

Single-objective evaluation

Fitness evaluation follows a technique used for noisy symbolic regression (Imada, 2009). The GP expression is interpreted by the stochastic π-calculus interpreter, resulting in a time series for each channel of interest. Selected feature values from Section 3 are computed for the time series. Then the sum of Euclidean distances between them and the target feature values for all channels (*ch*) is determined:

$$Distance = \sum_{j \in ch} \sqrt{\sum_{i \in features} \left(\frac{(v_{ij} - t_{ij})}{\sigma_{ij}} \right)^2}$$

where v_i is the computed feature value, t_i is the target value, and σ_i is the standard deviation for that feature as exhibited by the target process.

An option is to interpret an expression multiple times during fitness evaluation, and use the average of all the resulting distances. This may result in a more accurate estimation of behaviour.

Multi-objective evaluation

Solutions from multi-objective runs are determined in the following manner. We use *dominance ranking*, in which the rank of each individual is the number of other individuals that dominate it (Coello et al., 2007). As is usual for multi-objective evolution, the entire rank 1 set at the end of a run is saved as a set of candidate solutions. The rank 1 sets from all the runs are processed as follows:

1. The rank 1 sets from each run are combined into a single set. The set is re-ranked, yielding a new rank 1 set.

2. The new rank 1 set has duplicate expressions removed. This is done by translating each CFG tree to its equivalent π-calculus expression, and then deleting duplicates. Note that syntactic equivalence does not include associativity and permutativity of terms.

3. The remaining rank 1 solutions are each interpreted 100 times, and their feature scores as used in the fitness evaluation are determined. Then the zscores are computed and compared to those of the target expression features, which were predetermined by evaluating the target 100 times. Whenever a match is found between candidate and target score having a significance of $p \geq 90\%$, it is considered to be a feature match.

The final result of the above procedure is a set of usually unique process expressions, with zscore vectors indicating the proximity of feature matches with those of the target process. This feature matching analysis may indicate fairly precise matches with the target process behavior. Although behavioural equivalence here is most often assured with exact syntactic matches between solutions and target processes (including channel rates), often behavioural equivalence can involve different process expressions. The degree of precision required is dependent upon the particular process being considered.

Step 3 is also applied to the solutions from single-objective runs, in order to evaluate behavioural matches.

6.   Experiments

Process descriptions

A number of target processes were studied. All are taken from examples included with the SPIM system (Phillips, 2008).

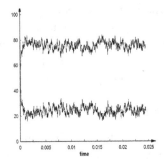

$$Na \; = \; !ionize.?deionize.Na$$
$$Cl \; = \; ?ionize.!deionize.Cl$$
$$\mathbf{NaCl} \; = \; 100@Na \mid 100@Cl$$
$$rate(ionize) = 100.0$$
$$rate(deionize) = 10.0$$

Figure 10-1.   NaCl: target process and plot.

A. NaCl: The process in Figure 10-1 models the ionization and deionization of salt molecules: $Na + Cl \Longleftrightarrow Na^+ + Cl^-$. The target expressions are the Na and Cl expressions, as well as the rates. The remaining expression is given to the GP in a wrapper, and is not evolved. The example time plot in Figure 10-1 shows the time series of the input terms only, for the ionize and deionize channels. The output channels behave nearly identically to the input channels. After running 100 simulations, the feature tests selected to represent this plot are: (i) ?ionize: mean (μ=24.63, σ=0.505), sd (μ=5.52, σ=0.407); (ii) ?deionize: mean (μ=75.37, σ=0.506), sd (μ=6.12, σ=0.261).

A number of different runs were performed (see Table 10-4 for a summary). (a) *Grammatical constraints*: To promote expressions with meaningful structure, a grammar is used that constrains process expressions, such as process definitions and expression complexity. These runs were compared to ones using the generic syntax from Table 10-1. (b) *Single- and multi-objective evaluation*: The single objective runs use the Euclidean distance evalation in Section 5.0. The multiobjective runs use 2 dimensions – one for the mean distance, and the other for the standard deviation distance – summed for all channels of concern. (c) *Partially and fully specified behaviours*: Target behaviours use either 2 (input) or 4 (input, output) channels. The 2 channel case is an underspecification, since the output channels are unconstrained.

B. Kna2Cl: The target process models the ionization and deionization of the KNa2Cl cotransporter: $K + Na + 2Cl \Longleftrightarrow K^+ + Na^+ + 2Cl^-$. This process uses 4 channels, and the plots are similar to the ones in Figure 10-1, except that there are 4 distinct curves. A portion of the Kna2CL process from (Phillips, 2008) is to be evolved, with the remaining expression put in a wrapper.

Processes are simulated to a time limit of 0.30 or 1000 ticks. The means and standard deviations, as well as σ's, were calculated for all channels.

$$Gene(a, b) = (delay(0.1).(Protein(a, b).0) \mid Gene(a, b))$$
$$+ (?a.delay(0.0001).Gene(a, b))$$
$$Protein(a, b) = !b.Protein(a, b) + delay(0.001)$$
$$\textbf{Repressilator} = Gene(x, y) \mid Gene(y, z) \mid Gene(z, x)$$
$$rate(x) = rate(y) = rate(z) = 1.0$$

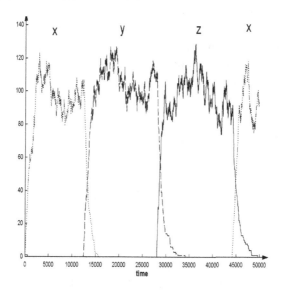

Figure 10-2. Repressilator: target process and plot.

C. Repressilator: The repressilator circuit is a genetic regulatory circuit that produces oscillating behaviour (Blossey et al., 2006). Figure 10-2 shows a stochastic π-calculus repressilator gate, as well as the wrapper circuit *Repressilator* that drives the circuit. The resulting oscillation behaviour is included.

The goal is to evolve expressions with behaviours equivalent to that of the Gene and Protein expressions in Figure 10-2. The features used are mean, standard deviation, serial correlation, chaos, and periodicity. The features are measured for $!x$, giving five dimensions for the multi-objective vector .

Other Genetic Programming Parameters

Table 10-3 shows GP parameters used for the experiments. A few parameters require explanation. Populations contain syntactically unique grammar trees. Lamarckian evolution (local search) is used in single-objective runs. First, a fitness "boost" is given to the initial population, by performing local search on

Table 10-3. GP Parameters

Parameter	NaCl	KNa2Cl	Repress
Initial popn.	1500	4000	4000
Running popn.	1000	1500	1500
Generations	30	40	30
Init max tree depth	8	8	8
Max tree depth	12	10	12
Tournament (sing obj)	4	4	4
Tournament (mult obj)	3	2	2
Elite migration (sing obj)	5	5	5
Elite migration (mult obj)	0	5	5

Parameter	Value
Unique popn	yes
Runs/experiment	20
Prob. crossover	0.90
Prob. mutation	0.10
Lamarckian boost (sing obj)	0.33 initial popn.
Lamarckian evol. (sing obj)	0.05 popn. every 7 gens

the weakest 33% of the population. As soon as a random mutation improves fitness, the stronger expression replaces the original. A total of 5 mutations are attempted per individual. Local search is performed on 5% of the population every 7 generations, by replacing trees with the best mutation found. Mutations are applied until 6 non-improvements occur.

7.　Results

A summary of results for the NaCl runs is in Table 10-4. The first columns indicate standard grammar or generic syntax, the number of channels for evaluation, and multi-objective evaluation. The next column is the size of the solution set considered. Single-objective experiments use 20 runs, while multi-objective set sizes are variable. H is the number of solutions whose textual expression matches the target NaCl expression in Table 10-1 (not including channel rate values). For the single objective runs (1-4), the number of solutions falling within the fitness range of the target solution are tallied. The target fitness range was determined by interpreting the solution expression 100 times, and recording the fitness values obtained. Tr is the fitness seen during evolution (training), while Te is the fitness obtained after run completion (testing). The remaining columns indicate the percentages of expression features that fall within the 90-percentile

Table 10-4. NaCl Results

Gr	Ch	MO	|S|	H	F range Tr	Te	F match % 0	1-50	100
1 std	2	n	20	5	20	12	60	35	5
2 std	4	n	20	14	15	10	50	40	10
3 gen	2	n	20	0	20	2	80	20	0
4 gen	4	n	20	0	0	0	60	40	0
5 std	2	y	3	3	-	-	33	66	0
6 std	4	y	2	1	-	-	50	0	50
7 gen	2	y	11	0	-	-	45	55	0
8 gen	4	y	16	0	-	-	63	38	0

of the corresponding target process features. These are determined following Section 5.0. The values given are percentages of the solutions who have the given percentages of features in which either (i) no features are matched; (ii) features match between 1% and 50% of the total features possible; and (iii) all the features.

The standard grammar runs (1, 2) found exact target expressions. Exact feature matches were found in both runs, meaning that both expressions and channel rates from the target NaCl were synthesized. Note that Experiment 1 seems to outperform 2 according to the fitness range values. Because this run was underspecified (2 channels), it is easier to satisfy the simpler specification. The generic grammar experiments (3 and 4) did not result in any expression hits, although some matched a few features.

Experiments 5 through 8 use multi-objective evaluation. The standard grammar experiments (5, 6) both found solution expressions, although only the 4-channel run also found an exact match with channel rates. The generic grammar performance was similar to the single-objective cases.

Table 10-5. Kna2CL and Repressilator Results

	MO	Ch	F	|S|	H	F range Tr	Te	F matches % 0	1-50	51-99	100
Kna2Cl	n	8	2	20	6	17	16	40	30	10	20
	y	8	2	21	6	-	-	48	38	0	14
Repress	n	1	5	20	0	20	19	55	35	10	0
	y	1	5	251	-	-	-	31	62	7	<1

Table 10-5 summarizes the Kna2Cl and repressilator runs. Both Kna2Cl experiments resulted in exact target matches. In the multi-objective case, these hits are "unique" expression instances (save for operator associativity, etc.), since duplicates are removed when the rank 1 sets are combined and re-ranked. In generaly, the single- and multi-objective runs show similar performance.

The repressilator resulted in a large number of rank 1 solutions (251 in total). The higher dimensionality for the fitness vector (5) increases the likelihood of solutions being undominated. Note that the *Hits* values were not determined for the multi-objective runs, due to the great number of solutions to examine. It is unlikely many exact hits arose, given the few 100% feature matches.

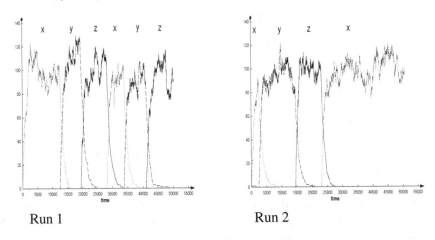

Run 1   Run 2

Figure 10-3. Best repressilator solution plots

One solution matched the target process in all 5 objectives ($p > 90\%$):

$$Gene(a, b) \; = \; ?a.delay(0.0001).Gene(a, b)$$
$$+ \; delay(0.1).(Protein(a, b) \; | \; Gene(a, b))$$
$$Protein(a, b) \; = \; !b + delay(0.001)$$

This expression is almost identical to the target in Figure 10-2, except for the following boldfaced term:

$$Protein(a, b) \; = \; !b.\mathbf{Protein(a, b)} + delay(0.001)$$

Two example plots of this near-solution are in Figure 10-3. The plots are almost indistinguishable from the target plot, which suggests that the feature tests have captured the essence of this process behaviour.

A few other plots from multi-objective repressilator solutions are in Figure 10-4. The process in (a) is one in which only 2 features matched ($p > 90\%$), those being chaos and periodicity. The process definition shows similarities to

$$Gene(a, b) = ?a.delay(0.001).Gene(a, b))$$
$$+delay(0.1).(Protein(a, b) \mid Gene(a, b))$$

$$Protein(a, b) = !b.!b.Protein(a, b)$$
$$+delay(0.001)$$

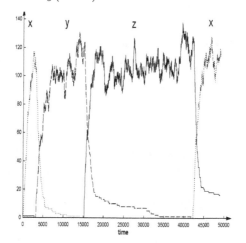

$$Gene(a, b) = delay(0.001).!a.Gene(a, b)$$
$$+delay(0.01).(Gene(a, b) \mid Gene(a, b))$$

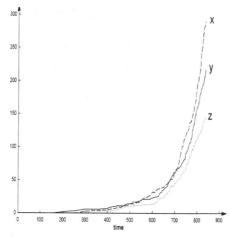

Figure 10-4. Other repressilator solutions

the target. On the other hand, although the process in (b) matches 4 of the 5 features, the feature not matched is periodicity. The Protein sub-process is not used, and is omitted. The great majority of solutions having 3 or 4 feature matches, but which does not include periodicity, generate plots similar to (b). Periodicity is a difficult feature to match. When examining the 173 solutions with feature matches ($p > 90\%$), only 6% of them matched periodicity. In comparison, standard deviation matched with 18%, chaos with 32%, serial correlation with 35%, and mean matched 54% of solutions. Periodicity is a challenging feature to fulfil, which is unfortunate, because it is *critical* of the repressilator. Expressions with a periodicity score somewhat in the desired range exhibit behaviour that is at least superficially similar to the target repressilator plot. Lacking this characteristic results in undesirable processes.

8.   Conclusion

When dealing with stochastic systems, the use of statistical feature tests as a means for characterizing behaviour is arguably the only sensible strategy. Statistical features are also used by Leier *et al.*, to evolve noisy oscillating bionetworks similar to the repressilator (Leier et al., 2006). Their set-based representation is similar to a process algebra, and their simulation environment also uses the Gillespie algorithm that we employ.

The automatic synthesis of stochastic processes is less tractable than deterministic process synthesis (Koza et al., 2003; Kitagawa and Iba, 2003). Deterministic process behaviours are defined by their start states, and this is exploitable by fitness strategies. The variability of stochastic processes makes them difficult to characterize, and which in turn results in a difficult search space for evolution. Interpreting a process multiple times, and for longer durations, will help in obtaining more accurate fitnesses (and possibly flatter search spaces). On the other hand, this can be prohibitively expensive.

Advantages of using multi-objective selection are that heterogeneous feature scores do not need to be artificially combined, and a set of candidates are generated for inspection after a run, hopefully producing a rich set of solutions. This has been exploited by others in similar problem domains. For example, Rodriguez-Vazquez and Fleming use multi-objective GP for evolving models of chaotic time series (Rodriguez-Vazquez and Fleming, 2005).

However, higher-dimension problems such as the repressilator resulted in too many outlier solutions. Statistical feature tests are not equal, as the periodicity score is crucial for the repressilator. Since the multi-objective environment treated all objectives democratically, periodicity was rarely dominant in solutions, given its technical difficulty compared to other features. This resulted in large numbers of useless solutions. Therefore, one cannot select features haphazardly, in hopes that a behaviour of interest will be adequately characterized. Search strategies such as multi-objective evaluation are effectively limited as to the number of dimensions used, and so the selection of lots of tests in the hope of possibly including effective ones is not feasible. Future work will consider more principled means for selecting features. Automatic feature selection is an active research problem (Liu and Motoda, 1998), and developments in those areas are of interest. The use of preference information in multi-objective strategies is worth considering (Coello et al., 2007).

Grammar-guided evolution is a useful tool in this application domain. The search space defined by stochastic π-calculus benefits with the use of syntactic constraints to help guide search towards good solutions.

Acknowledgements: Research supported by NSERC Operating Grant 138467, and an NSERC PGS A award.

References

Blossey, R., Cardelli, L., and Phillips, A. (2006). A Compositional Approach to the Stochastic Dynamics of Gene Networks. *Trans. in Comp. Sys. Bio (TCSB)*, 3939:99–122.

Borrelli, A., De Falco, I., Della Cioppa, A., Nicodemi, M., and Trautteura, G. (2006). Performance of genetic programming to extract the trend in noisy data series. *Physica A: Statistical and Theoretical Physics*, 370(1):104–108.

Bower, J.M. and Bolouri, H. (2001). *Computational Modeling of Genetic and Biochemical Networks*. MIT Press Kaufmann.

Chatfield, C. (2004). *The Analysis of Time Series: An Introduction*. Chapman and Hall/CRC.

Cho, D.-Y., Cho, K.-H., and Zhang, B.-T. (2006). Identification of biochemical networks by S-tree based genetic programming. *Bioinformatics*, 22(13):1631–1640.

Chu, D. (2007). Evolving genetic regulatory networks for systems biology. In Srinivasan, D. and Wang, L., editors, *Proc. CEC 2007*, pages 875–882, Singapore. IEEE Press.

Coello, C.A. Coello, Lamont, G.B., and Veldhuizen, D.A. Van (2007). *Evolutionary Algorithms for Solving Multi-Objective Problems*. Kluwer, 2 edition.

Drennan, B. and Beer, R.D. (2006). Evolution of repressilators using a biologically-motivated model of gene expression. In et al., L.M. Rocha, editor, *Artificial Life X: Proc. Tenth Intl. Conf. on the Simulation and Synthesis of Living Systems*, pages 22–27. MIT Press.

Gillespie, D.T. (1977). Exact stochastic simulation of coupled chemical reactions. *J. Phys. Chem*, 81:2340–2361.

Goldberg, D.E. (1989). *Genetic Algorithms in Search, Optimization, and Machine Learning*. Addison Wesley.

Hopcroft, J.E. and Ullman, J.D. (1979). *Introduction to Automata Theory, Languages, and Computation*. Addison Wesley.

Imada, J. (2009). Evolutionary synthesis of stochastic gene network models using feature-based search spaces. Master's thesis, Department of Computer Science, Brock University.

Imada, J. and Ross, B.J. (2008). Using Feature-based Fitness Evaluation in Symbolic Regression with Added Noise. In *Proc. GECCO 2008 Late Breaking Papers*.

Kitagawa, J. and Iba, H. (2003). Identifying Metabolic Pathways and Gene Regulation Networks with Evolutionary Algorithms. In Fogel, G.F. and Corne, D.W., editors, *Evolutionary Computation in Bioinformatics*, pages 255–278. Morgan Kaufmann.

Koza, J.R., Keane, M.A., Streeter, M.J., Mydlowec, W., Yu, J., and Lanza, G. (2003). *Genetic Programming IV: Routine Human-Competitive Machine Intelligence*. Kluwer Academic Publishers.

Leier, A., Kuo, P.D., Banzhaf, W., and Burrage, K. (2006). Evolving noisy oscillatory dynamics in genetic regulatory networks. In *et al.*, P. Collet, editor, *EuroGP 2006*, volume 3905 of *LNCS*, pages 290–299. Springer.

Liu, H. and Motoda, H. (1998). *Feature Selection for Knowledge Discovery and Data Mining*. Kluwer Academic Publishers.

Markowetz, F. and Spang, R. (2007). Inferring Cellular Networks - a Review. *MBC Bioinformatics*, 8:1–17.

Milner, R. (1989). *Communication and Concurrency*. Prentice Hall.

Milner, R. (1999). *Communicating and Mobile Systems: the Pi-calculus*. Cambridge University Press.

Nanopoulos, A., Alcock, R., and Manolopoulos, Y. (2001). Feature-based classification of time-series data. In *Information processing and technology*, pages 49–61. Nova Science Publishers, Inc., Commack, NY, USA.

Phillips, A. (2008). The stochastic pi machine. http://research.microsoft.com/ aphillip/spim/. Last accessed Dec 9, 2008.

Phillips, A. and Cardelli, L. (2004). A Correct Abstract Machine for the Stochastic Pi-calculus. In *Proc. Bioconcur'04*.

Priami, C. (1995). Stochastic pi-Calculus. *The Computer Journal*, 38(7):579–589.

Priami, C., Regev, A., Shapiro, E., and Silverman, W. (2001). Application of a stochastic name-passing calculus to representation and simulation of molecular processes. *Information Processing Letters*, 80:25–31.

Rodriguez-Vazquez, K. and Fleming, P. J. (2005). Evolution of mathematical models of chaotic systems based on multiobjective genetic programming. *Knowledge and Information Systems*, 8(2):235–256.

Ross, B.J. (2001). Logic-based Genetic Programming with Definite Clause Translation Grammars. *New Generation Computing*, 19(4):313–337.

Ross, B.J. and Imada, J. (2009). Evolving Stochastic Processes Using Feature Tests and Genetic Programming. In *Proc. GECCO 2009*.

Streichert, F., Planatscher, H., Spieth, C., Ulmer, H., and Zell, A. (2004). Comparing genetic programming and evolution strategies on inferring gene regulatory networks. In et al., K.Deb, editor, *GECCO-2004*, volume 3102 of *LNCS*, pages 471–480, Seattle, WA. Springer-Verlag.

Wang, X., Smith, K., and Hyndman, R. (2006). Characteristic-based clustering for time series data. *Data Min. Knowl. Discov.*, 13(3):335–364.

Whigham, P.A. (1996). *Grammatical Bias for Evolutionary Learning*. PhD thesis, School of Computer Science, University College, University of New South Wales, Australian Defence Force Academy.

Zhang, W., Yang, G., and Z.Wu (2004). Genetic Programming-based Modeling on Chaotic Time Series. In *Proc. 3rd Intl Conf. on Machine Learning and Cybernetics*, pages 2347–2352. IEEE.

Chapter 11

GRAPH STRUCTURED PROGRAM EVOLUTION: EVOLUTION OF LOOP STRUCTURES

Shinichi Shirakawa[1] and Tomoharu Nagao[1]

[1]*Graduate School of Environment and Information Sciences, Yokohama National University, 79-7, Tokiwadai, Hodogaya-ku, Yokohama, Kanagawa, 240-8501, Japan.*

Abstract   Recently, numerous automatic programming techniques have been developed and applied in various fields. A typical example is genetic programming (GP), and various extensions and representations of GP have been proposed thus far. Complex programs and hand-written programs, however, may contain several loops and handle multiple data types. In this chapter, we propose a new method called Graph Structured Program Evolution (GRAPE). The representation of GRAPE is a graph structure; therefore, it can represent branches and loops using this structure. Each program is constructed as an arbitrary directed graph of nodes and a data set. The GRAPE program handles multiple data types using the data set for each type, and the genotype of GRAPE takes the form of a linear string of integers. We apply GRAPE to three test problems, factorial, exponentiation, and list sorting, and demonstrate that the optimum solution in each problem is obtained by the GRAPE system.

Keywords: automatic programming, genetic programming, graph-based genetic programming, genetic algorithm, factorial, exponentiation, list sorting

1.   Introduction

This chapter introduces a new method for automatic programming. This new method, named **GRA**ph structured **P**rogram **E**volution (GRAPE), uses a graph structure to represent programs.

In standard genetic programming (GP), programs are represented as trees containing terminal and nonterminal nodes. Complex programs and hand-written programs, however, may contain several branches and loops. We believe that graph representation is the nearest representation to hand-written programs. Therefore, we adopt the graph structure to represent programs. In GRAPE programs, each program is constructed as an arbitrary directed graph of nodes

R. Riolo et al. (eds.), *Genetic Programming Theory and Practice VII*,
Genetic and Evolutionary Computation, DOI 10.1007/978-1-4419-1626-6_11,
© Springer Science + Business Media, LLC 2010

and a data set (index memory). The GRAPE program handles multiple data types using the data set for each type, and the genotype of GRAPE takes the form of a linear string of integers.

In the next section of this chapter, an overview of several related studies is presented. In Section 3, we describe our proposed method, GRAPE. Several experiments and results are described in Section 4. Finally, in Section 5, we describe our conclusions and future work.

2.   Related Works

Automatic programming is the method for generating computer programs automatically. Genetic programming (GP) proposed by Koza (Koza, 1992; Koza, 1994) is a typical example of automatic programming. GP evolves computer programs that usually have tree structures and searches for a desired program using a genetic algorithm (GA). Numerous extensions and improvements of GP have been introduced. Attempts were made to integrate modularity into the GP paradigm using automatically defined functions (ADF) (Koza, 1994) and module acquisition (Angeline and Pollack, 1993). Montana developed a strategy for incorporating multiple data types called strongly typed GP (Montana, 1995). In this approach, the user is required to specify the types of all values, function inputs, and function outputs, and the program generation, mutation, and crossover algorithms are modified to obey these type restrictions. It affects the shape of the program search space (e.g., by restricting crossover points).

Various representations for GP have been proposed thus far. GP with index memory (Teller, 1994) was introduced by Teller, and it has been proven to be Turing complete. This means that in theory, GP with indexed memory can be used to evolve any algorithm. Linear genetic programming (LGP) (Brameier and Banzhaf, 2001) uses a specific linear representation of computer programs. Instead of the tree-based GP expressions of a functional programming language (such as LISP), programs in an imperative language (such as C) are evolved. An LGP individual is represented by a variable-length sequence of simple C language instructions. Instructions operate on one or two indexed variables (registers) r or on constants c from predefined sets. The result is assigned to a destination register, e.g., $r_i = r_j * c$. Grammatical evolution (GE) (O'Neill and Ryan, 2003) is an evolutionary algorithm that can evolve computer programs in any language, and can be considered a form of grammar-based genetic programming. GE uses a chromosome of numbers encoded using eight bits to indicate which rule from the Backus-Naur form grammar to apply at each state of the derivation sequence, starting from a defined start symbol. Huelsbergen used machine language representation and evolved recursive sequences (sequences of squares, cubes, factorials, and Fibonacci numbers) (Huelsbergen, 1997). Yu and Clack proposed a structure of λ abstractions and implicit recursion with an effective mechanism to perform module creation and reuse for GP (Yu and Clack, 1998).

Recently, two interesting automatic programming techniques were proposed, PushGP (Spector and Robinson, 2002; Spector et al., 2005) and object oriented genetic programming (OOGP) (Agapitos and Lucas, 2006b; Agapitos and Lucas, 2006a). PushGP evolves programs using the Push language proposed by Spector et al. Push is a stack-based programming language. OOGP evolves object-oriented programs instead of programs in the form of a LISP parse tree. Both methods tackled the problem of generating recursive programs (e.g., factorial, Fibonacci sequence, exponentiation, list sorting, and so on) and obtained these programs automatically.

Various representations use a graph. Evolutionary programming (Fogel et al., 1995), which evolves a finite state machine, was first proposed by Fogel in 1960. Studies in the evolution of analog circuit and neural network topology often treat the evolution of graph structure (Koza et al., 1999; Mattiussi and Floreano, 2007; Gruau et al., 1996). Parallel algorithm discovery and orchestration (PADO) (Teller and Veloso, 1996) is a GP method based on graphs rather than a tree structure. PADO uses stack and index memory, and there are *action* and *branch-decision* nodes. It is executed from the start node to the end node in the network. PADO was applied to object recognition problems. Another graph-based GP is parallel distributed genetic programming (PDGP) (Poli, 1997). In this approach, the tree is represented as a graph with function and terminal nodes located over a grid. In this way, it is possible to directly execute several nodes concurrently. Cartesian genetic programming (CGP) (Miller and Thomson, 2000; Miller and Smith, 2006) was developed from a representation that was used for the evolution of digital circuits, and it represents programs as graphs. In certain respects, it is similar to PDGP. However, PDGP results were evolved without the use of genotype-phenotype mapping, and various sophisticated crossover operators were defined. In CGP, the genotype is an integer string that denotes a list of node connections and functions. This string is mapped into the phenotype of an index graph. Linear-Graph GP (Kantschik and Banzhaf, 2002) is the extension of Linear GP and Linear-Tree GP (Kantschik and Banzhaf, 2002). In Linear-Graph GP, each program is represented as a graph. Each node in the graph has two parts, a linear program and a branching node. Genetic network programming (Katagiri et al., 2001), which has a directed graph structure, is mainly applied to create the behavior sequences of agents and shows better performance than GP.

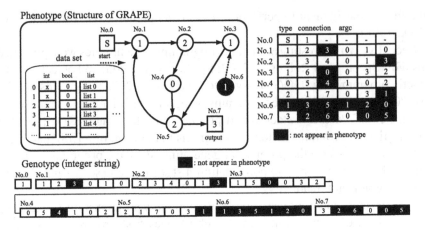

Figure 11-1. Structure of GRAPE (phenotype) and the genotype, which denotes a list of node types, connections, and arguments. No.6 is the inactive node.

3.   Graph Structured Program Evolution (GRAPE)

Overview

Various extensions and representations for GP have been proposed thus far. Complex programs and hand-written programs, however, may contain several loops and handle multiple data types. GRAPE (Shirakawa et al., 2007; Shirakawa and Nagao, 2007) constructs graph-structured programs automatically. These programs are composed of an arbitrary directed graph of nodes and a data set (index memory).

GRAPE's representation is different from that of PDGP, CGP, and Linear-Graph GP. These methods have some restrictions on connections (e.g., they restrict loops and allow only feed-forward connectivity). GRAPE's representation is an arbitrary directed graph of nodes. PADO is one of the methods similar to GRAPE. PADO has stack memory and index memory, and it is executed from the start node to the end node in the network. GRAPE is different from PADO in that GRAPE handles multiple data types using the data set for each type and adopts genotype-phenotype mapping.

The features of GRAPE are summarized as follows:

- Arbitrary directed graph structures

- Ability to handle multiple data types using a data set

- Genotype consisting of an integer string

Structure of GRAPE

Graph-structured programs are composed of an arbitrary directed graph of nodes and a data set (index memory). The data set flows through the directed graph and is processed at each node. Figure 11-1 illustrates an example of the structure of GRAPE. In GRAPE, each node has two parts, one for processing and the other for branching. The processing component executes several types of processing using the data set, e.g., arithmetic and Boolean calculations. After processing is complete, the next node is selected. The branching component decides the next node according to the data set.

Examples of nodes in GRAPE are shown in Figure 11-2. No.1 adds data[0] to data[1], substitutes it for data[0] using an integer data type, and selects No.2 as the next node. No.2 decides the next node using integer data[0] and data[1]; if data[0] is greater than data[1], connection 1 is chosen, else connection 2 is chosen. Special nodes are shown in Figure 11-1. No.0 is the start node, which is the equivalent of the root node in GP. It is the first node to be executed when a GRAPE program runs. No.7 is the output node. When this node is reached, the GRAPE program outputs data and the program terminates. In Figure 11-1, No.7 outputs integer data[0]. Although the GRAPE program has only one start node, it may have several output nodes.

Because GRAPE is represented by a graph structure, it can represent complex programs (e.g., branches and loops). Several data types are available in GRAPE programs, e.g., integer, Boolean, and list. The GRAPE program handles multiple data types using the data set for each type.

To adopt an evolutionary method, GRAPE uses genotype-phenotype mapping. This genotype-phenotype mapping method is similar to CGP. The GRAPE program is encoded in the form of a linear string of integers. The genotype is an integer string, which denotes a list of node types, connections, and arguments. The node connections are arbitrary, which is different from CGP. The length of the genotype is fixed and equals $N * (n_c + n_a + 1) + 1$, where N is the maximum number of nodes, n_c is the maximum number of connections, and n_a is the maximum number of arguments. Although the genotype in GRAPE is a fixed-length representation, the number of nodes in the phenotype can vary but is limited (not all nodes encoded in the genotype have to be connected). This allows the existence of inactive nodes. In Figure 11-1, No.6 is inactive, and the other nodes are active. In brief, GRAPE has *neutrality* (Harvey and Thompson, 1996; Miller and Thomson, 2000; Miller and Smith, 2006), as does CGP.

Genetic Operators and Generation Alternation Model in GRAPE

To obtain the optimum structure in GRAPE, an evolutionary method is adopted. The GRAPE genotype is a linear string of integers. Therefore, GRAPE

Examples of node

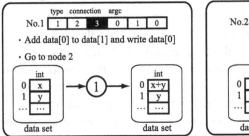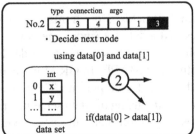

Figure 11-2. Examples of processing (left) and branching nodes (right).

is able to use a typical GA. GRAPE uses uniform crossover and mutation for a string of integers as genetic operators. The uniform crossover operator affects two individuals, as follows:

- Select several genes randomly according to the uniform crossover rate P_c for each gene.

- The selected genes are swapped between two parents, and generate offspring.

We use a low value (e.g., 0.1) of P_c to prevent destructive crossover. The mutation operator affects one individual, as follows:

- Select several genes randomly according to the mutation rate P_m for each gene.

- The selected genes are changed randomly.

It uses the minimal generation gap (MGG) model (Deb et al., 2002; Satoh et al., 1996; Tsutsui et al., 1999) as a generation alternation model. This is a steady-state model proposed by Satoh et al., having a desirable convergence property of being able to maintain the diversity of the population, and shows higher performance than other conventional models in a wide range of applications (especially real parameter optimization). The MGG model is summarized as follows:

1. Set the generation counter $t = 0$. Generate N individuals randomly as the initial population $P(t)$.

2. Select a set of two parents M by random sampling from the population $P(t)$.

3. Generate a set of m children C by applying the crossover and mutation operations to M.

Table 11-1. Parameters used in the experiments.

Parameter	Value
Number of evaluations	2500000 or 5000000 (list sorting)
Population size	500
Children size (for MGG)	50
Uniform crossover rate P_c	0.1
Crossover rate	0.9
Mutation rate P_m	0.02
Maximum number of nodes	10, 30, 50
Execution step limits	500 or 3000 (list sorting)

4. Select two individuals from set $M + C$. One is the elitist individual, and the other is an individual chosen by roulette wheel selection. Then replace M with the two individuals in population $P(t)$ to obtain population $P(t+1)$.

5. Stop when a certain specified condition is satisfied; otherwise, set $t = t + 1$ and go to step 2.

The MGG model localizes its selection pressure, not to the whole population as a simple GA or steady state does, but only to the family (children and parents).

4.   Experiments and Results

Several different problems have been tackled to verify GRAPE's effectiveness, including the computation of factorial $(n!)$, exponentiation (a^b), and list sorting. Evolution of these programs is difficult for standard GP, which must develop iterative or recursive mechanisms to solve these problems.

Experimental Settings

Table 11-1 lists the GRAPE parameters for the experiments. In our experiment, the maximum number of nodes in GRAPE is set as 10, 30, or 50. To avoid problems caused by nonterminating structures, we limited the execution steps to 500 (factorial and exponentiation) and 3000 (list sorting). When a program reaches the execution limit, the individual is assigned a fitness value of 0.0. These execution step limits are sufficient to solve the target problem. We prepared a data set of sufficient size to compute the problems. Initially, we set input and constant values of the data set. Therefore, GRAPE handles or creates constants within its programs. Table 11-2 shows the GRAPE node functions used in the experiments. We prepared simple node functions, arithmetic functions, and functions to swap and compare the elements of a list. We did not prepare special node functions such as iteration functions.

Table 11-2. GRAPE node functions for the experiments.

Name	# Connections	Arg(s)	Description
+	1	x, y, z	Use integer data type. Add data[x] to data[y] and substitute for data[z].
−	1	x, y, z	Use integer data type. Subtract data[x] from data[y] and substitute for data[z].
*	1	x, y, z	Use integer data type. Multiply data[x] by data[y] and substitute for data[z].
/	1	x, y, z	Use integer data type. Divide data[x] by data[y] and substitute for data[z].
=	2	x, y	Use integer data type. If data[x] is equal to data[y], choose connection 1; else, choose connection 2.
>	2	x, y	Use integer data type. If data[x] is greater than data[y], choose connection 1; else, choose connection 2.
<	2	x, y	Use integer data type. If data[x] is less than data[y], choose connection 1; else, choose connection 2.
SwapList	1	x, y	Use integer type and a list data. Swap list[data[x]] for list[data[y]].
EqualList	2	x, y	Use integer type and a list data. If list[data[x]] equals list[data[y]], choose connection 1; else, choose connection 2.
GreaterList	2	x, y	Use integer type and a list data. If list[data[x]] is greater than list[data[y]], choose connection 1; else, choose connection 2.
LessList	2	x, y	Use integer type and a list data. If list[data[x]] is less than list[data[y]], choose connection 1; else, choose connection 2.
OutputInt	0	x	Output data[x] and terminate the program.
OutputList	0	-	Output a list data and terminate the program.

Factorial

In this problem, we seek to evolve an implementation of the factorial function. We used integers from 0 to 5 to create a training set with the following input/output pairs (a, b): (0, 1), (1, 1), (2, 2), (3, 6), (4, 24), and (5, 120). We used the normalized absolute mean error of the training set as a fitness measure. The fitness function F used in the experiments is

$$F = 1 - \frac{\sum_{i=1}^{n} \frac{|Correct_i - Out_i|}{|Correct_i| + |Correct_i - Out_i|}}{n} \qquad (11.1)$$

where $Correct_i$ is the correct value for the training data i, Out_i is the value returned by the generated program for the training data i, and n is the size of the training set. The range of this fitness function was [0.0, 1.0]. A higher numerical value indicated better performance. If this fitness value is equal to 1.0, the program yields the perfect solution for the training set. If the fitness

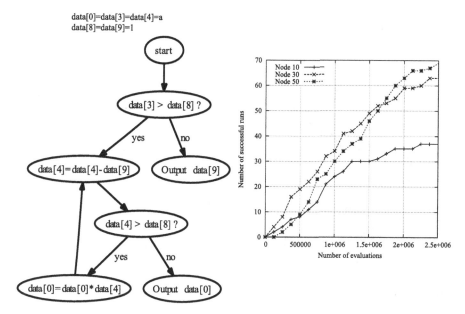

Figure 11-3. Example of factorial structure obtained by GRAPE (left) and transitions of the number of successful runs over 100 runs (right).

value in Equation 11.1 reaches 1.0, the fitness is calculated as follows:

$$F = 1.0 + \frac{1}{S_{exe}} \tag{11.2}$$

where S_{exe} is the total number of execution steps of the generated program. This fitness function indicates that fewer execution steps provide a better solution.

In the factorial experiment, integer data were used, and the integer data size in GRAPE was 10. Initially, we set the input value a for data[0] to data[4] and a constant value of 1 for data[5] to data[9]. The node functions used in this experiment are $\{ +, -, *, =, >, <, \text{OutputInt} \}$, as shown in Table 11-2.

Results of 100 runs with the same parameter set are provided. Figure 11-3 is an example of the obtained structure for factorial. This GRAPE program has a loop structure, and it calculates the factorial completely. Figure 11-3 also shows the transitions of the number of successful runs for the number of evaluations. When an individual whose fitness value is equal to or greater than 1.0 is found, the run is considered successful. We apply the most elite individual generated by GRAPE to the test data set for each run. The integers from 6 to 12 are used as the test set inputs. The number of correct programs for the test set appears in Table 11-3. When the number of nodes is 50, it shows best performance (training set: 69, test set: 59).

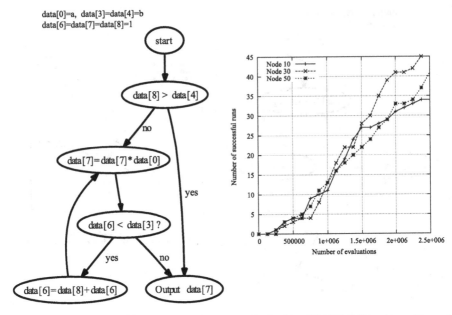

Figure 11-4. Example of exponentiation structure obtained by GRAPE (left) and transitions of the number of successful runs over 100 runs (right).

Exponentiation

In this problem, we seek to evolve an implementation of the integer exponential. The problem has two inputs. The training set (a, b, c) used in this experiment is (2, 0, 1), (2, 1, 2), (2, 2, 4), (3, 3, 27), (3, 4, 81), (3, 5, 243), (4, 6, 4096), (4, 7, 16384), and (4, 8, 65536). We also used the fitness functions in Equations 11.1 and 11.2 on the training set.

In the exponentiation experiment, the integer data type is used, and the integer data size is 9. Initially, we set the input value a for data[0] to data[2], input value b for data[3] to data[5], and the constant value of 1 for data[6] to data[8]. The node functions used in this experiment are { +, −, *, =, >, <, OutputInt }, as shown in Table 11-2.

Results of 100 runs with the same parameter set are provided. Figure 11-4 is an example of the obtained structure for exponentiation. This GRAPE program also calculates exponentiation completely. Figure 11-4 also shows the transitions of the number of successful runs for the number of evaluations. We apply the most elite individual generated by GRAPE to the test data set for each run. The test set inputs (a, b) are (5, 9), (5, 10), (5, 11), (4, 12), (4, 13), (4, 14), (3, 15) (3, 16), (3, 17), (2, 18), (2, 19), and (2, 20). The number of correct programs for the test set appears in Table 11-3. When the number of nodes is 30, it shows the best performance (training set: 45, test set: 44).

List Sorting

Several researchers have investigated the evolution of a general sorting algorithm. Kinnear evolved a general iterative sorting algorithm using GP (Kinnear, Jr., 1993b; Kinnear, Jr., 1993a). He prepared special functions for the sorting problem, such as the *iteration function*, which is an iterative operator. Spector et al. showed that PushGP evolved a general sorting algorithm (Spector et al., 2005). OOGP evolved a general recursive sorting algorithm using its recursive mechanism (Agapitos and Lucas, 2006a).

In this problem, we seek to evolve an implementation of the sorting algorithm. We provide a list of integers as input. A correct program returns a sorted input list of any length [e.g., input: (2, 1, 7, 5, 1), output: (1, 1, 2, 5, 7)]. The training data set is 30 random lists with lengths between 10 and 20. List elements are randomly chosen from the range of [0, 255]. The fitness function F used in this experiment is given in Equation 11.3. The range of this fitness function is [0.0, 1.0]. A higher numerical value indicates better performance. If this fitness value is equal to 1.0, the program yields the perfect solution for the training set.

$$F = 1.0 - \frac{\sum_{i=1}^{n} \frac{\sum_{j=0}^{l_i} (1 - \frac{1}{2^{d_{ij}}})}{l_i}}{n} \qquad (11.3)$$

where d_{ij} is the distance between the correct position and the return value position for the training data i for element j. l_i is the list length for the training data i, and n is the size of the training data set. If the fitness value in Equation 11.3 reaches 1.0, the fitness value is calculated using Equation 11.2. In this experiment, a list of integers and an integer data type were used, and the integer data size was 15. Initially, we set the size of the input list (the list length) for data[0] to data[4], a constant value of 0 for data[5] to data[9], and a constant value of 1 for data[10] to data[14]. The node functions used in this experiment are { +, −, *, /, =, >, <, SwapList, EqualList, GreaterList, LessList, OutputList } from Table 11-2.

Results are given for 100 different runs with the same parameter set. Figure 11-5 shows the transitions of the number of successful runs for the number of evaluations and an example of the obtained structure for list sorting, which is a general sorting algorithm. Figure 11-6 provides the transitions of the average fitness and the number of active nodes for the number of evaluations. In Figure 11-5, the number of successful runs increases greatly after 2,000,000 fitness evaluations, and finally reaches 75 when the number of nodes is 30. At the beginning of the evolution, the number of successful runs is 0 until about 1,000,000 fitness evaluations. This shows that the evolution of a sorting

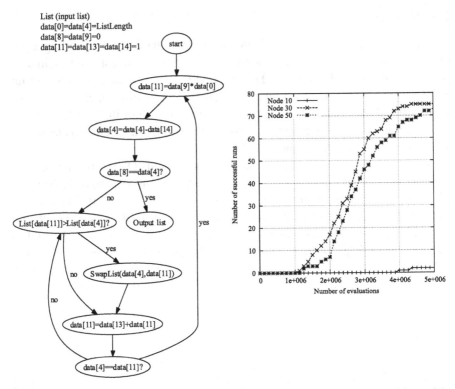

Figure 11-5. Example of list sorting structure obtained by GRAPE (left) and transitions of the number of successful runs over 100 runs (right).

algorithm is very difficult. Although the number of successful runs is 0 at the beginning of the evolution, the fitness increases gradually, as shown in Figure 11-6. Therefore, the evolutionary method is functionally effective. In Figure 11-6, the number of active nodes is about half of the maximum number of nodes when the maximum number of nodes is 30 or 50. Thus, the evolution of the GRAPE programs is efficient without *bloat* through the genotype of fixed integer string.

We apply the most elite individual generated by GRAPE to the test data set for each run. The test set is 500 random lists. We use lists between 20 and 50 items long as the test set. Table 11-3 provides the number of successful runs for the training and test sets. The results show a high number of successful runs (75 for "Node 30," the value with a maximum of 30 nodes, and 73 for "Node 50") for the training set, demonstrating that GRAPE is a powerful automatic programming technique. For the test set, "Node 50" shows best performance 31, and "Node 30" is 25. We can consider that these programs, which were successful for the test set, are a general sorting algorithm. When the number of nodes is 10, the result is not good (the number of successful runs is 2 for

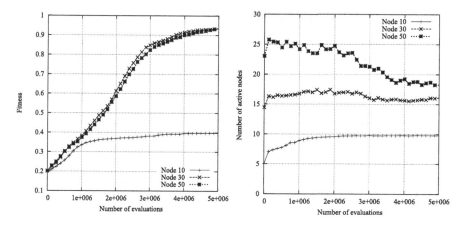

Figure 11-6. Transitions of the average fitness (left) and the number of active nodes (right) over 100 runs by GRAPE with a maximum number of nodes of 10, 30, and 50.

Table 11-3. Comparison of the number of successful runs for the training set with that of the test set.

	Factorial		Exponentiation		List sorting	
	Training set	Test set	Training set	Test set	Training set	Test set
Node 10	37	37	34	34	2	1
Node 30	63	57	**45**	**44**	**75**	25
Node 50	**69**	**59**	41	40	73	**31**

the training set and 1 for the test set). In the experiment, we use Equation 11.2 as the fitness function. For this fitness function, fewer execution steps mean a better solution. For this reason, GRAPE tends to construct an exclusive sorting algorithm for the training set. Thus, the fitness function and selection of the training set are very important for program evolution.

The obtained sorting program in Figure 11-5 has two loop structures and sorts any sequence of numbers. GRAPE successfully generates the sorting algorithm automatically, and the obtained structure is unique and completely solves the problem. This algorithm is similar to the *selection sort*.

Sorting algorithm programs can be represented using recursion. Several elegant and efficient sorting algorithms (e.g., merge sort, quick sort) are best expressed as recursive functions. Although we have not created a recursion function in this experiment, GRAPE has constructed the best programs using branches and loops. If we introduce recursion functions or modularity mechanisms [such as ADF (Koza, 1994)] to GRAPE, its performance may improve.

5.   Conclusions and Future Work

In this chapter, we propose a new method for automatic programming, Graph Structured Program Evolution (GRAPE). The representation of GRAPE is a graph structure. Each program is constructed as an arbitrary directed graph of nodes and a data set. The data set flows through the directed graph and is processed at each node. GRAPE adopts genotype-phenotype mapping. The genotype is an integer string that denotes a list of node types, connections, and arguments.

We applied GRAPE to three different problems, factorial, exponentiation, and list sorting, and confirmed that it obtained the optimum solution for each problem. As a result, we showed that the evolutionary method is functionally effective, and a maximum number of nodes of 30 or 50 shows better performance than a maximum number of 10. Therefore, we should prepare sufficient number of nodes to represent the programs. In experiments of factorial and exponentiation, the almost GRAPE programs that succeed with the training set also solve the test set. The programs of these problems can be represented simply using recursion. Although we have not prepared a recursion function in this chapter, the GRAPE system has constructed the optimum programs using branches and loops. If we introduce recursion functions or modularity mechanisms such as ADFs (Koza, 1994) to GRAPE, its performance may improve. In future, we will introduce recursion functions or modularity mechanisms to solve more complex problems.

The advantage of GRAPE compared to other automatic programming techniques is its ease of understanding and implementation. The GRAPE algorithm is relatively simple. It is easy to understand the evolved programs of GRAPE, owing to the graph representation. GRAPE is not compared to other techniques in this study. Several benchmark comparisons of performance, scalability, and speed would be highly useful future study.

Because the test problems in this work seem a bit simple, we plan to apply GRAPE to problems that are larger in scale and require more complex structures, for example, signal processing and agent control. Currently, we propose a method for evolving search algorithms using GRAPE (Shirakawa and Nagao, 2009). We apply GRAPE to construct search algorithms for benchmark function optimization and template matching problems, and show that the constructed search algorithms are effective for the utilized search spaces and also for several other search spaces.

References

Agapitos, Alexandros and Lucas, Simon M. (2006a). Evolving efficient recursive sorting algorithms. In *Proceedings of the 2006 IEEE Congress on Evolutionary Computation*, pages 9227–9234, Vancouver. IEEE Press.

Agapitos, Alexandros and Lucas, Simon M. (2006b). Learning recursive functions with object oriented genetic programming. In Collet, Pierre, Tomassini, Marco, Ebner, Marc, Gustafson, Steven, and Ekárt, Anikó, editors, *Proceedings of the 9th European Conference on Genetic Programming*, volume 3905 of *Lecture Notes in Computer Science*, pages 166–177, Budapest, Hungary. Springer.

Angeline, Peter J. and Pollack, Jordan (1993). Evolutionary module acquisition. In Fogel, D. and Atmar, W., editors, *Proceedings of the Second Annual Conference on Evolutionary Programming*, pages 154–163, La Jolla, CA, USA.

Brameier, Markus and Banzhaf, Wolfgang (2001). A comparison of linear genetic programming and neural networks in medical data mining. *IEEE Transactions on Evolutionary Computation*, 5(1):17–26.

Deb, Kalyanmoy, Anand, Ashish, and Joshi, Dhiraj (2002). A computationally efficient evolutionary algorithm for real-parameter optimization. *Evolutionary Computation*, 10(4):371–395.

Fogel, David B., Angeline, Peter J., and Fogel, David B. (1995). An evolutionary programming approach to self-adaptation on finite state machines. In *Proceedings of the Fourth Annual Conference on Evolutionary Programming*, pages 355–365. MIT Press.

Gruau, Frederic, Whitley, Darrell, and Pyeatt, Larry (1996). A comparison between cellular encoding and direct encoding for genetic neural networks. In Koza, John R., Goldberg, David E., Fogel, David B., and Riolo, Rick L., editors, *Genetic Programming 1996: Proceedings of the First Annual Conference*, pages 81–89, Stanford University, CA, USA. MIT Press.

Harvey, Inman and Thompson, Adrian (1996). Through the labyrinth evolution finds a way: A silicon ridge. In *Proceedings of the First International Conference on Evolvable Systems: From Biology to Hardware (ICES '96)*, volume 1259 of *LNCS*, pages 406–422. Springer-Verlag.

Huelsbergen, Lorenz (1997). Learning recursive sequences via evolution of machine-language programs. In Koza, John R., Deb, Kalyanmoy, Dorigo, Marco, Fogel, David B., Garzon, Max, Iba, Hitoshi, and Riolo, Rick L., editors, *Genetic Programming 1997: Proceedings of the Second Annual Conference*, pages 186–194, Stanford University, CA, USA. Morgan Kaufmann.

Kantschik, Wolfgang and Banzhaf, Wolfgang (2002). Linear-graph GP—A new GP structure. In Foster, James A., Lutton, Evelyne, Miller, Julian, Ryan, Conor, and Tettamanzi, Andrea G. B., editors, *Genetic Programming, Proceedings of the 5th European Conference, EuroGP 2002*, volume 2278 of *LNCS*, pages 83–92, Kinsale, Ireland. Springer-Verlag.

Katagiri, Hironobu, Hirasawa, Kotaro, Hu, Jinglu, and Murata, Junichi (2001). Network structure oriented evolutionary model – genetic network programming–and its comparison with. In Spector, Lee, Goodman, Erik D.,

Wu, Annie, Langdon, W. B., Voigt, Hans-Michael, Gen, Mitsuo, Sen, Sandip, Dorigo, Marco, Pezeshk, Shahram, Garzon, Max H., and Burke, Edmund, editors, *Proceedings of the Genetic and Evolutionary Computation Conference (GECCO-2001)*, page 179, San Francisco, California, USA. Morgan Kaufmann.

Kinnear, Jr., Kenneth E. (1993a). Evolving a sort: Lessons in genetic programming. In *Proceedings of the 1993 International Conference on Neural Networks*, volume 2, pages 881–888, San Francisco, USA. IEEE Press.

Kinnear, Jr., Kenneth E. (1993b). Generality and difficulty in genetic programming: Evolving a sort. In Forrest, Stephanie, editor, *Proceedings of the 5th International Conference on Genetic Algorithms, ICGA-93*, pages 287–294, University of Illinois at Urbana-Champaign. Morgan Kaufmann.

Koza, John R. (1992). *Genetic Programming: On the Programming of Computers by Means of Natural Selection*. MIT Press, Cambridge, MA, USA.

Koza, John R. (1994). *Genetic Programming II: Automatic Discovery of Reusable Programs*. MIT Press, Cambridge Massachusetts.

Koza, John R., Andre, David, Bennett III, Forrest H, and Keane, Martin (1999). *Genetic Programming 3: Darwinian Invention and Problem Solving*. Morgan Kaufman.

Mattiussi, Claudio and Floreano, Dario (2007). Analog genetic encoding for the evolution of circuits and networks. *IEEE Transactions on Evolutionary Computation*, 11(5):596–607.

Miller, Julian F. and Smith, Stephen L. (2006). Redundancy and computational efficiency in cartesian genetic programming. *IEEE Transactions on Evolutionary Computation*, 10(2):167–174.

Miller, Julian F. and Thomson, Peter (2000). Cartesian genetic programming. In Poli, Riccardo, Banzhaf, Wolfgang, Langdon, William B., Miller, Julian F., Nordin, Peter, and Fogarty, Terence C., editors, *Genetic Programming, Proceedings of EuroGP'2000*, volume 1802 of *LNCS*, pages 121–132, Edinburgh. Springer-Verlag.

Montana, David J. (1995). Strongly typed genetic programming. *Evolutionary Computation*, 3(2):199–230.

O'Neill, Michael and Ryan, Conor (2003). *Grammatical Evolution: Evolutionary Automatic Programming in a Arbitrary Language*, volume 4 of *Genetic programming*. Kluwer Academic Publishers.

Poli, Riccardo (1997). Evolution of graph-like programs with parallel distributed genetic programming. In Back, Thomas, editor, *Genetic Algorithms: Proceedings of the Seventh International Conference*, pages 346–353, Michigan State University, East Lansing, MI, USA. Morgan Kaufmann.

Satoh, Hiroshi, Yamamura, Masayuki, and Kobayashi, Shigenobu (1996). Minimal generation gap model for considering both exploration and exploitations. In *Proceedings of the IIZUKA '96*, pages 494–497.

Shirakawa, Shinichi and Nagao, Tomoharu (2007). Evolution of sorting algorithm using graph structured program evolution. In *Proceedings of the 2007 IEEE International Conference on Systems, Man and Cybernetics (SMC 2007)*, pages 1256–1261, Montreal, Canada. IEEE.

Shirakawa, Shinichi and Nagao, Tomoharu (2009). Evolution of search algorithms using graph structured program evolution. In Vanneschi, Leonardo, Gustafson, Steven, Moraglio, Alberto, De Falco, Ivanoe, and Ebner, Marc, editors, *Proceedings of the 12th European Conference on Genetic Programming, EuroGP 2009*, volume 5481 of *LNCS*, pages 109–120, Tuebingen. Springer.

Shirakawa, Shinichi, Ogino, Shintaro, and Nagao, Tomoharu (2007). Graph structured program evolution. In Thierens, Dirk, Beyer, Hans-Georg, Bongard, Josh, Branke, Jurgen, Clark, John Andrew, Cliff, Dave, Congdon, Clare Bates, Deb, Kalyanmoy, Doerr, Benjamin, Kovacs, Tim, Kumar, Sanjeev, Miller, Julian F., Moore, Jason, Neumann, Frank, Pelikan, Martin, Poli, Riccardo, Sastry, Kumara, Stanley, Kenneth Owen, Stutzle, Thomas, Watson, Richard A, and Wegener, Ingo, editors, *GECCO '07: Proceedings of the 9th annual conference on Genetic and evolutionary computation*, volume 2, pages 1686–1693, London. ACM Press.

Spector, Lee, Klein, Jon, and Keijzer, Maarten (2005). The push3 execution stack and the evolution of control. In Beyer, Hans-Georg, O'Reilly, Una-May, Arnold, Dirk V., Banzhaf, Wolfgang, Blum, Christian, Bonabeau, Eric W., Cantu-Paz, Erick, Dasgupta, Dipankar, Deb, Kalyanmoy, Foster, James A., de Jong, Edwin D., Lipson, Hod, Llora, Xavier, Mancoridis, Spiros, Pelikan, Martin, Raidl, Guenther R., Soule, Terence, Tyrrell, Andy M., Watson, Jean-Paul, and Zitzler, Eckart, editors, *GECCO 2005: Proceedings of the 2005 conference on Genetic and evolutionary computation*, volume 2, pages 1689–1696, Washington DC, USA. ACM Press.

Spector, Lee and Robinson, Alan (2002). Genetic programming and autoconstructive evolution with the push programming language. *Genetic Programming and Evolvable Machines*, 3(1):7–40.

Teller, Astro (1994). Turing completeness in the language of genetic programming with indexed memory. In *Proceedings of the 1994 IEEE World Congress on Computational Intelligence*, volume 1, pages 136–141, Orlando, Florida, USA. IEEE Press.

Teller, Astro and Veloso, Manuela (1996). PADO: A new learning architecture for object recognition. In Ikeuchi, Katsushi and Veloso, Manuela, editors, *Symbolic Visual Learning*, pages 81–116. Oxford University Press.

Tsutsui, Shigeyoshi, Yamamura, Masayuki, and Higuchi, Takahide (1999). Multi-parent re-combination with simplex crossover in real coded genetic algorithms. In *Proceedings of the Genetic and Evolutionary Computation Conference 1999 (GECCO '99)*, pages 657–664.

Yu, Tina and Clack, Chris (1998). Recursion, lambda-abstractions and genetic programming. In Poli, Riccardo, Langdon, W. B., Schoenauer, Marc, Fogarty, Terry, and Banzhaf, Wolfgang, editors, *Late Breaking Papers at EuroGP'98: the First European Workshop on Genetic Programming*, pages 26–30, Paris, France. CSRP-98-10, The University of Birmingham, UK.

Chapter 12

A FUNCTIONAL CROSSOVER OPERATOR FOR GENETIC PROGRAMMING

Josh Bongard[1]

[1]*Department of Computer Science, University of Vermont.*

Abstract   Practitioners of evolutionary algorithms in general, and of genetic programming in particular, have long sought to develop variation operators that automatically preserve and combine useful genetic substructure. This is often pursued with crossover operators that swap genetic material between genotypes that have survived the selection process. However in genetic programming, crossover often has a large phenotypic effect, thereby drastically reducing the probability of a beneficial crossover event. In this paper we introduce a new crossover operator, Functional crossover (FXO), which swaps subtrees between parents based on the subtrees' functional rather than structural similarity. FXO is employed in a genetic programming system identification task, where it is shown that FXO often outperforms standard crossover on both simulated and physically-generated data sets.

Keywords: homologous crossover, crossover operators, system identification

1. Introduction

Genetic programming (Koza, 1992) refers to a family of algorithms that employ various data structures to represent candidate solutions to a given problem. These genotypes either produce behavior directly that is then selected, or are directly or indirectly transformed into a phenotype that in turn exhibits behavior which is subjugated to selection pressure. The choice of genetic encoding, the genotype to phenotype mapping, and the variation operators have a significant impact on the system's evolvability (Wagner and Altenberg, 1996), or ability to continually improve solutions.

The choice of variation operators is of particular interest in that they significantly affect how the population moves through the search space. Mutation operators are designed to discover better variants of a single genotype;

R. Riolo et al. (eds.), *Genetic Programming Theory and Practice VII*,
Genetic and Evolutionary Computation, DOI 10.1007/978-1-4419-1626-6_12,
© Springer Science + Business Media, LLC 2010

crossover operators on the other hand should, when implemented properly, combine useful genetic substructure from multiple genotypes. Because most genetic programming instantiations are tree-based, crossover typically involves swapping subtrees between two parent trees, and this structural change often has a large phenotypic effect on the resulting genotypes. As originally articulated by Fischer (Fischer, 1930), the magnitude of the phenotypic effect of a genetic perturbation is inversely proportional to the probability of that perturbation being beneficial. For this reason it is often observed that random subtree crossover can adversely affect the performance of a genetic programming system. It may favor gradual increase in the size of genotypes over evolutionary time without providing any fitness benefit, a problem known as bloat (Langdon and Poli, 1997), and/or it may slow search by producing offspring that are less fit than their parents.

Several crossover operators have been proposed in the GP literature to improve their ability to combine useful genetic substructure from several parent genotypes. Headless chicken crossover (Jones, 1995) crosses subtrees between two GP trees in which one tree has survived selection while the second is created randomly in an attempt to introduce fresh genetic material into the population. Size fair crossover (Langdon, 1999) crosses subtrees between parent trees with a probability that is proportional to the size similarity between the selected subtrees. Homologous crossover refers to a family of crossover operators that attempt to preserve the context of the two crossed subtrees within their parent trees. D'haeseleer (D'haeseleer, 1994) has described deterministic and Langdon (Langdon, 1999) probabilistic homologous crossover operators that swap subtrees based on the similarity of their positions within their parent trees. Other homologous crossover operators based on syntactic similarity (Poli and Langdon, 1998; Nordin et al., 1999) have met with limited success.

Several researchers have argued that genetic material should be combined based on its semantic, rather than syntactic or structural similarity. Semantic crossover (Beadle and Johnson, 2008) uses standard (random) crossover between two trees and then retains the resulting trees only if they differ semantically from their parents. In enzyme genetic programming (Lones and Tyrrell, 2001), genotypes are composed of independent elements that attach to one another based on their input and output characteristics. Crossover is accomplished by injecting elements from a donor into an existing genotype; the donated components will only be incorporated into the new genotype if they can connect to existing components.

In this paper we introduce a crossover operator that swaps subtrees based on their functional (semantic) rather than structural (syntactic) similarity, in an attempt to reduce the magnitude of the phenotypic effect of the cross. The next section describes this functional crossover (FXO) operator and its application to a system identification task. Section 3 contrasts FXO with standard crossover and no crossover, and section 4 provides some concluding remarks.

2. GP-based system identification

In previous work (Bongard and Lipson, 2007) genetic programming was applied to the problem of nonlinear system identification, in which coupled, nonlinear systems composed of multiple state variables are modeled as sets of ordinary differential equations. The system is composed of two components: a modeling and testing component. The modeling component uses genetic programming to evolve a population of models to describe a subset of time series data extracted from the system under study. The testing component uses the model population to derive a new set of initial conditions with which to perturb the system, and thereby generate new useful training data.

The algorithm proceeds as follows. Initially, a random set of initial conditions is provided to the target system, which generates a short tract of time series data in response. The modeling phase then commences by creating 15 random models and training them against this training data for 200 generations. A model's fitness is determined as its ability to reproduce as closely as possible the behavior of the target system when integrated starting with the same set of initial conditions.

Model evolution is then paused, and the testing component commences by creating 15 random sets of initial conditions. Each initial condition is provided to each of the current models, and the fitness of each set of initial conditions is determined as the rate of divergence in the models' predictions about how the system would respond to these initial conditions. The initial conditions are optimized for 200 generations, and the most fit set of initial conditions is provided to the target system, which generates a second tract of time series data in response. This second tract is added to the training set, and the modeling component recommences evolution with the current set of models, and re-optimizes them against both time series tracts in the training set for 200 generations. This cycle of system interrogation, modeling and testing is repeated a set number of times during each experiment, and is summarized in Fig. 12-1.

During modeling, it was found previously that integrating all of the ODEs describing each state variable together, and then computing the fitness of the model as a whole has low evolvability: If there is coupling between a well-modeled and a poorly-modeled state variable in a model, then that model will obtain an overall low fitness because the poorly-modeled ODE will drag the well-modeled state variable off course, and this well-modeled component will be lost during evolution. In (Bongard and Lipson, 2007) a technique called *partitioning* was introduced in which each ODE is integrated and evaluated separately, even though there may be coupling between the variables. This is

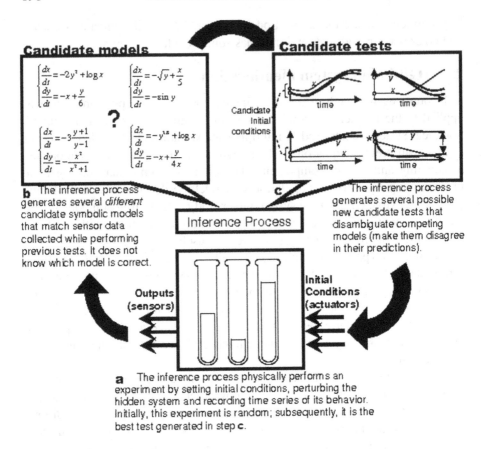

Figure 12-1. Overview of the GP-based system identification approach.

accomplished as follows. During each time step of the integration of the ODE describing a state variable, if there is a reference to another state variable in the GP tree then the value of that state variable generated by the target system, at that time step, is substituted into the terminal node. At the end of the modeling phase, the newly-optimized ODEs for each model are integrated back together to produce a full model. For more details about this methodology, please refer to (Bongard and Lipson, 2007).

Functional crossover

In the initial experiments using this system (Bongard and Lipson, 2007), crossover was not used as it was imperative to maintain variation in the population so that the testing component could induce disagreement amongst the predictions of the models for a given set of initial conditions, and it is well-known that crossover can reduce population hetereogeneity without necessarily conferring increased evolvability (e.g. (Bongard, 2007)). In order to improve the probability that crossover will incorporate useful genetic substructure into the receiving GP tree, a crossover operator that relies on semantic similarity between the two subtrees to be crossed was formulated and investigated here: functional crossover (FXO).

Given n state variables and 15 models, the population contains a total of $15n$ ODEs encoded as GP trees that are optimized. While each ODE is integrated, the minimum and maximum value that is passed upward by each node is recorded at that node. This process records the range of values experienced by each node during integration. After integration, the fitness of an ODE is computed as the error between the time series produced by the ODE and the time series produced by the target system for the corresponding state variable. A copy of each evaluated ODE is created, and the copy is mutated using standard GP mutation operators. The child ODE is integrated and evaluated: if its fitness is higher than its parent ODE, the parent is discarded and the child retained; otherwise, the child is discarded and the parent retained.

This experimental regime without crossover was contrasted to a second regime in which both mutation and standard GP crossover was employed. After all $15n$ ODEs are evaluated, they are copied and mutated. Within each of the n subgroups of 15 ODEs, a pair of the copies is chosen at random and crossed: a node is chosen at random in both trees, and the subtrees with those nodes as roots are swapped between trees. If either of the new trees is more fit than its parent, it is retained; otherwise, the new tree is discarded.

In the third regime, functional crossover is employed. Within each of the n subgroups of 15 ODEs, a pair of copies is chosen at random, and a node is chosen at random within the first tree. The node in the second tree is found that has the most similar range to that of the chosen node in the first tree, according to

$$\min_{j=1}^{t} \left(\frac{|i\text{min} - j\text{min}| + |i\text{max} - j\text{max}|}{2} \right)$$

where t is the number of nodes in the second tree, j is the index over the nodes being tested in the second tree, i is the index of the node chosen from the first tree, and i_{min} and i_{max} are the minimum and maximum values passed upward by node i during integration, respectively. After finding the most similar node in the second tree, the two subtrees are crossed. In all other respects the third regime is identical to the first and second regimes. Functional crossover is illustrated in Fig 12-2.

3. Results

The three regimes were used to model both synthetic and physical systems. The first set of synthetic systems is shown in Table 12-1, and is composed of eighteen coupled, nonlinear systems with from 2 to 7 state variables. For

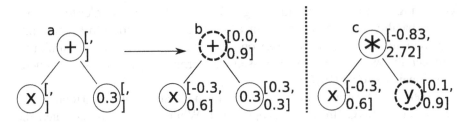

Figure 12-2. Functional crossover. While a GP tree is evaluated (a) the minimum and maximum values that pass through each node are recorded (b). If a node in the tree is then selected for crossover (b; dashed line), a second tree is chosen at random, and the node with the most similar range is found (c; dashed line), and those subtrees are then crossed as in standard GP crossover.

Table 12-1. The eighteen coupled nonlinear systems used for initial modeling.

	System 1	System 2	System 3
	a	b	c
$dx_1/dt =$	$-3x_1 - 3x_1x_2 + 2x_2x_2$	$-3x_1x_1 + 3x_1x_2 + 3x_2x_2$	$3x_1x_1 - x_1x_2 - x_2x_2$
$dx_2/dt =$	$-x_1x_1 - 3x_1x_2 - 2x_2x_2$	$-3x_1x_1 - 2x_1x_2 + 2x_2x_2$	$x_1x_1 + 3x_1x_2 - x_2x_2$
	d	e	f
$dx_1/dt =$	$-3x_1x3 - 2x_2x_3 - 3x_3x_3$	$-x_1x_2 + x_1x_3 - x_2x_3$	$-3x_1x_2 + x_1x_3 - x_3x_3$
$dx_2/dt =$	$-3x_1x_2 + x_1x_3 - 3x_2x_3$	$x_1x_1 + 2x_1x_2 + 2x_2x_3$	$-2x_1x_3 + 3x_2x_3 + 3x_3x_3$
$dx_3/dt =$	$3x_1x_2 + 3x_1x_3 - x_2x_3$	$-2x_1x_1 + x_1x_2 - 3x_2x_3$	$2x_1x_2 - 2x_1x_3 - 2x_2x_3$
	g	h	i
$dx_1/dt =$	$-x_1x_1 + 2x_2x_3 + 2x_3x_3$	$x_1x_4 + x_2x_4 + x_4x_4$	$-3x_1x_1 + 3x_1x_2 + 3x_2x_4$
$dx_2/dt =$	$x_1x_2 - 3x_1x_3 - 3x_2x_3$	$-3x_1x_2 - 2x_2x_3 - 3x_3x_4$	$-x_1x_1 - 2x_1x_3 - 3x_4x_4$
$dx_3/dt =$	$-x_1x_1 - x_2x_4 + 3x_4x_4$	$2x_1x_2 - x_1x_3 + 2x_2x_4$	$-2x_1x_4 + x_2x_2 - 3x_3x_4$
$dx_4/dt =$	$-3x_1x_2 - 3x_1x_4 - 3x_3x_4$	$x_1x_3 + 3x_2x_3 - x_3x_4$	$-x_1x_2 + 2x_1x_4 - 3x_3x_4$
	j	k	l
$dx_1/dt =$	$-3x_1x_5 + 3x_2x_3 - 3x_2x_5$	$-2x_2x_2 + 3x_3x_5 + 2x_4x_5$	$2x_1x_4 + 2x_2x_3 - x_2x_4$
$dx_2/dt =$	$-3x_1x_3 - 2x_3x_4 - x_4x_5$	$3x_1x_2 + x_1x_5 - 2x_2x_5$	$x_1x_3 + 3x_1x_4 + x_2x_4$
$dx_3/dt =$	$x_1x_1 - 3x_1x_4 + x_2x_4$	$x_1x_2 + 2x_2x_5 + 2x_4x_5$	$-2x_1x_1 + 2x_1x_2 - 3x_1x_3$
$dx_4/dt =$	$3x_1x_3 - 3x_1x_4 + 2x_2x_2$	$2x_1x_2 + 3x_1x_5 - x_4x_5$	$-3x_2x_5 + 3x_3x_4 - x_3x_5$
$dx_5/dt =$	$3x_1x_4 + 3x_3x_3 + 3x_3x_4$	$2x_1x_5 - x_2x_5 - 2x_5x_5$	$x_1x_1 + x_1x_5 + x_2x_3$
	m	n	o
$dx_1/dt =$	$-2x_1x_6 + x_2x_4 - 2x_2x_6$	$-2x_1x_3 - 3x_2x_4 + 2x_3x_6$	$x_1x_5 + x_1x_6 + x_4x_5$
$dx_2/dt =$	$x_1x_4 - x_1x_5 - 2x_4x_4$	$-3x_2x_4 + x_3x_4 - x_3x_6$	$-2x_2x_5 - 2x_2x_6 + 2x_3x_6$
$dx_3/dt =$	$2x_2x_5 - x_3x_4 + x_5x_5$	$-x_1x_2 - x_1x_3 + x_4x_6$	$-x_1x_5 - 2x_3x_4 + x_4x_4$
$dx_4/dt =$	$-3x_4x_5 - 2x_4x_6 + 2x_5x_5$	$-x_1x_4 + x_3x_5 - 2x_4x_6$	$3x_1x_2 + 3x_2x_3 - 2x_4x_5$
$dx_5/dt =$	$x_3x_6 - 2x_4x_4 - 3x_4x_5$	$3x_1x_2 - 3x_1x_6 - x_5x_6$	$-3x_1x_5 + x_2x_2 + 3x_2x_6$
$dx_6/dt =$	$x_3x_4 - x_3x_6 + 2x_4x_6$	$-3x_1x_3 - 2x_1x_6 - 3x_4x_6$	$-x_2x_5 - 2x_3x_5 - 3x_5x_6$
	p	q	r
$dx_1/dt =$	$-x_2x_2 - x_1x_2 + 3x_1x_1$	$-2x_2x_3 - 3x_1x_3 - 3x_3x_3$	$-3x_1x_1 + 3x_2x_2 + 3x_1x_2$
$dx_2/dt =$	$3x_1x_2 - x_2x_2 + x_1x_1$	$-3x_1x_2 - 3x_2x_3 + x_1x_3$	$-2x_1x_2 - 3x_1x_1 + 2x_2x_2$
$dx_3/dt =$	$2x_6x_7 - 2x_4x_4 + 3x_5x_7$	$3x_1x_3 - x_2x_3 + 3x_1x_2$	$-3x_4x_7 - 3x_3x_7 + 3x_4x_5$
$dx_4/dt =$	$x_3x_7 + 3x_3x_4 - 2x_4x_7$	$2x_5x_6 - x_4x_4 + 2x_6x_6$	$-2x_5x_6 - x_6x_7 - 3x_3x_5$
$dx_5/dt =$	$2x_4x_7 + 2x_6x_7 + x_3x_4$	$x_4x_5 - 3x_5x_6 - 3x_4x_6$	$x_4x_6 - 3x_3x_6 + x_3x_3$
$dx_6/dt =$	$3x_3x_7 - x_6x_7 + 2x_3x_4$	$3x_7x_7 - x_5x_7 - x_4x_4$	$2x_4x_4 + 3x_3x_5 - 3x_3x_6$
$dx_7/dt =$	$2x_3x_7 - 2x_7x_7 - x_4x_7$	$-3x_6x_7 - 3x_4x_5 - 3x_4x_7$	$3x_3x_6 + 3x_5x_5 + 3x_5x_6$

each system, initial conditions for a state variable could range between zero and unity. Two hundred independent trials of the first regime, 200 trials of the second regime and 200 trials of the third regime were applied to each system. Each experiment was conducted for 40 cycles. At the end of each pass through the modeling component, the objective error of the best model was calcuated: the physical system generates time series that the model was not trained on, and

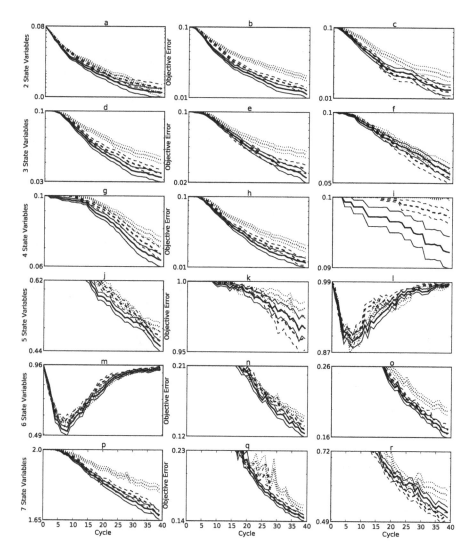

Figure 12-3. Relative modeling performance against the 18 synthetic systems using no crossover (dotted), random crossover (dashed), and functional crossover (solid). Thick lines indicate mean error; thin lines indicate one unit of standard error of the mean.

the error of the model is calculated. The relative errors of the models produced by the three regimes is shown in Fig. 12-3, and the sizes of those models in Fig. 12-4.

For 6 of the 18 systems, functional crossover led to signficantly more accurate models than when either no crossover or standard crossover was employed (Fig. 12-3a,b,d,g,i,j). It can be noted that for these systems, FXO also tended to produce more compact models (Fig. 12-4a,b,d,g,i,j), despite the fact that

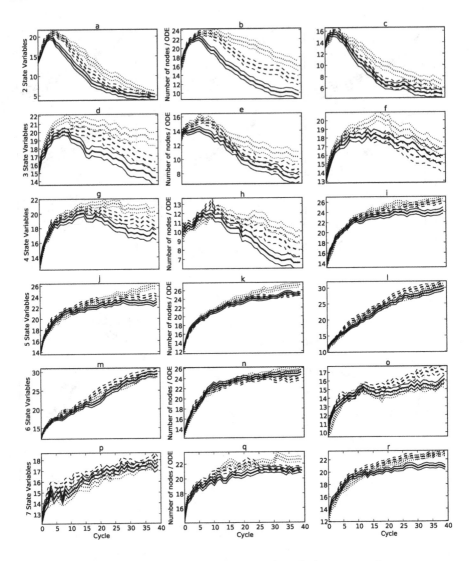

Figure 12-4. Relative model sizes resulting from the 18 synthetic systems using no crossover (dotted), random crossover (dashed), and functional crossover (solid).

there is no explicit selection pressure for smaller models. It is hypothesized that FXO produces more accurate and more compact models in these systems because FXO is able to swap out a large subtree that is an approximation of some function that can be expressed using fewer nodes, and therefore has a higher probability of swapping in a subtree from another tree that represents this function in a more compact way. For several of the other systems FXO

Table 12-2. The four synthetic target systems. a: A frictionless nondamped pendulum; b: two species competing for a common resource; c: a synthetic system with high degree; and d: a model of the Lac operon metabolic circuit in E. coli bacteria.

a: Pendulum	b: Lotka-Volterra
$d\theta/dt = \omega$	$dx/dt = 3x - 2xy - x^2$
$d\omega/dt = -9.8\sin(\theta)$	$dy/dt = 2y - xy - y^2$
c: High Degree	d: *Lac* operon
$dx/dt = -x^9 y^{11}$	$dG/dt = A^2/(A^2+1) - 0.01G + 0.001$
$dx/dt = -x^{11} y^9$	$dA/dt = G(L/(L+1) - A/(A+1))$
	$dL/dt = -GL/(L+1)$

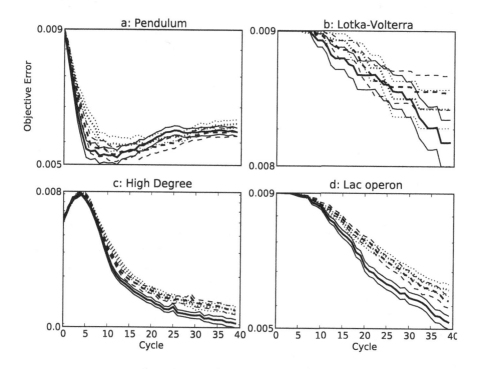

Figure 12-5. Relative modeling performance against the four target systems using no crossover (dotted), random crossover (dashed), and functional crossover (solid).

produced more accurate models but not significantly so (Fig. 12-3e,h,n,o,p,q), and for no systems did the other two regimes signficantly outperform FXO.

The three regimes were also applied to four target systems that are manually-derived models of nonlinear mechanical (Pendulum), ecological (Lotka-Volterra) and biological (Lac operon) systems (Table 12-2). The initial values

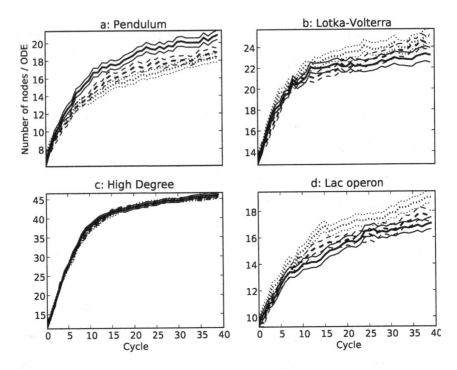

Figure 12-6. Relative model sizes resulting from the four target systems using no crossover (dotted), random crossover (dashed), and functional crossover (solid).

for each state variable in each system was restricted to the range $[0, 1]$. The models trained against the pendulum could be composed of algebraic and trigonometric functions; the Lotka-Volterra and high degree models were restricted to algebraic operators; and the Lac operon models were allowed algebraic functions and the Hill function $(x/(x+1))$. Terminal nodes were restricted to state variable references and floating-point constants. Fig. 12-5 reports the relative errors of the best models from 200 independent trials run using each of the three experimental regimes. Fig. 12-6 reports the relative sizes of these models.

As can be seen in Fig. 12-5, functional crossover signficantly outperforms the other two regimes when employed for modeling the system of high degree and the Lac operon (Fig. 12-5c,d), provides some advantage for the Lotka-Volterra system (Fig. 12-5b), and provides a slight advantage for the pendulum, as does standard crossover. Fig. 12-6 indicates that for two of the systems functional crossover produces larger trees (Fig. 12-6a,c) while for the other two systems produces more compact trees (Fig. 12-6b,d).

Finally, four physical systems were modeled by the three regimes. The first three systems are modifications of a physical pendulum, as shown in Fig. 12-7. Sensors in the pendulum's base record the angle of the arm relative to gravity,

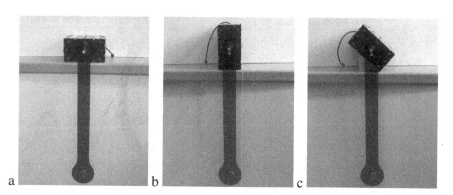

Figure 12-7. The pendulum was swung when it was in three different configurations, producing the data sets reported in Fig. 12-8a-c.

and angular velocity. The pendulum was swung and data was recorded when the base rested flat on a table (Fig. 12-7a); when the base was rotated 90 degrees counterclockwise (Fig. 12-7b), and rotated 138 degrees counterclockwise (Fig. 12-7c). The resulting data from these systems are reported as phase diagrams in Fig. 12-8a-c. The fourth physical system was a data set reflecting change in population for the Canadian lynx and artic hare, as estimated by numbers of pelts recorded per winter by the Hudsons Bay Company (Odum and Odum, 1971). The data set indicates oscillations in both populations over a 100-year period (Fig. 12-8d).

Unlike the systems investigated so far, it is assumed that data has been previously generated by these systems, so the testing components cannot perturb the system based on model disagreement. Rather, the testing component searches for a time index within the existing data from the system for which, when the values for the state variables at that index are supplied to the models and the models are integrated, the models diverge in their predictions about future time indices. After a short period of optimization, the time index that induces maximum model disagreement, and the subsequent four time indices, are added to the training set.

For two of the data sets, crossover slows evolutionary search such that the regime with no crossover produces more accurate models (Fig. 12-9b,d). For the flat pendulum, there is no difference in model accuracy across the three experimental regimes. However for the pendulum when rotated 138 degrees counterclockwise, functional crossover significantly outperforms the other two regimes. Unlike for the previous systems, functional crossover enlarges the size of models, compared to the other two experimental regimes.

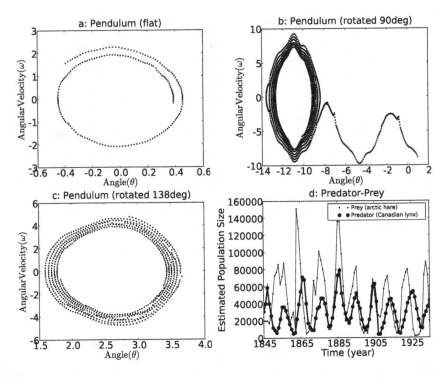

Figure 12-8. The four data sets produced by the four modeled physical systems. The data sets produced by the pendulum (a-c) are represented as phase diagrams; the ecological data set is drawn as a raw time series.

4.   Discussion and conclusions

In general, it was found that functional crossover helped to produce significantly more accurate models across a total of 26 synthetic and physical coupled, nonlinear systems. It is hypothesized that FXO confers an advantage because the phenotypic effect of a cross is less severe than a random crossover event. Because the two selected subtrees return values in a similar range, the newly-grafted subtree will return values similar to those returned by the original subtree, and will therefore impact the overall behavior of its parent tree less than if random crossover is employed. As has been known for some time (Fischer, 1930), a genetic perturbation has a higher probability of conferring an advantage the more mild the phenotypic effect of that perturbation is. It seems likely that this dynamic is the cause of the observed benefit of FXO, however more detailed investigation is required to validate this hypothesis.

It was found that for the first set of 18 systems, FXO tended to produce more accurate and more compact models. It is hypothesized that this is a result of FXO's ability to swap out a large subtree that approximates a function that can be expressed with fewer nodes, and has a higher probability of swapping in a

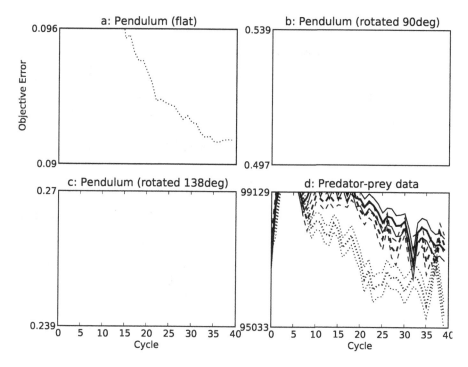

Figure 12-9. Relative modeling performance against the four physical systems using no crossover (dotted), random crossover (dashed), and functional crossover (solid).

subtree from another tree that encodes this function more compactly, compared to random crossover. However, increased model accuracy was not accompanied by model compactness in the other systems. In particular for the physical systems, increased model accuracy (Fig. 12-9) was accompanied by an increase in model size (Fig. 12-10). It is believed that for the physical pendulum, an equation that would describe its friction may not be easily modelable, so the trees grow in size in an attempt to account for this.

Despite this, FXO was able to significantly outperform the no crossover and random crossover regimes for one of the pendulum arrangements (Fig. 12-9c). It seems likely the reason for this is that more data was collected for this arrangement compared to the data set associated with the flat pendulum (12-8a), and there is less noise present than in the data set collected from the pendulum rotated 90 degrees counterclockwise, which rotated over the top (12-8b).

Trees with similar structure may encode very different functions, which suggests that structural crossover operators for genetic programming may be of limited utility. Conversely, trees with very different structure may encode similar functionality as neutral genetic structure tends to be prevalent in such systems, and the commutative properties of many operators admits to alternative

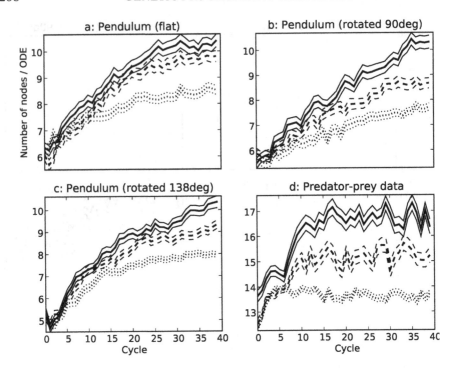

Figure 12-10. Relative model sizes resulting from the four physical systems using no crossover (dotted), random crossover (dashed), and functional crossover (solid).

encoding possibilities. The one current limitation of semantics-based crossover operators is that they are somewhat domain specific: tree structure tends to be similar across GP implementations, but the behavior of those trees is domain specific. That being said, FXO can still be employed in any GP system if trees are employed to compute a numerical function. It would also be relatively straightforward to develop semantic similarity metrics for other problem domains. For example, in the Central Place Food Foraging problem (Koza, 1992), a subtree describes a subset of an agent's behavior. During the evaluation of a tree, the area traversed by an agent as a result of each subtree may be recorded. FXO may then cross subtrees based on geometric similarities between the areas traversed by agents controlled by different trees.

Future work is planned in which this crossover operator will be compared directly to existing syntactic and semantic crossover opeators. Also, a probabilistic version of FXO (P-FXO) will be investigated in which subtrees are chosen from the second parent probabilistically, rather than deterministically based on nodes' functional similarity. Finally, rather than comparing minimum and maximum values experienced by nodes in different trees, probability distributions will be employed to better compare functional similarity between genetic substructure from different members of the population.

Acknowledgment

This work is supported in part by a 2007 Microsoft New Faculty Fellowship, and National Science Foundation grant EPS-0701410.

References

Beadle, Lawrence and Johnson, Colin (2008). Semantically driven crossover in genetic programming. In Wang, Jun, editor, *Proceedings of the IEEE World Congress on Computational Intelligence*, pages 111–116, Hong Kong. IEEE Computational Intelligence Society, IEEE Press.

Bongard, J. (2007). Action-selection and crossover strategies for self-modeling machines. In *Proceedings of the 9th annual conference on Genetic and evolutionary computation*, pages 198–205. ACM New York, NY, USA.

Bongard, J. and Lipson, H. (2007). Automated reverse engineering of nonlinear dynamical systems. *Proceedings of the National Academy of Sciences*, 104(24):9943.

D'haeseleer, Patrik (1994). Context preserving crossover in genetic programming. In *Proceedings of the 1994 IEEE World Congress on Computational Intelligence*, volume 1, pages 256–261, Orlando, Florida, USA. IEEE Press.

Fischer, R.A. (1930). *The Genetical Theory of Natural Selection*. Clarendon.

Jones, T. (1995). Crossover, macromutation, and population-based search. In *Proceedings of the Sixth International Conference on Genetic Algorithms*, pages 73–80. Morgan Kaufmann.

Koza, John R. (1992). A genetic approach to the truck backer upper problem and the inter-twined spiral problem. In *Proceedings of IJCNN International Joint Conference on Neural Networks*, volume IV, pages 310–318. IEEE Press.

Langdon, W. B. (1999). Size fair and homologous tree genetic programming crossovers. In Banzhaf, Wolfgang, Daida, Jason, Eiben, Agoston E., Garzon, Max H., Honavar, Vasant, Jakiela, Mark, and Smith, Robert E., editors, *Proceedings of the Genetic and Evolutionary Computation Conference*, volume 2, pages 1092–1097, Orlando, Florida, USA. Morgan Kaufmann.

Langdon, W. B. and Poli, R. (1997). Fitness causes bloat. Technical Report CSRP-97-09, University of Birmingham, School of Computer Science, Birmingham, B15 2TT, UK.

Lones, Michael A. and Tyrrell, Andy M. (2001). Enzyme genetic programming. In *Proceedings of the 2001 Congress on Evolutionary Computation, CEC 2001*, pages 1183–1190, COEX, World Trade Center, 159 Samseong-dong, Gangnam-gu, Seoul, Korea. IEEE Press.

Nordin, Peter, Banzhaf, Wolfgang, and Francone, Frank D. (1999). Efficient evolution of machine code for CISC architectures using instruction blocks and homologous crossover. In Spector, Lee, Langdon, William B., O'Reilly, Una-May, and Angeline, Peter J., editors, *Advances in Genetic Programming 3*, chapter 12, pages 275–299. MIT Press, Cambridge, MA, USA.

Odum, E.P. and Odum, H.T. (1971). *Fundamentals of Ecology*. Saunders Philadelphia.

Poli, Riccardo and Langdon, William B. (1998). Schema theory for genetic programming with one-point crossover and point mutation. *Evolutionary Computation*, 6(3):231–252.

Wagner, G.P. and Altenberg, L. (1996). Complex adaptations and the evolution of evolvability. *Evolution*, 50(3):967–976.

Chapter 13

SYMBOLIC REGRESSION OF CONDITIONAL TARGET EXPRESSIONS

Michael F. Korns[1]

[1]*Freeman Investment Management, 1 Plum Hollow, Henderson, Nevada, 89052 USA.*

Abstract   This chapter examines techniques for improving symbolic regression systems in cases where the target expression contains conditionals. In three previous papers we experimented with combining high performance techniques from the literature to produce a large scale, industrial strength, symbolic regression-classification system . Performance metrics across multiple problems show deterioration in accuracy for problems where the target expression contains conditionals. The techniques described herein are shown to improve accuracy on such conditional problems. Nine base test cases, from the literature, are used to test the improvement in accuracy. A previously published regression system combining standard genetic programming with abstract expression grammars, particle swarm optimization, differential evolution, context aware crossover and age-layered populations is tested on the nine base test cases. The regression system is enhanced with these additional techniques: pessimal vertical slicing, splicing of uncorrelated champions via abstract conditional expressions, and abstract mutation and crossover. The enhanced symbolic regression system is applied to the nine base test cases and an improvement in accuracy is observed.

Keywords: Abstract Expression Grammars, Differential Evolution, Genetic Programming, Particle Swarm, Symbolic Regression

1.   Introduction

This chapter examines techniques for improving symbolic regression systems in cases where the target expression contains conditionals. In three previous papers (Korns, 2006; Korns, 2007; Korns and Nunez, 2008) our pursuit of industrial scale performance with large-scale, symbolic regression problems, required us to reexamine many commonly held beliefs and, of necessity, to borrow a number of techniques from disparate schools of genetic programming and "recombine" them in ways not normally seen in the published literature.

R. Riolo et al. (eds.), *Genetic Programming Theory and Practice VII*,
Genetic and Evolutionary Computation, DOI 10.1007/978-1-4419-1626-6_13,
© Springer Science + Business Media, LLC 2010

The evolutionary techniques, as of the three previous papers, vetted for efficacy in symbolic regression are as follows:

- Standard tree-based genetic programming

- Vertical slicing and out-of-sample scoring during training

- Grammar template genetic programming

- Abstract expression grammars utilizing swarm intelligence

- Context aware cross over

- Age-layered populations

- Random noise terms for learning asymmetric noise

- Bagging

While the above techniques, described in detail in (Korns and Nunez, 2008), produce a symbolic regression system of breadth and strength, performance metrics across multiple problems show deterioration in accuracy for problems where the target expression contains conditionals. Using the nine base test cases from (Korns, 2007) as a training set, to test for improvements in accuracy, we enhanced our symbolic regression system with these additional techniques which we will show improve accuracy:

- Pessimal vertical slicing

- Splicing

- Abstract mutation and crossover

For purposes of comparison, all results in this paper were achieved on two workstation computers, specifically an Intel Core 2 Duo Processor T7200 (2.00GHz/667MHz/4MB) and a Dual-Core AMD Opteron Processor 8214 (2.21GHz), running our Analytic Information Server software generating Lisp agents that compile to use the on-board Intel registers and on-chip vector processing capabilities so as to maximize execution speed, whose details can be found at *www.korns.com/Document_Lisp Language_Guide.html*. Furthermore, our Analytic Information Server is in the founding process of becoming an open source software project.

Testing Regimen

Our testing regimen uses only statistical best practices out-of-sample testing techniques. We test each of the nine test cases on matrices of 10000 rows (samples) by 5 columns (input variables) with no noise, and on matrices of 10000 rows by 20 columns with 40% noise, before drawing any performance conclusions. Taking all these combinations together, this creates a total of 18 separate test cases. For each test a training matrix is filled with random numbers between -50 and +50. The target expression for the test case is applied to the training matrix to compute the dependent variable and the required noise is added. The symbolic regression system is trained on the training matrix to produce the regression champion. Following training, a testing matrix is filled with random numbers between -50 and +50. The target expression for the test case is applied to the testing matrix to compute the dependent variable and the required noise is added. The regression champion is evaluated on the testing matrix for all scoring (i.e. out of sample testing).

Fitness Measure

Standard regression techniques often utilize least squares error (LSE) as a fitness measure. In our case we normalize by dividing LSE by the standard deviation of "Y" (dependent variable). This normalization allows us to meaningfully compare the normalized least squared error (NLSE) between different problems.

Of special interest is combining fitness functions to support both symbolic regression and classification of common stocks into long and short candidates. Specifically we would like to measure how successful we are at predicting the future top 10% best performers (*long candidates*) and the future 10% worst performers (*short candidates*).[1]

Briefly, let the dependent variable, Y, be the future profits of a set of securities, and the variable, EY, be the *estimates* of Y. If we were prescient, we could automatically select the best future performers *actualBestLongs, ABL,* and worst future performers *actualBestShorts, ABS,* by sorting on Y and selecting an equally weighted set of the top and bottom 10%. Since we are not prescient, we can only select the best future estimated performers *estimatedBestLongs, EBL,* and estimated worst future performers *estimatedBestShorts, EBS,* by sorting on EY and selecting an equally weighted set of the top and bottom 10%. If we let the function *avgy* represent the average y over the specified set of fitness cases, then clearly the following will always be the case.

---

[1] The concept of long short tail classification is described in detail in (Korns, 2007).

- -1 <= ((avgy(EBL)-avgy(EBS))/(avgy(ABL)-avgy(ABS))) <= 1

We can construct a fitness measure known as tail classification error, TCE, such that

- TCE = ((1-((avgy(EBL)-avgy(EBS))/(avgy(ABL)-avgy(ABS))))/2)

and therefore

- 0 <= TCE <= 1

A situation where TCE < 0.50 indicates we are making money speculating on our short and long candidates. Obviously 0 is a perfect score (we might as well have been prescient) and 1 is a perfectly imperfect score (other traders should do the opposite of what we do). Clearly, considering our financial motivation, we are interested in achieving superior regression fitness measures; but, we are also interested in superior classification. In fact, even if the regression fitness (NLSE) is poor but the classification (TCE) is good, we can still have an advantage, in the financial markets, with our symbolic regression-classification tool.

Since both the TCE and NLSE fitness measures are normalized, we can make standard interpretations of results across a wide range of experiments. In the case of NLSE, any score of 0.30 or less is very good (meaning the average least squared error is less than 0.30 of the standard deviation of Y), while a score of less than 0.50 is okay, NLSE scores greater than 0.50 indicate increasingly poor regression results. Our system automatically averages the estimates of the ten top champions *(bagging)* whenever the training NLSE of the top champion is greater than 0.50. Finally, a TCE score of less than 0.20 is excellent. A TCE score of less than 0.30 is good; while, a TCE of 0.30 or greater is poor.

2.   Previous Results on Nine Base Problems

The previously published results (Korns and Nunez, 2008) of training on the nine base training models on 10,000 rows and five columns with no random noise and only 20 generations allowed, are shown in Table 1-1.[2]

In general, training time is very reasonable given the difficulty of some of the problems and the limited number of training generations allowed. Average percent error performance varies from excellent to poor with the *linear* and *cubic* problems showing the best performance. Extreme differences between training error and testing error in the *mixed* and *ratio* problems suggest over-fitting.

Surprisingly, long and short classification is fairly robust in most cases with the exception of the *ratio*, and *mixed* test cases. The salient observation is the

[2]The nine base test cases are described in detail in (Korns, 2007).

Table 13-1. Result For 10K rows by 5 columns with 0% Random Noise

Test	Minutes	Train-NLSE	Test-NLSE	Test-TCE
linear	0	0.01	0.01	0.00
cubic	0	0.00	0.00	0.00
cross	107	0.37	0.39	0.02
elipse	0	0.00	0.00	0.00
hidden	3	0.00	0.05	0.00
cyclic	4	0.04	0.14	0.06
hyper	369	0.00	0.00	0.00
mixed	123	0.24	1.65	0.13
ratio	6	0.03	1.05	0.50

Table 13-2. Result for 10K rows by 20 columns with 40% Random Noise

Test	Minutes	Train-NLSE	Test-NLSE	Test-TCE
linear	10	0.11	0.11	0.00
cubic	10	0.11	0.11	0.00
cross	9	0.80	0.80	0.19
elipse	12	0.45	0.46	0.05
hidden	10	0.99	0.99	0.45
cyclic	8	0.39	0.91	0.18
hyper	9	0.96	0.96	0.36
mixed	12	0.69	1.85	0.07
ratio	26	0.95	1.18	0.46

relative ease of classification compared to regression even in problems with this much noise. In some of the test cases, testing NLSE is either close to or exceeds the standard deviation of Y (not very good); however, in many of the test cases classification is below 0.20. (very good).

The previously published results (Korns and Nunez, 2008) of training on the nine base training models on 10,000 rows and twenty columns with 40% random noise and only 20 generations allowed, are shown in Table 1-2.

Clearly the symbolic regression system performs most poorly on the test cases *hidden*, *mixed* and *ratio* with conditional target expressions. There is evidence of over-fitting shown by the extreme differences between training error and testing error. Plus, the testing TCE is very poor in both ratio test cases. Taken together, these scores portray a symbolic regression system which is not ready to handle industrial strength problems containing conditional target expressions.

Enhancements which will improve our regression scores on the two conditional base test cases, without also greatly reducing the efficiency of the symbolic regression system on the other test cases, is the subject of the remainder of this chapter.

3.   Pessimal Vertical Slicing

In (Korns, 2006) we describe an out-of-sample testing procedure we call *vertical slicing*, wherein the rows (samples) in the training matrix X are sorted in ascending order by the dependent values, Y. Then the sorted rows in X are subdivided into S *vertical slices* by selecting every S-th row to be in each vertical slice. Thus the first vertical slice is the set of training rows as follows *X[0], X[S], X[2*S], ...* .

Since Y represents the *behavior* of the system to be learned, sorting X by Y insures that each vertical slice contains training examples equally distributed across the range of behaviors of the system. We train on a single vertical slice, but score across every fitness example in X.

Vertical slicing reduces training time (which in multiple regression and swarm grammars can be time consuming); while simultaneously reducing over fitting by scoring fitness over all slices (out-of-sample testing).[3]

Our normal vertical slicing sampling size is one out of every hundred training cases. Of course with difficult conditional target expressions, while this sampling size reduces training time, it also reduces accuracy. So we face a conundrum. Increasing the sampling rate increases accuracy; but, also greatly increases the time to manage easier test cases.

One solution is to leave our normal sampling size as it is (one out of every hundred training cases) until an emergency is declared. If we get to the end of the first training epoch (currently set to ten generations) and the champion NLSE is .50 or higher, then we declare an emergency. The emergency sampling rate is one out of every four training cases. Increasing the emergency sampling rate increases accuracy for the difficult problems; and, has no impact on the easier test cases.

For complete training coverage, we intersperse randomly selected vertical training slices with pessimally selected vertical training slices with respect to the current best-of-breed champion. The pessimal vertical slice, with respect to the current best-of-breed champion, is the vertical slice on which the current champion has the worst fitness scores. Regardless of which vertical slice is selected, as the training subset, we still score across every fitness example in X. Choosing randomly selected training subsets forces complete training

---

[3] The implementation of Vertical Slicing is described in detail in (Korns, 2006).

coverage while still maintaining the out-of-sample scoring so important for avoiding overfitting. Choosing the pessimal training subset forces the system to learning those test cases which have been difficult for the current champion while still maintaining the out-of-sample scoring.

4.   Splicing *Background*

Our system uses a technique known as *aged-layered population structure* (ALPS), devised to minimize premature population convergence.[4] During the course of an ALPS training run we keep track of an elitist pool of all-time champions. As an enhancement, to support splicing, we simultaneously keep track of a second elitist pool of all-time champions *which are uncorrelated to the champions in the elitist pool.* Unfortunately managing the uncorrelated champion pool requires that we perform a standard statistical correlation test for every new champion above a certain NLSE. This process is not free, and therefore it will degrade the performance on the easier test cases to some extent. Nevertheless maintaining an uncorrelated champion pool will allow us to splice uncorrelated champions together using conditional abstract expressions.

Before we can reasonably describe the splicing process in detail, we must provide a brief background on abstract expression grammars as they are used in this symbolic regression system.

In the literature, informal and formal grammars have been used in genetic programming to enhance the representation and the efficiency of a number of applications including symbolic regression - see overviews in (O'Neill and Ryan, 2003) and (Poli et al., 2008). Using a hybrid combination of tree-based GP and formal grammars, where the head of each s-expression is a grammar rule, the standard genetic programming population operators of mutation and crossover can be used without alteration. We use standard mutation and crossover operations (Koza, 1992) and support both simple regression and multiple regression.

A Concrete Expression Grammar

A simple concrete expression grammar suitable for use in most symbolic regression systems would be a C-like grammar with the following basic elements.

- **Real Numbers**: 3.45, -.0982, and 100.389

- **Row Features**: x1, x2, and x5.

- **Operators**: $+, *, /, \%, <, <=, ==, !=, >=, >$

- **Functions**: sqrt(), log(), cube(), sin(), tan(), max(), etc.

---

[4]The implementation of age-layered population structure is described in detail in (Hornby, 2006).

- **Conditional**: (expr1 < expr2) ? expr3 : expr4

Our numeric expressions are JavaScript-like containing the variables **x1** through **xm** (where *m* is the number of columns in the regression problem), real constants such as **2.45** or **-34.687**, with the following operators **+**, **-**, **/**, **%**, *****, **<**, **<=**, **==**, **! =**, **>=**, **>**, and binary functions **expt**, **max**, **min**, and unary operators **abs, cos, cosh, cube, exp, log, sin, sinh, sqrt, square, tan, tanh**, and the ternary conditional expression operator (...) **?** (...) **:** (...);

Our symbolic regression system creates its regression champion using mutation, and cross over; but, the final regression champion will be a compilation of a basic concrete expression such as:

- (*E1*): f = (log(x3)/sin(x2*45.3))>x4 ? tan(x6) : cos(x3)

Computing an NLSE score for f requires only a single pass over every row of X and results in an attribute being added to f by executing the "Score" method compiled into f as follows.

- f.NLSE = f.score(X,Y).

Abstract Constants

Suppose that we are satisfied with the form of the expression in (E1); but, we are not sure that the real constant 45.3 is optimal. The standard genetic programming algorithm does not provide a mechanism for optimizing the real constant, 45.3, other than running the symbolic regression system for more iterations; and, then we are not guaranteed of receiving an improved answer in the same form as in (E1). We can enhance our symbolic regression system with the ability to optimize individual real constants by adding abstract constant rules to our built-in algebraic expression grammar.

- *Abstract Constants*: c1, c2, and c10

Abstract constants represent placeholders for real numbers which are to be optimized by the symbolic regression system. To further optimize f we would alter the expression in (E1) as follows.

- (*E2*): f = (log(x3)/sin(x2***c1**))>x4 ? tan(x6) : cos(x3)

The compiler adds a new real number vector, C, attribute to f such that f.C has as many elements as there are abstract constants in (E2). Optimizing this version of f requires that the built-in Score method compiled into f be changed from a single pass to a multiple pass algorithm in which the real number values in the abstract constant vector, f.C, are iterated until the expression in (E2) produces an optimized NLSE. This new score method has the side effect that executing f.score(X,Y) also alters the abstract constant vector, f.C, to optimal real number choices. Clearly the particle swarm (Eberhart et al., 2001) and differential evolution algorithms provide excellent candidate algorithms for optimizing f.C and they can easily be compiled into f.score by common compilation techniques currently in the main stream. Summarizing, we have a new grammar term, c1, which is a reference to the 1st element of the real number vector, f.C (in C language syntax c1 == f.C[1]). The f.C vector is optimized by scoring f, then altering the values in f.C, then repeating the process iteratively until an optimum NLSE is achieved. Two important features of abstract expression grammars are worth mention here. The overall genetic programming algorithms within the nonlinear regression system do not have to be altered because the swarm and differential learning enhancements are hidden inside the Score method by the abstract expression compiler when appropriate. Furthermore, as Riccardo Poli (Poli et al., 2008) has pointed out, a new population operator can be defined which converts abstract expressions into their concrete counterparts. For instance, if the regression champion agent in (E2) is optimized with:

- f.C == $< 45.396 >$

Then the optimized regression champion agent in (E2) has a concrete conversion counterpart as follows:

- f = (log(x3)/sin(x2***45.396**))>x4 ? tan(x6) : cos(x3)

Since abstract expressions are not grammatically excessively different than concrete expressions, the genetic programming logic in the symbolic regression system will be able to apply the same type of operations (crossover, mutation, etc.) on either type of expression. At different stages in the evolutionary process population operators can be introduced which convert abstract expressions into their optimized concrete counterparts, or even new mutation operators which convert concrete expressions into abstract expressions.

Abstract Features

Suppose that we are satisfied with the form of the expression in (E1); but, we are not sure that the features, x2, x3, and x6, are optimal choices. The standard genetic programming algorithm does not provide a mechanism for optimizing these features other than running the symbolic regression system for more iterations; and, then we are not guaranteed of receiving an improved answer in the same form as in (E1). We can enhance our symbolic regression system with the ability to optimize individual features by adding abstract feature rules to our built-in algebraic expression grammar.

- *Abstract Features*: v1, v2, and v10

Abstract features represent placeholders for features which are to be optimized by the nonlinear regression system. To further optimize f we would alter the expression in (E1) as follows.

- (*E3*): f = $(\log(\mathbf{v1})/\sin(\mathbf{v2}*45.3))>\mathbf{v3}$? $\tan(\mathbf{v4})$: $\cos(\mathbf{v1})$

The compiler adds a new integer vector, V, attribute to f such that f.V has as many elements as there are abstract features in (E3). Each integer element in the f.V vector is constrained between 1 and M, and represents a choice of feature (in x). Optimizing this version of f requires that the built-in Score method compiled into f be changed from a single pass to a multiple pass algorithm in which the integer values in the abstract feature vector, f.V, are iterated until the expression in (E3) produces an optimized NLSE. This new score method has the side effect that executing f.score(X,Y) also alters the abstract feature vector, f.V, to integer choices selecting optimal features (in x). Clearly the genetic algorithm (Man et al., 1999), discrete particle swarm (Eberhart et al., 2001), and discrete differential evolution (Price et al., 2005) algorithms provide excellent candidate algorithms for optimizing f.V and they can easily be compiled into f.score by common compilation techniques currently in the main stream. Summarizing, we have a new grammar term, v1, which is an indirect feature reference thru to the 1st element of the integer vector, f.V (in C language syntax v1 == x[f.V[1]]). The f.V vector is optimized by scoring f, then altering the values in f.V, then repeating the process iteratively until an optimum NLSE is achieved. For instance, the regression champion agent in (E3) is optimized with:

- f.V == < 2, 4, 1, 6 >

Then the optimized regression champion agent in (E3) has a concrete conversion counterpart as follows:

- f = $(\log(\mathbf{x2})/\sin(\mathbf{x4}*45.396))>\mathbf{x1}$? $\tan(\mathbf{x6})$: $\cos(\mathbf{x2})$

Abstract Functions

Similarly, we can enhance our nonlinear regression system with the ability to optimize individual features by adding abstract functions rules to our built-in algebraic expression grammar.

- *Abstract Functions*: f1, f2, and f10

Abstract functions represent placeholders for built-in functions which are to be optimized by the nonlinear regression system. To further optimize f we would alter the expression in (E2) as follows.

- (*E4*): f = (**f1**(x3)/**f2**(x2*45.3)))>x4 ? **f3**(x6) : **f4**(x3)

The compiler adds a new integer vector, F, attribute to f such that f.F has as many elements as there are abstract features in (E4). Each integer element in the f.F vector is constrained between 1 and (number of built-in functions available in the expression grammar), and represents a choice of built-in function. Optimizing this version of f requires that the built-in Score method compiled into f be changed from a single pass to a multiple pass algorithm in which the integer values in the abstract function vector, f.F, are iterated until the expression in (E4) produces an optimized NLSE. This new score method has the side effect that executing f.score(X,Y) also alters the abstract function vector, f.F, to integer choices selecting optimal built-in functions. Clearly the genetic algorithm (Man et al., 1999), discrete particle swarm (Eberhart et al., 2001), and discrete differential evolution (Price et al., 2005) algorithms provide excellent candidate algorithms for optimizing f.F and they can easily be compiled into f.score by common compilation techniques currently in the main stream. Summarizing, we have a new grammar term, f1, which is an indirect function reference thru to the 1st element of the integer vector, f.F (in C language syntax f1 == funtionList[f.F[1]]). The f.F vector is optimized by scoring f, then altering the values in f.F, then repeating the process iteratively until an optimum NLSE is achieved. For instance, if the valid function list in the expression grammar is

- f.functionList = < log, sin, cos, tan, max, min, avg, cube, sqrt >

And the regression champion agent in (E4) is optimized with:

- f.F = < 1, 8, 2, 4 >

Then the optimized regression champion agent in (E4) has a concrete conversion counterpart as follows:

- $f = (\mathbf{log}(x3)/\mathbf{cube}(x2*45.3)) > x4$? $\mathbf{sin}(x6) : \mathbf{tan}(x3)$

The built-in function argument arity issue is easily resolved by having each built-in function ignore any excess arguments and substitute defaults for any missing arguments. Furthermore random noise functions, such as in (Schmidt and Lipson, 2007), can easily be added to the list of available built-in functions in the expression grammar.

5. Splicing *Details*

Assume that we have reached the end of the first training epoch and the best of breed NLSE is so high that we declare an emergency. What action do we take to address this declared emergency?

Our approach is to introduce an end-of-epoch splicing algorithm to fit together uncorrelated champions using abstract conditional expressions. Selecting the fittest champion, *G*, from the elitist all-time champion pool and selecting the fittest champion, *H*, from the uncorrelated champion pool, we create several new candidate champions by splicing together the well formed formulas *G.wff* and *H.wff* via various predefined abstract conditional expressions as follows.

- *B1*: $y = (\mathbf{v1} > \mathbf{c1})$? G.wff : H.wff

- *B2*: $y = (\mathbf{c1} > \mathbf{v1})$? G.wff : H.wff

- *B3*: $y = (\mathbf{v1} > \mathbf{v2})$? G.wff : H.wff

- *B4*: $y = (\mathbf{f1}(\mathbf{v1},\mathbf{v2}) > \mathbf{c1})$? G.wff : H.wff

- *B5*: $y = (\mathbf{f1}(\mathbf{v1},\mathbf{v2}) < \mathbf{c1})$? G.wff : H.wff

- *B6*: $y = (\mathbf{f1}(\mathbf{v1},\mathbf{v2}) > \mathbf{v3})$? G.wff : H.wff

- *B7*: $y = (\mathbf{f1}(\mathbf{v1},\mathbf{v2}) < \mathbf{v3})$? G.wff : H.wff

- *B8*: $y = (\mathbf{f1}(\mathbf{v1},\mathbf{v2}) < \mathbf{f2}(\mathbf{v3},\mathbf{v4}))$? G.wff : H.wff

Finally, at the end of each epoch, the splicing algorithm introduces each of the above abstract expressions into the evolutionary pool trying to improve the NLSE over that of the current best of breed champion. Each of the above splicings is optimized and their ***optimized concrete conversions*** are stored in the appropriate population.

For example, suppose our target expression is shown in (E5) below, our best of breed champion is such that *G.wff* = *tan(x6)*, and our best uncorrelated champion is such that *H.wff* = *cos(x3)*, then we have final training situation as follows.

- (*E5*): f = (log(x3)>x4) ? tan(x6) : cos(x3)

- G.wff = tan(x6)

- H.wff = cos(x3)

Clearly, given the above situation, the splicing algorithm would attempt to train the following several spliced abstract conditional champions.

- *B1*: y = (**v1>c1**) ? tan(x6) : cos(x3)

- *B2*: y = (**c1>v1**) ? tan(x6) : cos(x3)

- *B3*: y = (**v1>v2**) ? tan(x6) : cos(x3)

- *B4*: y = (**f1(v1,v2)>c1**) ? tan(x6) : cos(x3)

- *B5*: y = (**f1(v1,v2)<c1**) ? tan(x6) : cos(x3)

- *B6*: y = (**f1(v1,v2)>v3**) ? tan(x6) : cos(x3)

- *B7*: y = (**f1(v1,v2)<v3**) ? tan(x6) : cos(x3)

- *B8*: y = (**f1(v1,v2)<f2(v3,v4)**) ? tan(x6) : cos(x3)

If the splicing algorithm is behaving optimally, we would expect the final concrete conversion of the fully trained (B6) to be as follows.

- *B6 (concrete)*: y = (log(x3)>x4) ? tan(x6) : cos(x3)

This is of course the correct answer.

6.   Abstract Mutation and Crossover

In standard mutation and crossover, random segments of program code are selected for mutation and swapping. In abstract mutation and crossover, these randomly selected segments are *abstracted*. In both abstract mutation and abstract crossover, a set of simple rules define the process of abstracting an expression segment, as follows:

- *Real Numbers*: **3.45, -.0982** *are converted to* **c1, c2**

- *Row Features*: **x1, x4** *are converted to* **v1, v2**

- *Operators*: **+, *** *are converted to* **f1(), f2()**

- *Functions*: **sqrt(), log()** *are converted to* **f1(), f2()**

Using these simple rules, the abstract mutation population operator works as in the following example:

- $f = (\log(x3)/\mathbf{sin(x2*45.3)}))>x4$? $\tan(x6) : \cos(x3)$

- The selected segment $\mathbf{sin(x2*45.3)}$ is abstracted into $\mathbf{f1(f2(v1,c1))}$

- where f1 = sin, f2 = *, v1 = x2, and c1 = 45.3

- which is then inserted below

- $f = (\log(x3)/\mathbf{f1(f2(v1,c1))}))>x4$? $\tan(x6) : \cos(x3)$

Similarly, the abstract crossover population operator selects two random segments from two expressions such as:

- $dad = (\mathbf{log(x3)}/\sin(x2*45.3))$

- $mom = (\tan(x3)/\mathrm{cube}(\mathbf{x2*45.3}))$

- The selected segments are first swapped and then "abstracted" as follows:

- $dad = (\mathbf{x2*45.3})/\sin(x2*45.3))$ *abstracted as* $= (\mathbf{f1(v1,c1)})/\sin(x2*45.3))$

- $mom = (\tan(x3)/\mathrm{cube}(\mathbf{log(x3)}))$ *abstracted as* $= (\tan(x3)/\mathrm{cube}(\mathbf{f1(v1)}))$

After abstract mutation or crossover, the new abstract expressions are optimized by the regression system. Only their ***optimized concrete conversions*** are saved in the proper evolutionary populations. In the enhanced system, 5% of all mutations are abstract mutations and 5% of all crossovers are abstract crossovers.

From first principles, abstract mutation and crossover are compelling because it is less likely that **45.3** will be optimal in a new mutation or location; and, more likely that **c1** will find a local optimum in the new mutation or location. Similar arguments are put forward for **v1**, and **f1**.

7.   Enhanced Results on Nine Base Problems

The enhanced results of training on the nine base training models on 10,000 rows and five columns with no random noise and only 20 generations allowed, are shown in Table 1-3 in order of difficulty.

The enhanced results of training on the nine base training models on 10,000 rows and twenty columns with 40% random noise and only 20 generations allowed, are shown in Table 1-4 in order as shown in Table 1-3.

Clearly, in time-constrained training (only 20 generations), the enhanced symbolic regression system is an improvement over the previously published

Table 13-3. Result For 10K rows by 5 columns no Random Noise

Test	Minutes	Train-NLSE	Train-TCE	Test-NLSE	Test-TCE
linear	1	0.00	0.00	0.00	0.00
cubic	1	0.00	0.00	0.00	0.00
cross	145	0.00	0.00	0.00	0.00
elipse	1	0.00	0.00	0.00	0.00
hidden	3	0.00	0.00	0.00	0.00
cyclic	1	0.02	0.00	0.00	0.00
hyper	65	0.17	0.00	0.17	0.00
mixed	233	0.94	0.32	0.95	0.32
ratio	229	0.94	0.33	0.94	0.32

Table 13-4. Result for 10K rows by 20 columns with 40% Random Noise

Test	Minutes	Train-NLSE	Train-TCE	Test-NLSE	Test-TCE
linear	82	0.11	0.00	0.11	0.00
cubic	59	0.11	0.00	0.11	0.00
cross	127	0.87	0.25	0.93	0.32
elipse	162	0.42	0.04	0.43	0.04
hidden	210	0.11	0.02	0.11	0.02
cyclic	233	0.39	0.11	0.35	0.12
hyper	163	0.48	0.06	0.50	0.07
mixed	206	0.90	0.27	0.94	0.32
ratio	224	0.90	0.26	0.95	0.33

Table 13-5. Result for 10K rows by 5 columns with 0% Random Noise

Test	Minutes	Train-NLSE	Train-TCE	Test-NLSE	Test-TCE	Gens
mixed	233	0.94	0.32	0.95	0.32	20
mixed	9866	0.87	0.24	0.88	0.25	200
mixed	15148	0.85	0.23	0.87	0.26	400
ratio	229	0.94	0.33	0.94	0.32	20
ratio	10324	0.87	0.23	0.87	0.25	200
ratio	14406	0.82	0.19	0.82	0.20	400

results. While the enhanced system performs poorly on the two test cases *mixed* and *ratio* with conditional target expressions, the obvious over fitting, determined by the extreme differences between training error and testing error in the previously published results, has vanished. In addition, the testing TCE scores indicate that we can perform some useful classification even in the difficult conditional problems with noise added.

As an acid test of the value of the system enhancements, it would be helpful to know how well the enhanced symbolic regression system performs on the two test cases *mixed* and *ratio* with conditional target expressions when the training is not time-constrained. For instance, do added training generations improve the training NLSE and TCE scores? Does added training time also improve the testing NLSE and TCE scores, or does the harmful over fitting reappear once again?

The results of training on the two test cases *mixed* and *ratio*, with conditional target expressions, on 10,000 rows and five columns with 0% random noise and allocating additional training generations, are shown in Table 1-5.

Clearly removing the time constraint on training, by adding additional training generations, steadily improves the results. There is obvious incremental improvement in the training NLSE and TCE scores for both problems as the number of training generations increases. Furthermore, the testing NLSE and TCE scores for both problems also improve steadily as the number of training generations increases. There is no evidence of a limit on training improvement nor any evidence of over fitting at least up to 400 training generations.

Taken together, these results portray a symbolic regression system which is ready to handle some industrial strength problems containing conditional target expressions.

Summary

Genetic Programming, from a corporate perspective, is ready for industrial use on *some* large scale, symbolic regression-classification problems. Adapting the latest research results, has created a symbolic regression tool whose efficiency is improving especially on the more difficult test cases.

Financial institutional interest in the field is growing while pure research continues at an aggressive pace. Further applied research in this field is absolutely warranted. We are using our nonlinear regression system in the financial domain. But as new techniques are added and current ones improved, we believe that the system has evolved to be a domain-independent tool that can provide superior regression and classification results for industrial scale nonlinear regression problems.

Clearly we need to experiment with even more techniques which will improve our performance on the conditional test cases. Primary areas for future research should include: experimenting with statistical and other types of analysis to help build conditional WFFs for difficult conditional problems with large amounts of noise; and experimenting with techniques to remove training time constraints while increasing training generations, for instance parallelizing the system on a cloud environment.

References

Eberhart, Russell, Shi, Yuhui, and Kennedy, James (2001). *Swarm Intelligence*. The Morgan Kaufmann Series in Artificial Intelligence. Morgan Kaufmann, New York.

Hornby, Gregory S. (2006). ALPS: the age-layered population structure for reducing the problem of premature convergence. In Keijzer, Maarten, Cattolico, Mike, Arnold, Dirk, Babovic, Vladan, Blum, Christian, Bosman, Peter, Butz, Martin V., Coello Coello, Carlos, Dasgupta, Dipankar, Ficici, Sevan G., Foster, James, Hernandez-Aguirre, Arturo, Hornby, Greg, Lipson, Hod, McMinn, Phil, Moore, Jason, Raidl, Guenther, Rothlauf, Franz, Ryan, Conor, and Thierens, Dirk, editors, *GECCO 2006: Proceedings of the 8th annual conference on Genetic and evolutionary computation*, volume 1, pages 815–822, Seattle, Washington, USA. ACM Press.

Korns, Michael F. (2006). Large-scale, time-constrained symbolic regression. In Riolo, Rick L., Soule, Terence, and Worzel, Bill, editors, *Genetic Programming Theory and Practice IV*, volume 5 of *Genetic and Evolutionary Computation*, chapter 16, pages –. Springer, Ann Arbor.

Korns, Michael F. (2007). Large-scale, time-constrained symbolic regression-classification. In Riolo, Rick L., Soule, Terence, and Worzel, Bill, editors, *Genetic Programming Theory and Practice V*, Genetic and Evolutionary Computation, chapter 4, pages 53–68. Springer, Ann Arbor.

Korns, Michael F. and Nunez, Loryfel (2008). Profiling symbolic regression-classification. In Riolo, Rick L., Soule, Terence, and Worzel, Bill, editors,

Genetic Programming Theory and Practice VI, Genetic and Evolutionary Computation, chapter 14, pages 215–229. Springer, Ann Arbor.

Koza, John R. (1992). *Genetic Programming: On the Programming of Computers by Means of Natural Selection*. MIT Press, Cambridge, MA, USA.

Man, Kim-Fung, Tang, Kit-Sang, and Kwong, Sam (1999). *Genetic Algorithms: Concepts and Designs*. Advanced Textbooks in Control and Signal processing. Springer Verlag, New York.

O'Neill, Michael and Ryan, Conor (2003). *Grammatical Evolution: Evolutionary Automatic Programming in a Arbitrary Language*, volume 4 of *Genetic programming*. Kluwer Academic Publishers.

Poli, Riccardo, Langdon, William B., and McPhee, Nicholas Freitag (2008). *A field guide to genetic programming*. Published via http://lulu.com and freely available at http://www.gp-field-guide.org.uk. (With contributions by J. R. Koza).

Price, Kenneth, Storn, Rainer, and Lampinen, Jouni (2005). *Differential Evolution: A Practical Approach to Global Optimization*. Natural Computing Series. Springer Verlag, New York.

Schmidt, Michael D. and Lipson, Hod (2007). Learning noise. In Thierens, Dirk, Beyer, Hans-Georg, Bongard, Josh, Branke, Jurgen, Clark, John Andrew, Cliff, Dave, Congdon, Clare Bates, Deb, Kalyanmoy, Doerr, Benjamin, Kovacs, Tim, Kumar, Sanjeev, Miller, Julian F., Moore, Jason, Neumann, Frank, Pelikan, Martin, Poli, Riccardo, Sastry, Kumara, Stanley, Kenneth Owen, Stutzle, Thomas, Watson, Richard A, and Wegener, Ingo, editors, *GECCO '07: Proceedings of the 9th annual conference on Genetic and evolutionary computation*, volume 2, pages 1680–1685, London. ACM Press.

Index